GLOBAL SECURITY WATCH

LEBANON

Recent Titles in
Global Security Watch

Global Security Watch—Korea: A Reference Handbook
William E. Berry, Jr.

Global Security Watch—Iran: A Reference Handbook
Thomas R. Mattair

Global Security Watch—Egypt: A Reference Handbook
Denis J. Sullivan and Kimberly Jones

Global Security Watch—Turkey: A Reference Handbook
Mustafa Kibaroglu and Aysegul Kibaroglu

Global Security Watch—Russia: A Reference Handbook
Richard Weitz

GLOBAL SECURITY WATCH
LEBANON

A Reference Handbook

David S. Sorenson

PRAEGER SECURITY INTERNATIONAL
An Imprint of ABC-CLIO, LLC

A B C 🔖 C L I O

Santa Barbara, California • Denver, Colorado • Oxford, England

Library of Congress Cataloging-in-Publication Data

Sorenson, David S., 1943–
   Global security watch—Lebanon : a reference handbook / David S. Sorenson.
      p. cm. — (Global security watch)
   Includes bibliographical references and index.
      ISBN 978-0-313-36578-2 (hard copy : alk. paper) — 978-0-313-36579-9 (ebook) 1. Lebanon—
Politics and government—1946- 2. Lebanon—Economic conditions. 3. Lebanon—Population. 4.
Lebanon—Foreign relations. 5. National security—Lebanon. 6. National security—United States. I.
Title. II. Title: Lebanon.
DS87.S63   2010
956.9204′3—dc22   2009038380

14 13 12 11 10   1 2 3 4 5

This book is also available on the World Wide Web as an eBook.
Visit www.abc-clio.com for details.

ABC-CLIO, LLC
130 Cremona Drive, P.O. Box 1911
Santa Barbara, California 93116-1911

This book is printed on acid-free paper ∞

Manufactured in the United States of America

For Jonah, Bill, Fred, and Jennie
My friends

Contents

Preface

Lebanon is one of those countries that too often make headlines, mostly for tragic reasons. In 2006, television news viewers throughout the world watched as Israeli bombs obliterated apartment buildings in Beirut and elsewhere, and as Hezbollah and Israeli forces traded explosives across the border that divides Lebanon from Israel. The screams of ambulance sirens punctuated the scenes, as aid workers laid victims, usually civilians, onto stretchers and rushed them away in ambulances. The casualties in Lebanon's wars, either inside or adjacent to its borders, usually are civilians, partly because many of Lebanon's wars are fought in cities such as Beirut. The images of 2006 recalled earlier portraits of Lebanese violence, as rival militias systematically turned much of Beirut to rubble during Lebanon's civil war in the 1970s and 1980s, or of U.S. Marines digging out their compatriots from the rubble of their barracks near the Beirut airport, attacked by a suicide bomber in 1983.

It is one of Lebanon's tragedies that it is remembered this way. Lebanon is also a land of white beaches, lofty mountain peaks, and a modern capital that was once regarded as the "Paris of the Orient" by European visitors. Lebanon is also heir to an extraordinary past, whose ancient cities of Baalbek, Sidon, Tyre, Byblos, and others remain as magnets for tourists and historians alike. Lebanon once had a vibrant economy, with a banking infrastructure that moved funds throughout the Middle East and an agricultural sector that supplied everything from apples to silk. It managed to avoid the attraction of Arab nationalism and Arab socialism, which offered so much in the early 1950s and ultimately delivered so little, finally to die in the wake of lost wars and inept political systems too frequently marred by cronyism and corruption. Lebanon certainly had its share of corruption and mismanagement, but it was not shackled to a set of ideas that largely died after the Middle East's 1967 War. Lebanon is a unique and special country that deserves its own book about its security issues.

Lebanon fascinates me, and as I traveled all around it, I frequently tried to gain access. While in Israel in 1986, I attempted to get permission to enter Lebanon, but was refused by an American consular official whose face went white at the prospect of yet another American held hostage by militia forces in Beirut. Later, I flew over the coast and looked at Lebanon's snow-capped peaks as the plane crossed over the country on its way to Damascus. I then drove with a Syrian driver to within five miles of the Lebanese-Syrian border. The day was cold and sleet blew from the north, which I hoped would hide my effort to sneak across the border, but an Austrian peace-keeper loomed out of the mist and informed me that we were in a UN-controlled area and my Syrian driver was not allowed any farther. I was scheduled to finally get to Lebanon with my students from the U.S. Air War College in the spring of 2004, but just before we were to arrive, an assassin's bomb took the life of former prime minister Rafiq Hariri, so the U.S. ambassador to Lebanon finally decided to cancel the trip after he realized that a delegation of Americans arriving at a tense time when Syrian intelligence agents were following embassy personnel around Beirut would be unwise. Several years later I wistfully looked into Lebanon from the Israeli side, as the country beckoned through the yellow gate that announced "off limits." In the fall of 2008 I tried again, but by February 2009 the U.S. embassy officially denied a visit, partly because I bring my students with me, and there was no room to lodge us at the embassy. Maybe someday.

I have thus relied on sources from Lebanon as well as on outside interpretations. I have been inspired by those who are either Lebanese citizens or those who have done extensive fieldwork there. I thus stand on the shoulders of Augustus Richard Norton, Samir Makdisi, Kamal Salab, Samir Khalaf, and countless others who have lived in Lebanon, or call Lebanon home, and who have often lived both its pain and its pleasures.

SPELLINGS

Lebanon is an Arab-speaking country (though some Maronite Christians prefer to use other languages even though their native language may be Arabic), and thus much of the written work from and about Lebanon is in Arabic. The Arabic language does not translate easily into English; thus rules are necessary for consistency. I have chosen to simplify as much as possible, to enable non-Arabic speakers to follow my text without having to consider proper pronunciation. I use spellings that are more commonly used in news sources (so "Hussein" rather than the more proper "Husayn," and "sheik" rather than "sheikh"or "shaikh," or the Turkish form, "şeyh"). Still, there are differences between the most common form and direct quotes from original sources, and thus readers will find that the Lebanese political/militia group "Hezbollah" can also be "Hizbollah" or "Hisbollah" or "Hesbullah" or "Hizballah," depending on pronunciation, and the Arabic form of the name does not distinguish between regional pronunciation across different Arab countries (North African Arabic is pronounced differently than is Eastern Mediterranean Arabic, for example). Readers need to be advised that spellings may not be consistent, because one form may occur in the text and one in a quote. I also avoid complex transliteration that distinguishes between different versions of the same letter (the letter "H," for example, has different versions with different sounds). I do use a ' to designate the hamza, which gives a pronunciation glottal stop. Thus "Shi'a" is pronounced as if it had a dash, "Shi-a." In short, I have tried to engineer a trade-off between proper pronunciation and ease of reading.

STUDYING THE MIDDLE EAST: PERSPECTIVES

The study of the Middle East is contentious at best. Some of the debate on Middle East studies revolves around charges and countercharges involving "Orientalism," a concept popularized by the late Edward Said, a professor of literature at Columbia University, and defined as "a Western Style for dominating, restructuring, and having authority over the Orient."[1] The argument underscoring Orientalism was that the scholars and writers who often denigrated the "Orient" were from imperial or postimperial societies, and the results of their works could justify crude notions of "the White Man's burden." Said concentrated his discussion largely on Western literature, though he also reserved criticism for groups such as the Middle East Studies Association, and U.S. government-funded institutes such as the RAND Corporation, and the Hudson Institute, along with individual scholars such as Raphael Patai (author of *The Arab Mind* and other works), P. J. Vatikiotis, and Bernard Lewis who retain, according to Said, "the traditional Orientalist outlook which had been developed in Europe."[2] Others joined Said's commentary on Orientalism, arguing that it continued to influence American policy toward the region throughout the Cold War and after.[3] Zachary Lockman maintains that an Orientalist thread led to the Bush II administration image and consequent policy on Iraq since 2003.[4]

Orientalist challenges to scholarship have predictably generated a countermovement, which has provided both intellectual and structuralist challenges to the Orientalist narrative. One leading figure is Martin Kramer, who argues that some Middle East scholars tried to avoid the taint of Orientalism by "whitewashing their studies of Islam in particular. Kramer cites work by John Esposito, John Voll, Richard Bulliet, and Michael Hudson, and others, who, according to Kramer, sought to portray Islamic politics as inherently democratic and essentially peaceful, and thus "failing" to explain the resurgence of Islamic violence in the Middle East and elsewhere.[5] Kramer does not mince words,

In a sentence, post-Orientalist Middle Eastern studies underestimated the rising power of Islamism, and overestimated the potential of civil society. The new mandarins predicted revolutionary change by progressive forces, the very forces admired and promoted by Edward Said; the Middle East instead got Islamism, whose trajectory the academic experts plotted erroneously. The right politics or the right ethnicity, or the right combination of the two, didn't provide protection against error. In fact, it may have invited it, by shutting out consideration of other possibilities.[6]

Said himself drew considerable criticism for his scholarship and his political activism; beyond his arguments in *Orientalism* he was an advocate of various Palestinian political causes. Some Middle East scholars such as Bernard Lewis (criticized by Said in *Orientalism*), Nikki Keddie, and Albert Hourani countered Said's positions on the dominance of European influence in the Orient. Said was called "anti-American," held responsible for creating a "thuggish environment" at Columbia University, and placed under surveillance by the FBI (Federal Bureau of Investigation), which created a 238-page file on him.[7]

The controversy over Orientalism and professed bias in the Middle East studies field has grown beyond Said and his critics to foster new institutions purportedly dedicated to the protection of academic freedom against alleged infringement of academic freedom. New organizations have appeared, including the "Association for the Study of the Middle East and Africa" (ASMEA), founded in late 2007, which lists, among others, Bernard Lewis and Fouad Ajami as members of its Academic Council. The ASMEA, on its official Web site, claims to be, "first and foremost, a community of scholars concerned to protect academic freedom and promote the search for truth to reach new heights in inquiry."[8] But in a linked Web site to "InsideHigherEd," Lewis was more specific: "Because of various political and financial pressures and inducements, the study of the Middle East and of Africa has been politicized to a degree without precedent."[9] This was apparently a veiled reference to the Middle East Studies Association (MESA), which ASMEA president Mark Clark described as "kind of a closed circle" of people with similar views," and he claimed, "We're going to have a greater mix of perspectives than MESA ever had," prompting Laurie A. Brand, head of MESA's academic freedom committee to counter, "I don't disagree that there's been tremendous politicization, but it's been coming from the folks establishing this new organization." "I see these people as part of the problem. They can speak from experience about introducing politics to the agenda."[10] Both Lewis and Ajami had advised the Bush administration to launch the invasion of Iraq in 2003, drawing sharp criticism from those such as Brand who argued that it was they who had politicized Middle East studies.

There was also Campus Watch, founded in 2002 by Daniel Pipes, a historian and critic of the Orientalist position on Middle East studies. According to Campus Watch, it "reviews and critiques Middle East studies in North America with an aim to improving them. The project mainly addresses five problems:

analytical failures, the mixing of politics with scholarship, intolerance of alternative views, apologetics, and the abuse of power over students."[11] Campus Watch reports on academics who, in its view, have been improperly critical of Israel, or supportive of political Islam, or the Palestinian position in the Palestinian-Israel conflict. Other scholars accuse Campus Watch of McCarthyism (named after the Wisconsin senator who made a campaign out of identifying people in government he suspected of communist affiliation during the 1950s). Said Hamid Dabashi of Columbia University, "This is about McCarthyism, freedom of expression. It's very important that it not be made into a Jewish-Muslim kind of thing. I am most concerned for my Jewish students, that they might feel that they shouldn't take my class, that the atmosphere would be intimidating, or that they couldn't express their opinions."[12]

I discuss this rancorous debate because it has clouded perspectives on Middle East studies. Criticism is a valid part of scholarship, as is the formation of controversial and unpopular interpretations, but the purpose of scholarship should be to evaluate facts and consider the possible conclusions that both facts and analysis present. Thus the aim of this book is to offer unbiased evaluations of Lebanon and its neighborhood. I am not seeking to varnish any of the participants (including my own country, the United States), but I also understand that the modern play called "Lebanon" has a diverse cast of characters, who can easily be portrayed as heroes or villains, but the primary purpose here is to evaluate actions, policies, and events while reserving judgment based on "Western" standards. Thus I have drawn upon scholarship that is critical of certain parties and actions and tried to counter its messages with counterinterpretations. I have used a variety of sources while recognizing that each source has a limited perspective and may well be swayed by the writer's biases. I do not have a dog in the Lebanese political ring and am not trying to build on the passions of those who do, or who are rooting for a particular dog. This book is about analysis to find the most accurate answers to the varied puzzles of Lebanon. That assignment is difficult enough without adding emotion or bias to it.

I have benefited greatly from the willingness of colleagues to read draft chapters, and I specifically thank Evelyn Early, Elyane Tarazi, and Christopher Hemmer for insightful comments. Any remaining errors are my own.

Finally, I am an employee of the United States Government. That has never stopped me from expressing my own conclusions and views, even if they are contrary to U.S. official policy, because my employer, the Air War College, the U.S. Air Force's senior service school, values academic freedom, so as long as I indicate that the analysis and conclusions in this book represent my own views, and not necessarily those of any U.S. government agency, I may continue to enjoy academic freedom.

NOTES

1. Edward W. Said, *Orientalism* (New York: Pantheon Books, 1978), p. 3.

2. Ibid., p. 295, see also pp. 308–328.

3. Douglas Little, *American Orientalism: The United States and the Middle East since 1945* (Chapel Hill, NC: University of North Carolina Press, 2002).

4. Zachary Lockman, *Contending Visions of the Middle East: The History and Politics of Orientalism* (Cambridge: Cambridge University Press, 2004), 248–251.

5. Martin Kramer, *Ivory Towers on Sand: The Failure of Middle Eastern Studies in America* (Washington, DC: The Washington Institute for Near East Policy, 2001).

6. Martin Kramer, "Middle East Studies: What Is the Debate About?" Campus Watch, April 14, 2005, http://www.campus-watch.org/article/id/1941.

7. Lawrence Davidson, "The Attack on Middle East Studies: A Historical Perspective," *Middle East Policy* 15 (Spring 2008): 152.

8. "Welcome to the Association for the Study of the Middle East and Africa," http://www.asmeascholars.org/.

9. "A Different View of the Middle East," InsideHigherEd, http://www.insidehighered.com/news/2007/11/02/mideast.

10. Ibid.

11. Campus Watch Web site, http://www.campus-watch.org/. The organization appeared to lean toward Republican politics, running a story, for example, on its Web page linking Senator Barak Obama to 1960's radical William Ayers as Republican campaign literature was also doing in the fall of 2008. "Evidence Mounts: Ayers Co-Wrote Obama's Dreams [incl. Rashid Khalidi], http://www.campus-watch.org/article/id/5878.

12. "Website Fuels Debate on Campus Anti-Semitism," *New York Times*, September 27, 2002.

Introduction

The very name "Lebanon" evokes mystery, as there is some debate about its origins. Some argue that it stems from "white" (*laabaan* in Arabic), referring to the milky color of its snow-capped mountains. Some argue that the name dates to pre-Arabic languages, though the root (LBN, or ل ن ب) is similar. The name Lebanon stems from the larger "Mount Lebanon," historically a Maronite Christian area, and some argue that its choice for the name of the nation of Lebanon marginalizes the other provinces and their religious groups that were annexed to form Lebanon in 1920.[1] Lebanon is the only country in the Arab world whose territory has more mountains than desert, and its majestic mountains are its most distinctive geological feature. Its tall peaks were once covered with forest, and Lebanon's distinctive cedar trees became its national symbol; today their remains can be seen in underground tombs in Egypt's Valley of the Kings and in the Egyptian Antiquities Museum in Cairo. Their majesty remains on Lebanon's flag and on the tails of Lebanon's Middle East Airlines' planes. But the mountains are one of many features that render Lebanon as a distinct entity in the Middle East. It is the only country in the region with a significant Christian population. It is the only country in the Middle East with a "confessional" government, where religious distinctions apportion political and social power (though the post-Saddam Hussein Iraq is moving in that direction). It is one of only a few Arab countries to have a significant Shi'a population, around 40 percent (lower than Bahrain's 70 percent or Iraq's perhaps 60 percent, but higher than any other Arab country). It is the only Middle Eastern country where members of the Druze faith have played a significant social and political role in the life

of the country. It is one of a very few countries in the largely desert Middle East to
have a water surplus.

Lebanese popular culture has its own unique character: in the summer of
2008, the top song on the play list of the month on *Beirut Nights*, an Internet
radio show, was by a transsexual Israeli singer, while one of the most famous of
all music festivals occurs at Baalbek each summer, drawing some of the most
famous singers, orchestras, and theater troupes in the world. Lebanon's popular
culture also includes a significant role for soothsayers and astrologers, who are
usually banned in Muslim countries as un-Islamic. But in Lebanon, requests
for a glimpse into one's personal fortune are eclipsed by queries into the political
future of the country, a testament to the tumultuous nature of Lebanese politics.[2]

Lebanon has other peculiarities. It was the only Arab country in the vicinity of
Israel to not join the Arab cause in 1948. It was not directly involved in the 1967
or 1973 wars. Its conflicts with Israel came separately, in 1976, for example, and
in the years following 1983, when Israeli forces crossed into Lebanon either in
pursuit of terrorists and Syrian forces, according to one view, or pursuit of land
and water, according to another view. Those repeated incursions, and counterat-
tacks from Lebanon into Israel, had profound effects on both countries that continue to this day. Lebanon was also the scene of one of the greatest single
tragedies to face the United States Marine Corps since World War II, when
149 Marines died in the bombing of their barracks in 1983, attacked by a smiling
suicide bomber whose identity remains a mystery to this day. Lebanon is also one
of a very few countries to be claimed by another country, Syria, which lost
Lebanon through French influence in the 1920s. Syria historically did not
maintain an embassy in Beirut because that would imply sovereign recognition
of Lebanon, which Syria considered a part of "Greater Syria." Syria maintained
troops in Lebanon, and influenced the Lebanese economy, to Syria's benefit.
Syrian intelligence agents stand accused of numerous assassinations of prominent
Lebanese officials, including former Prime Minister Rafiq Hariri. Syria finally
withdrew its military forces from Lebanon after that assassination in 2005, but
Syrian influence remains, and Syrian troops still mobilize along the Syrian-
Lebanese border when troubles stir in Lebanon.

Lebanon's civil war in the 1970s and 1980s was particularly vicious, with its
horrific scenes beamed into living room televisions around the world. Entire
blocks of Beirut became rubble as militias turned heavy weapons on rival neighborhoods, and the sight of the wounded being carried to minibuses pressed into
ambulance service by stretcher carriers became daily fare. By some estimates, over
150,000 Lebanese died in the struggle, around the same as the violent Algerian
Civil War of the 1990s, except that Lebanon's population is much smaller than
Algeria's (34 million to 4 million in 2009). Saudi Arabia brokered an end to
the war in November 1989, and the subsequent rebuilding process turned barren
neighborhoods back into modern spaces comparable to those in southern

Europe. The wars would erupt again, and the country seemed unable to rise above the ethnic and religious divisions that had historically been its burden.

Lebanon is a small country in a tense region, and much of that tension has spilled over into Lebanon itself. Israel, according to some historians, sought what is now the southern part of Lebanon to gain access to the Litani River. Whether or not those beliefs are accurate, Israel has periodically invaded and occupied the region up to the Litani River, either to claim it, or to prevent Israel's enemies from using the area to launch attacks into Israel. Syria has long-standing ties to Lebanon, which was actually a part of "Greater Syria" until 1923, when France cleaved it off, allegedly to protect the then-majority Maronite Christian population. The move also gave France a position of influence in the eastern Mediterranean, placing it next to Britain, which controlled Palestine and the Suez Canal. Syria retains a grievance over the French action, and thus Syrian maps at the Damascus International Airport still show the area of Lebanon as a part of Syria. Syria exercised a heavy hand over Lebanese affairs until 2004, when the "Cedar Revolution" reduced the Syrian role, though it still remains.

THE FOCUS OF THIS BOOK

This book concentrates on Lebanon as a security interest, given the emphasis of the Praeger series "Global Security Watch." "Security" is a very broad term, though, to encompass matters of both internal and regional instability. Security threats emerge when a country becomes plagued with internal disorder that attracts outside forces, which further complicates its disarray. Security issues also develop when external parties or countries attempt to control other countries against the will of significant members of its population. Security problems emerge when insurgencies use a particular country to operate training camps and to obtain resources for their operations.

So in every sense of the term, Lebanon poses a security challenge to its own population, to the region, and beyond. "Beyond" can be a long way—in the early 1990s, Lebanese-based Hezbollah reportedly bombed two targets in Argentina, a Jewish community center and the Israeli embassy, killing over 120 persons. In 2002, Singapore accused Hezbollah of trying to recruit terrorists to attack ships in the Singapore Strait. Lebanon was under Syrian control until 2004, and Syrian influence reportedly still remains. Syrian intelligence agents formed vast secret networks into many centers of Lebanese power, and it is difficult to believe that they left with the Syrian soldiers. Israel has attacked into Lebanon several times, often with bloody consequences. Attacks against Israel have come from behind Lebanon's northern border, including one from a motorized hang glider pilot who flew into an Israeli military camp and killed six Israeli soldiers before the camp's defenders shot him dead. In 2006, rockets rained into Israel from Hezbollah positions in Lebanon, killing hundreds of Israelis, as Israeli military power responded back, killing thousands of Lebanese in the process. Hezbollah, sustained by Iranian money and weapons, strengthened its position, not only in Lebanon, but through much of the world, even winning praise from its normal rival, al-Qaeda. There are few countries in the world where security issues loom as large as they do in Lebanon.

There are many ways to unravel security issues. The most thorough is through the recognition that security is deeply rooted in cultural, political, economic, and cultural factors, and sometimes carries religious overtones. To understand the security situation of a particular country, it is necessary to understand its history, its political system, its patterns of economic development, and its cultural heredity. History is often a neglected element in understanding insecurity, but it is a vital one. The case of Algeria is instructive. In the 1990s and the early 2000s, Algeria underwent a tragic spasm of violence that probably claimed over 150,000 lives, often taken in ruthless fashion. Several scholars have argued that Algeria's violent past, to include its revolution against French rule, contributed to the continuing violence that followed independence.[3] Israel presents another case where images of security have been profoundly shaped by history, as Idith Zertal documents in her study of the impact of the Holocaust on Israeli perceptions of security, particularly after the poignant reminder of that event with the arrest of Nazi war criminal Adolf Eichmann in 1960.[4]

The political and economic climates of the country also factor into an understanding of its security issues. It has become almost axiomatic that democracies are less likely to engage in wars of choice than autocracies, though the issue continues to draw debate in academic circles. Democracies are also considered less likely to allow for terrorists to make them a base for operations, though F. Gregory Gause III has offered a challenge to this thesis.[5] Starting with the Carter administration, the United States has supported the development of democracies, particularly in areas regarded as instable. Democratization as a U.S. policy grew in the Bill Clinton and George W. Bush administrations, and Lebanon was held as a model for other countries in the Middle East in particular to emulate. In the 1990s, Lebanon appeared to be on the cusp of a modern democracy, but the confessional system and the scars of the civil war, along with outside influence, have made Lebanon's democracy almost unworkable. In a similar way, the remarkable rebuilding of Lebanon after its civil war became a model for postwar reconstruction, as modern apartment buildings and public squares replaced Beirut's war rubble. But while Beirut and its surrounding environs are much improved over the wreckage of the 1970s and 1980s, the improvement has not led to a more civil society or a working political system, or a mechanism to pay off the national debt, one of the highest in the world. So security is impacted, as urban bombs continue to kill high-profile figures, including alleged members of terrorist groups, a former and possible future prime minister, and the dozens of innocent bystanders, bodyguards, and the like who often also perish in political murders. Israeli bombs, some made in the United States, pulverized parts of Beirut and the surrounding areas in 2006, sadly providing jobs to underpaid construction workers who often came from Syria to rebuild war damage.

Security issues also stem from the regional neighborhood of the country under study. Instability, political and social ideas, commerce, and peace efforts rarely respect borders, nor can they in an age of globalization. Lebanon's neighborhood is no exception. Lebanon is next to Syria and Israel, and the home of hundreds of Palestinian refugees, and thus the problems of the neighborhood have become Lebanon's problems. Indeed Israel and Syria have fought proxy wars in Lebanon, and hundreds of thousands of Lebanese have perished in these wars. Lebanon's Palestinian population has grown increasingly restive, with the desire to return to its native home in what is now Israel and its second-class standing in Lebanon, fueling Palestinian anger. In many ways, Lebanon may not become more peaceful or stable until the problems of its environs are either resolved or lessened.

LEBANESE IN THE WORLD

One of Lebanon's particularities is that many of its citizens have left the country, either permanently or on extended absence. Many migrated to the United States over decades, and that influence shows in the United States. There are at least 35 cities, towns, townships, or counties named "Lebanon" or some derivative ("South Lebanon," for example) in the United States. There are over 3 million Lebanese-Americans, including former Senator James Abourezk of South Dakota, Spencer Abraham, former senator and energy secretary, Ambassador Philip Habib, Secretary of Transportation Ray Lahood (a relative of former Lebanese President Emile Lahoud), Governor Jeanne Shaheen of New Hampshire (elected to the U.S. Senate in November 2008), John E. Sununu, Republican Senator from New Hampshire (son of John N. Sununu, former White House Chief of Staff, and defeated in the November 2008 election by Jeanne Shaheen), perennial presidential candidate and consumer activist Ralph Nader, Helen Thomas, dean of the White House Press Corps, former Central Command commander General John Abizaid, former National Football League quarterbacks John Elway and Doug Flutie, race car driver and Indianapolis 500 winner Bobby Rahal, John Mack, former CEO of Morgan Stanley, Jack Nasser, former president of the Ford Motor Company, Stephen P. Yokich, eighth president of the International Union, United Automobile, Aerospace and Agricultural Implement Workers of America, and artistic performers including Paul Anka, Sammy Haggar, Harold Ramis, Danny Thomas, Marlo Thomas, Tony Shalhoub, Frank Zappa, and Keanu Reeves, among many.[6] Many if not most of their families migrated to the United States from Lebanon during the nineteenth century, and not all maintain much connection with their ancestral homeland. Such connections hardly end with the United States. Notable Lebanese have set down roots in other parts of the world, including Jordan's former Queen Noor, Carlos Ghosn, president of Renault, and Carlos Slim Helú of Mexico, listed as the world's third wealthiest person in 2009.

Most of Lebanon's expatriates are not wealthy or notable, but instead are common people who have migrated to other parts of the world in search of a better life. There are large communities of Lebanese in the Caribbean and South America, in sub-Saharan Africa, in Europe, Asia, other parts of the Middle East, and elsewhere. While some of these Lebanese have left permanently, many others return to retain their citizenship while operating shops or other businesses outside of the country. They often send funds back home to their families, becoming a significant source of revenue. However, they do not often get involved in their new countries in support of Lebanese politics. Surprisingly, in the United States, the land of interest groups, there are very few Lebanese (or Arab, for that matter) lobbies to push for policies favoring their country. During the 2006 Israel-Hezbollah War, small actions by the Arab American Institute (a pan-Arab American group, not specifically Lebanese) were all that marked a counter to the large-scale political activity in the United States to support Israel.

The next chapter concentrates on Lebanon's modern history, though the real history of Lebanon dates back for thousands of years. While Lebanon's recent (post–World War I) history has the most significant impact on modern Lebanon, the continuity of its older past is also a strong factor in shaping Lebanon's identity.

NOTES

1. Roschanack Shaery-Eisenlohr, *Shi'ite Lebanon: Transnational Religion and the Making of National Identities* (New York: Columbia University Press, 2008), 21.

2. "Boom Market for Lebanon's Soothsayers," *New York Times*, January 30, 2007.

3. Martin Stone, *The Agony of Algeria* (New York: Columbia University Press, 1997); Martin Evans and John Phillips, *Algeria: Anger of the Dispossessed* (New Haven, CT: Yale University Press, 2007).

4. Idith Zertal, *Israel's Holocaust and the Politics of Nationhood* (Cambridge: Cambridge University Press, 2005).

5. F. Gregory Gause III, "Can Democracy Stop Terrorism?" *Foreign Affairs* 84 (September/October 2005): 62–76.

6. Not all of these individuals come from pure Lebanese parentage; many have mixed ancestry, as is the case for most Americans.

CHAPTER 1

The Modern History of Lebanon

There are few places in the world that have a more storied history than does Lebanon. It was the home of the ancient Phoenicians, and the word "Bible" may come from the Lebanese city of Byblos (which is Greek for "papyrus," the material on which early sacred books were published). Its history goes back much further, to Neolithic peoples who inhabited Lebanon as early as 50,000 BCE,[1] and it has marched on steadily, but not without tragedy and violent conflict. Modern Lebanon is a child of that tragic but rich history.[2]

LEBANON'S EARLY HISTORY

It is difficult to know exactly what early peoples populated Lebanon, but the Canaanites were probably the first to leave behind writings that allowed a window into their history. They may have arrived as early as 4,000 BCE, taking advantage of Lebanon's rich alluvial soil to raise crops and its natural harbors to start seafaring. The Hyksos came next, using Lebanon to invade their neighbors, sweeping into Egypt in the second millennia BCE, until Egypt finally drove them out after centuries of rule. Egyptian forces would later do battle with the Hittites, who came to Lebanon from modern Turkey, at one point doing battle with Rameses II at a remote place called Kadish; though the details of the conflict are vague, Rameses decorated his mortuary temple with depictions of Hittite severed body parts as symbols of Egypt's victory over them.

According to some legends, the Greeks referred to Lebanon's Canaanites as "Phoenicians" from a Greek word for crimson, referring to the purple dye extracted from the murex mollusks that the Phoenicians used to color their clothing. The Phoenicians were traders, sailing large ships from ports at Sidon, Byblos, Tyre, and other places to ply the Mediterranean. As their trade expanded, the Phoenicians built an empire that spread across North Africa, established the city of Carthage in modern Tunisia, and reportedly sailed as far as the British Isles for tin, and down the coast of Africa. In Lebanon's Beqaa Valley, the Phoenicians added to previous buildings to enhance the city of Baalbek, which has become one of the popular tourist destinations in the Middle East. Phoenicia declined after the Assyrians conquered the area around 875 BCE. A steady stream of conquerors followed, as the Babylonians replaced the Assyrians in 685, followed by Cyrus the Great from Persia, who conquered the eastern Mediterranean in 539 BCE, forcing some of its population to migrate to Carthage, which remained a powerful nation until the Second Punic War from 218 to 201 BCE. Alexander the Great swept out of Greece and took the eastern Mediterranean in 332 BCE, using the area to launch an imperial war that would bring much of the known world under his sway. Alexander brought Greek influence to the world he conquered, and there are remains of the Greek presence in Lebanon, along with the Roman influence that followed the Roman invasion in 64 CE. The Roman Empire divided in 395 CE, and the eastern part, containing modern Lebanon, became the Christian Byzantine Empire. That empire gradually fell to a combination of corruption and constant war with the Persian Sassanid Empire, and in 636 Byzantine forces lost to a Muslim army at the Battle of Yarmouk, opening the door for Muslim conquest of the eastern Mediterranean. Lebanon came under the rule of the Umayyad Caliphate, with its capital in Damascus, until 750, when a revolt led by a distant relative of the Prophet Muhammad, Ali Abbas, toppled the Umayyad and replaced it with the Abbasid Caliphate, which lasted until the Mongol sack of Baghdad in 1258. Under the Abbasids, Lebanon became a restive place with numerous revolts, including a major uprising in 759. Several regions declared independence from Abbasid rule, and many of the remote mountain areas never came under full Abbasid control, instigating a pattern of Lebanese local independence that persists to this day.

In 1099, the Crusaders crossed through Lebanon on their way to Jerusalem, and their two-century presence in the eastern Mediterranean was yet another layer of history impacting Lebanon, marking it with castles and fortifications that remain tourist attractions now. The Crusaders realized that their ability to take and hold Palestine depended on their taking control of Mediterranean seaports, and thus different Crusader armies and naval forces conquered Tripoli in 1109, Beirut in 1110, Sidon in 1111, and Tyre, which capitulated to a combined Crusader-mercenary force in 1111.[3] After the final defeat of the Crusaders by a Muslim army in 1290, control of Lebanon reverted to the Egyptian Mamlukes. In 1512 Mamluke troops went into battle against the Ottoman Turks as the Ottomans penetrated into Mamluke-controlled Syria, threatening the Mamluke capital of Cairo. The Mamlukes believed that proper soldiers fought with piercing weapons and not firearms and went into battle equipped with fine swords and spears. However, the Ottomans had other ideas about warfare, and their muskets shredded the Mamluke army, whose tattered remnants marched back to Cairo some years later, having yielded most of the Middle East, including Lebanon, to the Ottoman victors.

LEBANON UNDER OTTOMAN RULE

Ottoman rule divided modern Lebanon into three provinces, or *vilayets.* To the north was the *vilayet* of Tripoli, to its east was the *vilayet* of Damascus, and the *vilayet* of Sidon was in the south. The Ottomans largely ruled through a feudal system that allowed powerful regional families to actually govern. As Karen Barkey notes, Ottoman imperial strategy stressed a combination of negotiated power across social networks in the conquered areas, coupled with repression where core Ottoman power came under challenge.[4] In Lebanon's case, autonomy divulged to family and region as long as local leaders did not stray from deference to Ottoman overall control.

Thus Lebanon's place in the Ottoman world did not break the power of local dynasties. As Ussama Makdisi explains, rank in Lebanese society was much more important than was religious identity.[5] The Druze Jumblatt family, for example, dominated the Shuf region between 1711 and 1825.[6] The Shi'a Harfoush family was prominent in the Beqaa Valley for centuries, supplying Baalbek with at least three governors. The Himadah family was another prominent Shi'a family that dates back to at least the fifteenth century.[7] Significant Maronite families included the Shihab family, the al-Kazen family, the Gemayel family, the Aoun family, and the Chamoun family, among many others. The regional influence of these and other families allowed the Ottomans to play one clan against another, but never allowing one family to become powerful enough to unite the region against Turkish rule.

Despite titular Ottoman control, France was an interested party in Lebanese affairs. During the seventeenth century, French King Louis XIV and King Louis XV ordered their ambassadors in Istanbul (then Constantinople) to protect the interests of Lebanon's Maronite Christians. French trade with the Maronite communities grew, particularly after Sidon opened its port to European commerce, and trade between France and Lebanon ranged from 1 to 2 million French francs per year in the seventeenth and eighteenth centuries.[8] French influence would grow considerably in Lebanon in the centuries to follow. The Ottoman rulers did not object, perhaps remembering that France and Turkey had signed an alliance in the sixteenth century when France was at war with the Hapsburg Empire and that French commercial relations with Lebanon's Maronites might help them to prosper.

OTTOMAN RULE AND LEBANON'S SECTS

The Ottomans were usually content to collect revenues in Lebanon while leaving governance to local authorities. There were also periods of peaceful relations between religious sects, though foreign interference could provoke violence across the schisms, as was the case when Egypt's ruler, Muhammad Ali, pressured Abdalla Pasha to execute Druze leader Bashir Jumblatt in 1825, ending a pattern of collaboration across religious identities. As Maroun Kisirwani tells it, "the end of Bahsir Janbulat (Jumblatt) was the beginning of a radical change in Lebanese society. The old political rivalries were replaced by sectarian factions grouping the Maronites on one side and the Druses on the other."[9] As Farid el Khazen indicates, between the sixteenth and nineteenth centuries, Maronite power and influence in Lebanon expanded considerably, enhanced by the Maronite church's outward reach to Europe.[10] Ibrahim Pasha's perceived favoritism for Lebanon's Christian population also led to deadly clashes between the Maronites and the Druze in 1841.[11] As a consequence, the Ottoman rulers divided Lebanon into two districts, a Christian area in the north and a Druze area in the south, a partition referred to as the Double Qaimaqamate, which created a council system to apportion power between Christian and Druze groups. However, the partition assumed religious homogeneity in the country, when in fact many areas of Lebanon had mixed populations. Moreover, the Sunni population was not included because many had objected to the separation of their spiritual home of Greater Syria. Less than 20 years after partition, violence broke out again between the Druze and the Maronite populations, with considerable loss of life on both sides. A clash between Druze and Christians in the village of Beit Meri quickly spread throughout the mountains and all the way to Damascus, where mobs attacked Christian areas, massacring thousands. The Damascus violence drew in the French, who sent an occupying force to Lebanon in July 1860, remaining for a year.[12] Key European powers, France in particular, which had encouraged partition in 1841, now called for reunification after the 1860 violence (which claimed the lives of over 10,000 Maronites), and thus the Ottomans joined the country back together under a Christian governor, advised by a multi-sectarian council. After this reunification, Lebanon remained in relative peace between 1860 and 1914. The Ottoman authorities tried to preserve this tranquility by trying to avoid more outside influence; when American Protestant missionaries tried to convert Maronite Christians during the nineteenth century, the Ottomans denounced the efforts, yet took pains to recognize the Protestant faith as one of Lebanon's religions as the missionaries succeeded in converting a very few to their faith (though in the end the Protestants failed to gain the penetration into the Middle East that they had hoped for).[13]

The comparatively peaceful period ended with the start of World War I, when Turkey, Lebanon's occupying power, joined Germany and Austria-Hungary as a part of the triple alliance. Turkey, realizing the strategic significance of the eastern Mediterranean theater, replaced the Armenian administrator of Lebanon with a Turk, Jamal Pasha, known for his harsh military rule. In 1915, Turkish forces attacked the British Army, which was guarding the Suez Canal. Frustrated by the failure of the attack, Turkey established a blockade of the eastern Mediterranean to prevent supplies from reaching British forces fighting in the Middle East Theater. The blockade caused shortages of food, and thousands of Lebanese died from starvation, while tourists stopped coming, and remittances from Lebanese working abroad dried up. Turkish troops felled Lebanon's mulberry trees for fuel and imposed military conscription, as they did across the Arab world. Turkish troops executed 21 Lebanese in Beirut, allegedly for anti-Turkish activities, and today Martyrs' Square stands in Beirut as a reminder. In all, Samir Khalaf estimates that 100,000 of a population of 450,000 Lebanese died under World War I Ottoman rule.[14] Turkey's days as the occupier of Lebanon were numbered, though, and the surrender of the triple alliance in November 1918 not only ended the alliance itself, but also marked the demise of Ottoman Turkey, which transformed into the new Turkish Republic in 1925. The end of World War I also meant the creation of the League of Nations, an international body whose mission was to transform the state-centered system to a world order where states could negotiate away the conflicts that often spawned war. Instead, the League of Nations was captured by the victorious European nations who used its mandate to further their own imperial ambitions, particularly in the Middle East.

MODERN LEBANESE HISTORY

In September 1920, the League of Nations, dividing the territory of the losing powers in World War I, awarded Greater Syria to France, with Britain gaining Palestine, giving approval to a French decision to partition Lebanon away from Syria the month before. The creation of Lebanon was the result of the long-standing ties between the Maronite Christians and France (enhanced by France's role in mediating the crisis of 1860, noted above), but the Lebanon that France created also included the Muslim areas of Beirut, the coastal cities of Sidon, Tyre, and Tripoli and the Beqaa Valley, all of which had a predominately Shi'a population. Initially, the Sunni Muslim populations did not want to be a part of a Maronite-dominated polity and agitated for inclusion with Syria. However, by the 1930s, many Lebanese Muslims realized that they might have more political and economic power in Lebanon despite its then-Maronite majority than they would if they had to compete with the long-entrenched Muslim elites in Damascus and Aleppo. Thus even though they still wanted union with Syria, they worked in the political bargaining process in Lebanon to create niches of power for themselves.[15]

The loss of Lebanon contributed heavily to the narrative of Syrian nationalism, spawning peals of outrage over the perfidy of imperialism and allowing the ruling Damascus Ba'ath to bolster its claim to rule Syria with demands that Lebanon be reunited with the mother country.[16] For Syrian nationalists, the separation of Lebanon from Syria represented the dangers of foreign influence that would later form the rallying cry of Ba'athist socialism. Syria would also find ways to continue de facto control over Lebanon, something that the Ta'if Accord of October 1989 finally allowed it to accomplish.

In 1926, France drafted a constitution for Lebanon, modeled after the constitution of the French Third Republic then in power. Article 95 of that constitution provided for something that differed from the French constitution, a "balanced" confessional government based on religious differentiation. The president was to be a Maronite Christian, the prime minister a Sunni Muslim, and the speaker of the Chamber of Deputies a Shi'a Muslim. The Chamber of Deputies would have six Christian members for every five Muslim members. However, despite the language of the constitution, which applied a limited Lebanese sovereignty, the French high commissioner actually held supreme power. It was this influence that led to the selection of Charles Dabbas, a Greek Orthodox, as president, despite the provision that the president should be a Maronite Christian. Since the constitution called for one six-year term for the president, Dabbas was technically eligible to hold the office after 1932. However, the two most powerful Maronite candidates divided the chamber of deputies, and thus a Muslim, Muhammad al-Jisr, was named as a compromise candidate. To prevent a Muslim president (also a violation of the 1926 understanding), the French high commissioner extended Dabbas's term for a year. In 1936, the chamber selected Maronite Émile Eddé as president, but the French again suspended the constitution in 1939 as the clouds of World War II appeared.

In 1940, France fell to Nazi Germany, and the Nazis placed France under the rule of the pro-Nazi Vichy Party, presided by World War I marshal Philippe Pétain. The Vichy regime appointed General Henri-Fernand Dentz as high commissioner of Lebanon, but Vichy rule in Lebanon ended in July 1941 when British and Free French forces invaded Syria and Lebanon, fearing that the Vichy forces would turn the region over to German forces. In November 1941, the Free French, inheriting the mantle of Lebanese rule, declared Lebanon independent. Despite this declaration, France continued to interfere with Lebanese political affairs, arresting President Bishara al-Khoury, Prime Minister Riyad as-Sulh, and other elected leaders for amending the constitution in a way that eliminated the French Mandate of Lebanon provisions. Lebanese factions united in response to the arrest, and that, along with pressure from the United States, some Arab countries, and Britain, combined to release the political prisoners, which they did on November 22, 1943, now considered the Lebanese day of independence.

THE IMMEDIATE POSTINDEPENDENCE PERIOD

Following genuine independence, President Khoury and Prime Minister Sulh codified the informal agreement of 1926, crafting the National Pact in the summer of 1943, which became the basis of Lebanon's government. The National Pact set into agreement the unwritten understandings that Khoury and Sulh had used briefly and reflected their understanding that Lebanon must have a government that reflected the divided religious identities of its population while at the same time becoming free of the foreign influence that often accentuated those differences. Lebanon's Muslim population feared the possible European (and American) influence that Lebanese Christians had used in the past to keep their protected status. Lebanon's Christians were a small population surrounded by Arabs, both in Lebanon and in the larger Arab world, and feared that the currents of pan-Arab nationalism might marginalize them in a pan-Arab arrangement that could be largely Islamic. Leadership on both sides of the religious split realized that Lebanon's future rested on reassuring both populations that their worst fears would not be realized.

Thus the National Pact was designed to ensure that Lebanese independence would be complete, with Christians promising to cut connections to Christian Europe, and the Muslim groups promising not to seek ties to the Arab world. The National Pact also sanctified the confessional system of the 1926 Constitution, distributing power on the basis of the 1932 census with its six-to-five ratio of Christians to Muslims. That census, the last ever taken, has considerable significance for contemporary Lebanon. However, like most censuses, the 1932 Lebanese census was driven by partisan politics. As Rania Maktabi shows, powerful Maronite actors shaped the census rules so that they not only excluded certain non-Maronite Lebanese (particularly the Shi'a), but, more significantly, counted emigrant Lebanese even though many were actually citizens of the countries to which they had migrated.[17] Thus even today the questionable validity of the founding census casts a question over Lebanese politics and society.

The fact that the National Pact was never actually recorded indicated just how fragile the results were. Some Pact supporters saw it as a temporary measure to allow for the growth of a true Lebanese identity that would pull Lebanon's population away from their primary religious community identification. That did not happen, though, for numerous reasons. Lebanon's population was partially divided by geography, with a large portion of Sunni Muslims living in the north of the country, in pockets in the eastern part on the Syrian border, and in the south central region. The Shi'a were located mostly in the Beqaa Valley in the east, and in the south, north of the Israeli border. The Druze lived in the Shuf region in central Lebanon, and in proximity with a Greek Orthodox population in the south, north of the Shi'a areas. The primary Maronite Christian area was north of Beirut in the Mount Lebanon region, with smaller areas in the Shuf,

while Greek Catholics shared the Shuf with other populations, and the Greek
Orthodox lived largely in the far north around Tripoli. While there were areas
of mixed population (particularly in and around Beirut), most of Lebanon's
population formed isolated communities without much contact with their
neighbors, thus impeding national identity.

The 1948 War and Its Aftermath

Beginning in the nineteenth century, Jewish refugees from Poland, Russia, and
other parts of Europe streamed into Palestine, seeking a Jewish homeland free
from the persecution that they often faced in Europe. Seeking the believed safety
of their ancestral home, waves (or *aliyas*) of Jewish immigrants fled to Palestine,
from where Rome had exiled them around 70 CE. During the first *aliya*, over
25,000 Jews arrived in Palestine from Russia between 1882 and 1903. They were
joined by 40,000 additional Russian Jews in the second *aliya* between 1904 and
1914, and a third group of around 25,000, also from Russia, arrived in Palestine
immediately after World War I. The final *aliya* and the largest yet, consisting of
60,000 Polish Jews, landed in Palestine between 1923 and 1926. These Jews
bought land from Palestinians in some cases, or expropriated land in other situa-
tions, and started the kibbutzim, or rural commune, that sowed the seeds of
modern Zionism. Thousands of other Jews would later follow the example of
these early Jewish settlers in the aftermath of the Nazi Holocaust, setting the stage
for one of the Middle East's most intractable problems.

These Jewish settlers had little organization to guide them in Palestine, but
currents in Europe would change that. European Jewish writers and organizers
founded the Zionist movement in the early 1800s, drawn from one of the early
names for Jerusalem. Writings by Rabbi Yehuda Hai Alkalay and Rabbi Zvi
Hirsch Kalisher, who observed a loss of faith among Jews worldwide in the nineteenth century, inspired Zionism, and the movement gained momentum in the
mid-nineteenth century, and European Jews began organizing to return to
Palestine, the site of the ancient Hebrew kingdoms. The most notable of these
organizers was Theodor Herzl, a journalist who wrote of his plan for a Jewish
state in Israel to serve as a refuge for Jews who were coming under increasing persecution in Europe. Herzl and his followers met in Basel, Switzerland, in
August 1897, chartering the first World Zionist Congress. The momentum of
the Basel Conference carried over into Herzl's dealings with Great Britain, which
issued the Balfour Declaration in November 1917, calling for the creation of a
Jewish homeland.

There was already a growing population of Jews in Palestine, fueled by po-
groms in Russia and Poland, starting around 1882, bringing in hundreds of
thousands of European Jews who bought or expropriated land from the resident
Palestinians. These numbers would swell in the aftermath of the Holocaust,

when hundreds of thousands of European Jews fled to Palestine, pushing away a British effort to keep them out. The United Nations attempted to defuse a growing regional crisis by devising a partition plan that would have divided the old British Mandate of Palestine into separate Jewish and Arab states, but the regional Arab countries rejected the proposal. They argued that the Jewish settlers got a disproportionate share of the land, including the best arable land in the Galilee region and complete access to the Sea of Galilee, or Lake Tiberias, the largest body of fresh water in the area. Israel's leadership stepped into the resulting political vacuum and unilaterally declared the State of Israel. Arab states in the vicinity declared the act unacceptable and declared war. The consequence was the 1948 Arab-Israeli War, fought by Israel on one side, and Syria, Jordan, and Egypt on the other. There was little coordination among the Arab armies, or, for that matter, among Arab leaders, who were pursuing somewhat different objectives. King Abdullah I of Jordan had wanted control over all of Palestine, and both Egypt and Syria wanted to prevent such a takeover.

The Israelis also faced internal disunity (the *Haganah*, or self-defense force, the *Irgun Zvai Leumi*, and the *Lohamei Herut Yisrael* had differing objectives), but Arab disunity and the skills of the Israeli armies (who outnumbered their Arab foes) won the day for Israel. The result was that a massive influx of Palestinian refugees, driven from their homeland, could not return to it. Over 700,000 Palestinians sought shelter in neighboring Arab countries, and over 110,000 fled to Lebanon (the actual figure is disputed, with some authorities placing it higher). Most remained in Lebanon, housed in refugee camps, ineligible for Lebanese citizenship (as in most Arab countries), and existing on the margins of Lebanese society.

The 1948 War stoked Arab nationalism, with pro-Arab unity movements sweeping out the regimes in Syria and Egypt, and a Palestinian assassinated King Abdullah I of Jordan in 1952. Lebanese political leaders understood that a divided Lebanon would be torn asunder if it became involved in the regional unrest, and thus Muslim and Christian leaders agreed to keep Lebanon neutral. Lebanon did not participate in the 1948 War (except for a brief skirmish) and maintained neutrality during most of the period of Israeli-Arab conflict. That nonaligned status was limited, however. The Lebanese regime, after strident debates between Muslim and Christian factions, decided not to oppose operations by the Arab Liberation Army (ALA) from bases in Lebanon, and in May 1948, ALA members pushed south from Lebanon into the abandoned village of al-Malikiyya, which lay on the Lebanese-Palestine border.[18] They drove out elements of the Jewish Palmah, one of the volunteer forces fighting for Israeli independence. The Palmah units counterattacked and succeeded in blockading Malikiyya, until the Lebanese Army broke the blockade and recaptured the town from the Palmah units.[19] It was the Lebanese Army's only success in the 1948 War, but it was enough. The legend of Malikiyya became a backstop for the

Lebanese Army, and it endured for decades as a symbol of Lebanon's pan-Arab spirit, even though in reality Lebanon largely abstained from the 1948 War.

Lebanon eschewed the rise of Arab socialism that grew in much of the Arab world, with its state planning and state-run economies, instead maintaining a free market system, and a fairly pluralistic democracy. Consequently, Lebanon prospered, drawing funds for its increasingly powerful banks, and tourists flocked to Lebanon's beaches during the daytime and to Beirut's vibrant night life after the sun went down. The consequences for the rejection of Arab socialism meant that Lebanon did not have to later suffer the consequences of it, including the bloated bureaucracies, the inefficient state-run factories, and the maintenance of wasteful job-creation schemes. However, Lebanon's dynamic style of capitalism also pushed the boundaries of income inequality and maintained the power of the leading commercial families, perpetuating their claim to the dominance of Lebanon's political spaces.

LEBANON'S NASCENT POLITICAL SYSTEM FORMS

In September 1943, Bishara al-Khoury, one of the architects of the National Pact, became Lebanon's first postindependence president. He entered office with strong nationalist credentials, having been jailed by French officials for opposing the French Mandate. His administration presided over economic growth, but charges of corruption, including favoritism for family members, dogged his rule, and in September 1952 the presidency shifted to Camille Chamoun. Chamoun was unabashedly pro-Western, believing that Lebanon's future lay with closer ties to Europe and the United States. However, Chamoun found that his preferences for the West and strong Maronite influence in national politics was getting in the way of the more traditional role of neutrality played by the Lebanese president. As Michael C. Hudson described the situation, the president "is not only the balancer but a representative of the most influential group in the country. There is therefore a danger that a president will act as though he were the Maronite patriarch. President Chamoun played such a role in 1958."[20] Thus Chamoun found himself backing into the buzz saw of Arab nationalism that had first kindled decades before, but was energized by the continuing influence of the West in the Middle East as the Cold War increasingly pulled both the West and the Soviet Union into Middle East affairs.

ARAB NATIONALISM BECKONS

In 1958, Egyptian president Gamal Abdul Nasser expanded his vision of Arab nationalism by creating the United Arab Republic, bringing Syria and Egypt together in what he hoped was the first step in a united Arab nation. The marriage did not last long, though, as Syrian leaders increasingly discovered Nasserite officers gaining influence in Syria and broke off the union in 1961. When Nasser nationalized the Suez Canal in 1956, provoking war with Britain, France, and Israel, President Chamoun refused to support the operation and maintained ties with the two European countries, compounding the anger among Lebanon's Muslim leaders for Chamoun's support of the pro-West Baghdad Pact the year before.[21] As Nasser reached out to Lebanon, insurrection broke out against the Chamoun government, led by Kamel Jumblatt (father of current Druze leader Walid Jumblatt) and Saeb Salam (a Sunni Muslim and former and future prime minister), prompting Chamoun to request American peace-keepers. Given the instability in nearby Iraq, with the Saudi Arabian monarchy of King Faisal overthrown in a bloody coup that seemed to have Soviet hands on it, President Dwight D. Eisenhower dispatched U.S. Marines, who waded ashore in July 1958, surprising the sunbathers on Beirut's beaches. U.S. Army troops later joined the Marines, and the force grew to almost 20,000 personnel. President Eisenhower also dispatched Ambassador Robert Murphy to Lebanon, who ultimately persuaded Chamoun to resign, thus ending the crisis, though American fears of the spread of a Soviet-inspired Marxist revolution from Iraq were never justified by events, because the conflict, as most in Lebanon, revolved largely around Lebanese issues.

THE PALESTINIAN ISSUE GROWS

One consequence of Arab nationalism in Lebanon was tepid support for Lebanon's refugee Palestinian population, elements of which began to organize against Israel following the creation of the Palestinian Liberation Organization by the Arab League in the 1960s. Palestinians of different factions launched sporadic border raids south into Israel from their refugee camps, and while such raids got some sympathy support from Lebanese across the religious spectrum, that support waned when Israeli forces retaliated against both Palestinian and Lebanese sites, including a commando operation against Beirut International Airport in December 1968. Negotiations between the Lebanese government, representatives of Lebanese Palestinians, and the Egyptian government brokered the Cairo Agreement in November 1969 to regulate Palestinian operations both inside and outside of Lebanon, but adherence by all sides was problematic. The situation would only grow worse because of events in Jordan, as noted below.

FOUAD CHEHAB AND THE 1958 CRISIS

Fouad Chehab took office at a critical time for Lebanon, serving as president between 1958 and 1970. A former commander of the Lebanese military, Chehab had briefly served as prime minister in the crisis of 1952. His predecessor, Camille Chamoun, saw his presidency tattered by the events of 1958, and

Chehab succeeded him, carrying considerable good will into the office from Muslims and Christians alike. Chehab is best known for his efforts to reform Lebanese political and administrative institutions, making them more efficient and available to ordinary Lebanese. Khazen describes the period well:

> The heyday of Chehabism was during Chehab's six-year presidential term. This is when comprehensive administrative reforms were introduced and the process of institution-building was initiated. That Chehab was the quintessential professional military man and the most reform-minded leader in Lebanon was no mere coincidence. The process of balancing state authority and reform was the key element behind the success of the Chehab regime. A minimal dose of authoritarianism was inevitable in the process, something that Lebanese politicians were not used to tolerating.[22]

Indeed it was the very resistance to the Chehab way of rule that empowered his opposition, and by 1970 he believed that he had knighted his chosen successor, Elias Sarkis, but Sarkis lost by one parliamentary vote to Suleiman Frangieh, who rapidly found his way back to the old way of doing things in Lebanese politics.

In the summer of 1970, events in Jordan spilled over into Lebanon, when the Palestinian Liberation Organization (PLO) launched operations that threatened the survival of the Jordanian Hashemite monarchy, culminating in the takeover of the industrial city of Irbil. The Jordanian military responded with force, killing thousands, and, after several failed cease-fires, evicted the remainder of the PLO from Jordan in mid-1971. Most PLO members and their families crossed into Lebanon, moving into the southern border area next to the Israeli border. They entered into an uneasy relationship with the largely Shi'a population who lived there. Some long-time residents were startled to find that the Palestinians quickly penetrated the economic life of the region, infiltrating the illegal trade in particular. They took over gold and drug smuggling routes inside of Lebanon and often set up roadblocks along rural roads, charging motorists to pass through. Some PLO members also launched raids into southern Israel, drawing Israeli retaliation, which started in 1973 with targeted assassinations of Palestinian leaders in Lebanon and escalated from that point. The Shi'a population who were often hit in these raids compounded their anger over them with the dismay over Palestinian takeovers of the local economy, and clashes between the Shi'a and the Palestinians became more frequent.

THE LEBANESE CIVIL WAR

On April 13, 1975, a group of Christian militiamen killed four members of the rival Christian Phalangist militia during an assassination attempt on former President Pierre Gemayel. In the mistaken belief that the attackers were Palestinians, Phalangist gunmen retaliated by shooting up a bus containing 26 Palestinians. The fighting, kindled by decades of smoldering resentment between Christians and Muslims, quickly escalated. Soon images of blasted buildings and bloody bodies filled the world's television screens as the violence became both more frequent and more complicated. Short-lived cease-fires came about largely as a means of allowing the various militias to rearm and reequip their forces for the next round of shooting. The armament itself got heavier and deadlier with each round. Militia members fired truck-mounted multiple-barreled antiaircraft guns against buildings and rival fighters, and the shabbily constructed apartment buildings in Beirut crumbled under their shells. As rubble piled up in the streets, all public services stopped. Police and fire protection disappeared, and armed militia fighters took over their jobs. Medical care consisted of stretcher-bearers with a bloodstained victim on their stretchers dashing toward minivans pressed into service as ambulances. Garbage piled high on the streets, providing ready-made material for barricades. Civilians unfortunate enough to live in the neighborhoods punctuated by fighting were reduced to living like prisoners in their basements. The apocalyptic nature of the situation was evidenced by a militia vehicle speeding down a Beirut highway dragging a dead enemy body behind, with the passengers casually waving to a rival militia vehicle coming the other way, also with a body bouncing along behind it. None of the passing motorists paid either vehicle any attention.

The kindling for the war's fires came from the simmering tensions between the various religious factions, made more combustible by the influx of Palestinians, by frequent Israeli raids, and by Lebanon's political structure. The internal situation between the Maronite and Palestinian factions alone was an explosive force, as Khalaf holds,

> The two major combatants—the Christian Phalange and their allies and the Palestinians and the Muslim-left coalition—behaved as if their very existence was at stake. Little wonder that the fighting quickly descended into the abyss of a zero-sum deadly rivalry, where the perceived victory of one group can be realized only by annihilating the other.[23]

The chameleon-like nature of Lebanon's many political parties also contributed to the agony. As Khazen comments,

> Most (Lebanese) parties were predisposed politically and ideologically to transform themselves into militia forces in crisis situations linked to regional turmoil . . . On the eve of the war in 1975, all active parties—with the exception of the National Bloc Party led by Raymond Eddé—acquired weapons and party members underwent military training as part of the military mobilization that culminated in war.[24]

Khazen also notes that as the war continued, the parties became increasingly dependent on external support, drawing even more fuel into the conflict and often fragmenting militias who shared the same faith but drew on different patrons. This only increased the intensity of the war.[25]

A year after the conflict started, Syria made its first effort to intervene in the civil war. Hoping for a stalemate in the fighting, the Syrians advanced a proposal for general political reform. But in order to even discuss reform, the conflict had to abate. However, new combustible material was added to the fire when the

Lebanese Army virtually fell apart, and many of its members joined a militia group called the Lebanese Arab Army. They attacked parts of Christian Beirut and forced President Suleiman Frangieh to flee to the Shouf region. In response, Syrian forces intervened directly against the Lebanese National Movement, but took heavy casualties before withdrawing from the struggle. However, the withdrawal did not dampen Syrian ambitions for Lebanon. Syria wanted a pro-Syrian government in Lebanon, dominance over the PLO, and Arab recognition of Syria's paramount role in Lebanese politics.[26] The Israelis themselves also intervened in south Lebanon in 1976, moving forces up to the Litani River before turning the area over to the South Lebanon Army.

When President Frangieh's term expired in September 1976, the Chamber of Deputies elected Elias Sarkis to replace him. Sarkis had ties to Syria and to Syria's attempt to impose its own solution to Lebanon's civil war. Thus the Druze under Kemal Jumblatt opposed Sarkis for just this reason, because Jumblatt feared that a Syrian-imposed peace would lead to Syrian domination of Lebanese politics. He had reason for his concerns.

Earlier, in May, Syrian forces again took on the Lebanese National Movement and this time almost crushed it. The move allowed the opportunity for a peace effort, and thus Syria joined an Arab-led peace conference in Riyadh, Saudi Arabia, in October 1976. The Arab League also held a conference on Lebanon in October to try to build a consensus for stopping the bloodshed. That conference agreed to dispatch an Arab Deterrent Force (ADF) to Lebanon, which arrived in Lebanon in January 1977. Despite the name, the real power in the force was Syria, which contributed 27,000 of the 30,000-person force. The Syrians were effective peace enforcers, setting up checkpoints on the so-called "Green Line" dividing Muslim and Christian neighborhoods in Beirut. They did not hesitate to use force against those trying to cross the checkpoints, and they fanned out into local areas searching for violators. Most importantly, Syria became a greater political force in Lebanese politics through its actions.

ADF forces stayed out of the southern part of Lebanon, which remained home to Palestinian refugee groups. Several Palestinian factions established bases in south Lebanon from which they launched guerrilla raids into Israel. In March 1978, around 25,000 Israeli troops drove into the area in retaliation for a bus attack by Palestinians in Tel Aviv in March 1978. The Israelis rolled up to the Litani River and remained there for three months before returning the area to Major Saad Haddad, a renegade Lebanese Army officer of Greek Catholic origin, who left (or was thrown out of) the Lebanese military and started the South Lebanon Army (SLA). The invasion caused over 1,000 deaths, mostly Shi'a. The invasion helped to empower the Shi'a group Amal, which formed militia to help protect against both the Israelis and the Palestinian *fida'iyin*, or guerrilla fighters.[27] Relations between the Palestinians and the Shi'a followers of Amal were reflected in a comment by one Shi'a villager, "We gave the Palestinians everything and they give us back insults, corpses, and a lesson in corruption."[28] Anger between Lebanese citizens and the PLO in particular escalated, and the Lebanese Army began large-scale operations against Palestinian bases in 1973; however, without Lebanese Muslim support for the army, Frangieh was powerless to really weaken the PLO as Jordan had done, further setting the stage for the civil war that would follow.

The United Nations Security Council responded by authorizing the United Nations Interim Force in Lebanon (UNIFIL) to help stabilize south Lebanon, but that force was unable to bring about agreements among the various factions there.[29] Intense fighting continued among Palestinians, Christians, and several Shi'a militias. PLO militants also used the region to lob shells and rockets into northern Israel, setting the stage for another Israeli intervention in 1982.

In Beirut, the situation deteriorated when the ADF fought both the Lebanese Army and the Christian population, culminating in a massive shelling of the Christian part of the capital. Sarkis resigned in protest, but soon returned to the palace, now unable to control his Syrian occupiers. Twice, in 1980 and again in 1981, Syria acted to curb the actions of the Christian Phalange Party, now headed by Bashir Gemayel. These actions, south of Beirut, alarmed the Israelis, who feared the loss of the Phalange would strengthen Syria's position in Lebanon. Israeli aircraft downed two Syrian helicopters, prompting Syria to introduce antiaircraft missiles into Lebanon, further escalating the crisis.

Israel decided to seek support from the South Lebanon Army. For the Israelis, the purpose of the SLA was to keep Palestinian terrorists away from the Israeli border, although for Hadad it was a source of power and resources as he took on the role of a *za'im*. While the SLA continued to fight with other militias in south Lebanon, Hadad also avoided fights that might bleed off his supplies and potentially weaken his position. Clashes continued between the Shi'a Amal militia and the militant wing of the PLO, Fatah. The Christian militias also intensified their infighting, with the Gemayel Phalangist militia gaining the upper hand in July 1980 over the rival Chamoun militia.

The Battlefield Expands: Israel and Syria Fight in Lebanon

The Palestinians' new base in Lebanon was bound to draw the attention of Israel. For Israel, Lebanon had become a base for both Palestinian guerrilla groups and for the Syrian military. While Israel viewed it as a tacit alliance between the Palestinian PLO and Syria, the facts on the ground were quite different. Syria's president, Hafiz al-Asad, had maintained an uneasy peace with Lebanon's Christian community, and after the eruption of the Lebanese civil war in April 1975 (though its actual beginning is difficult to trace), Syria found that the loose federation of Muslim forces was gaining ground over the Maronite Christian coalition, and in June 1976, Asad dispatched Syrian forces to aid the

Maronites. Syrian armored units moved into the Beqaa Valley and Tripoli, encountering stiff resistance that effectively halted the Syrian drives. Syrian reinforcements arrived and gradually secured the Beirut-Damascus highway, giving Syria a base of operations and a supply line.[30] Syrian forces then moved against the coastal city of Sidon, which would give them access to the coastal roads leading to Beirut. They subdued the city after taking heavy casualties and then moved on to Beirut in October. They could not entirely pacify the city, but Syria still gained positions in Lebanon that would enable them to exercise some political influence in later years.

Syrian ploys divided the Maronite communities, with some families choosing to support Syria, particularly the Frangieh family. When the rival Gemayel family suffered an assassination of a member by someone they believed was sent by the Frangiehs, they dispatched Samir Geagea and his militia to take revenge, which resulted in the death of Tony Frangieh in 1978. Geagea, wounded in the attack, would later use its legendary status to climb to power at the head of his Lebanese Forces militia. The blood feuds between Maronite families often led to both bitter tit-for-tat violence, but also alliances with non-Maronite groups, including Muslim factions, in order to gain power in interfamily Maronite disputes. Israel was hardly a disinterested spectator in this expanded drama. Israel, too, had supported the Maronites, hoping, among other things, that Maronite forces would limit the Palestinian's ability to strike into Israel from Lebanon. Israeli forces periodically struck into Lebanon to hit Palestinian targets, and Israel funneled arms and other supplies to the Maronites.

Israel's activity in Lebanon expanded in 1978, following a PLO Fatah attack from Lebanon that landed on an Israeli beach and hijacked a civilian bus, resulting in 6 Palestinian and 34 Israeli deaths. Israel countered by sending over 20,000 troops into Lebanon in an operation that drove most non-Maronite civilians from areas in south Lebanon. Those who remained were caught in a strip of land occupied periodically by the SLA, Amal, and the UNIFIL peace-keepers, who joined the unarmed observers from the original United Nations Truce Supervision Organization, sent to Lebanon in 1948 to monitor the truce lines from the 1948 war. The UNIFIL troops, who were initially to be deployed for a six-month period, wound up remaining for years. As a result of their presence, some villages in the area prospered from 4,500 UN troops spending money for food and other goods, as soldiers came from the Republic of Ghana, Ireland, Norway, and India, among other places. They remained so long that the villagers of Qantara learned some passable Finnish from the peace-keepers nearby.[31]

The border between Israel and Lebanon remained tense as Palestinian guerrillas took advantage of Lebanon's inability to police its southern area. They fired rockets into Israeli villages and towns in northern Galilee, slipped through border defenses to shoot settlers, and, in one bold move, infiltrated silently at night in a hang glider. PLO guns in south Lebanon shelled the northern Galilee area, and in July 1981, Israeli warplanes responded by bombing PLO buildings in Beirut, killing over 300 PLO members and adjacent civilians. As PLO provocations continued, Israeli warplanes bombed the PLO headquarters in Beirut, killing over 300 people. The next year, responding to a land mine attack that killed an Israeli officer, Israeli jets struck Damour on the Lebanese coast, killing 23. Israel apparently hoped that its strategy of disproportionate retaliation for PLO attacks (often killing 10 or sometimes 100 for every 1 Israeli killed) would deter PLO attacks against Israeli targets. But the violence continued, though not always from the PLO.

THE 1982 ISRAELI INVASION

In a sense, the June 1982 Israeli invasion of Lebanon was an escalation of previous conflict, which was only briefly and ineffectively interrupted by peace efforts. In early June 1983, an assailant belonging to the violent Abu Nidal group (a Palestinian terrorist organization opposed by the PLO) shot and wounded Israel's ambassador to Great Britain, Shlomo Argov.[32] Though Israeli leaders knew that the PLO was not responsible for the assassination attempt, they had their justification for an all-out military operation into Lebanon.[33]

For Zeev Maoz, the PLO was exercising restraint on the Lebanese-Israeli border, and the Israeli operations into Lebanon came at the behest of Minister of Defense Ariel Sharon and Prime Minister Menachim Begin.[34] In early June 1982, Israeli forces streamed across the Lebanese border and quickly drove north toward Beirut, even after U.S. President Ronald Reagan pleaded with Begin to limit the conflict. Israel stated that its goals were just to clear a security zone to put Israeli settlements out of the range of Palestinian artillery. Both Syria and Israel attempted to avoid military contact in Lebanon, given the bloody conflicts of the past. Syria kept its forces in northern Lebanon, but the Israeli forces rapidly moved north. Syria began to move forces south, and the United States demanded an immediate cease-fire. However, U.S. officials claimed to have limited leverage to pressure Israel. The UN peacekeeping force in south Lebanon could not block the Israeli move northward. Israeli and Syrian pilots clashed the next day, in an air battle where the Israelis shot down 82 Syrian aircraft with no losses to their own forces. That prompted Hafiz al-Asad to ask for Soviet assistance in evicting the Israelis from Lebanon, and Soviet leader Leonid Brezhnev in turn contacted President Reagan to demand that the United States do everything in its power to stop the Israeli operation. In July, Israeli forces entered the suburbs of Beirut and destroyed much of the western part of the city with both air and artillery attacks. In August, the parties achieved a cease-fire, and PLO units agreed to evacuate Beirut.

Partially out of concern over greater Soviet involvement in the defense of Syria, the United States and France sent in peacekeeping forces in August 1982. They were withdrawn after a brief period in September, with assurances that the Israelis, too, would withdraw. President Reagan increased pressure on Israel to withdraw from the outskirts of Beirut, which they gradually began to do. Bashar Gemayel became Lebanon's president on August 21, 1982, but his tenure was short-lived. Like so many other Lebanese leaders, a bomb planted in the Phalangist headquarters in western Beirut killed Bashar and 25 others. Unlike so many other assassinations, authorities arrested a culprit, Habib Tanios Shartouni, a Maronite Christian sympathetic to the Syrian Socialist National Party. His collaborators fled to Syria, and thus Bashar Gemayel's supporters widely blamed Syria for the murder. This was the second assassination effort against Bashar Gemayel; a 1980 attempt on his life with a bomb killed his daughter instead. For Syria, the assassination made sense given Bashar's support for the Israeli invasion, and his death ended the façade of Lebanese support for the Israeli operation.[35] Supporters of Gemayel apparently believed that the Palestinians were responsible for killing him and carried out the massacre of civilian Palestinian refugees in two camps, Shatila and Sabra, in late September. Ariel Sharon had directed Israeli forces to surround the Sabra and Shatila camps and allowed Phalangist and South Lebanon Army militia soldiers to enter the camps, allegedly to hunt for terrorists. Instead, the militia members massacred the mostly women and children residents of the camps, killing somewhere between 300 and over 3,000 civilians in their squalid camp setting.

The attack triggered a horrified response in both the United States and France, with both countries ordering the return of their peacekeeping forces to Lebanon, after they initially departed following the evacuation of the PLO from Beirut. Small contingent British and Italian forces joined them. The United States established its base around the Beirut airport and engaged in limited Marine patrols. However, danger was never far away. In April, a bomb destroyed much of the U.S. embassy, killing 63 people, including 17 Americans. On October 23, a truck bomb with around 2,000 pounds of high explosives rammed the U.S. Marine barracks, killing 241 troops. It was the worst loss of life for the U.S. Marine Corps in a single day since the Pacific campaigns of World War II. At almost the same moment, another bomber attacked French headquarters, and 59 French soldiers died in the rubble. In November Israeli troops were also bombed, with a loss of 30. Those attacks paved the way for a complete withdrawal of French and American peace-keepers and Israeli withdrawal to the so-called and self-proclaimed "Security Zone" in south Lebanon, where they remained until June 2000, when Prime Minister Ehud Barak withdrew them.

In response to outrage both inside and outside of Israel over the Sabra and Shatila massacres, the Israeli foreign ministry commissioned a study, the Kahan Commission, whose report minced few words on Israeli responsibility:

In our view, everyone who had anything to do with events in Lebanon should have felt apprehension about a massacre in the camps, if armed Phalangist forces were to be moved into them without the I.D.F. (Israeli Defense Force) exercising concrete and effective supervision and scrutiny of them. All those concerned were well aware that combat morality among the various combatant groups in Lebanon differs from the norm in the I.D.F. that the combatants in Lebanon belittle the value of human life far.[36]

The Kahan Commission also found several high-ranking Israel Defense Forces (IDF) officers culpable for the actions at Sabra and Shatila and recommended the firing of Defense Minister Ariel Sharon, who did step down after over 300,000 Israelis took the to streets of Tel Aviv to demand his dismissal in February 1983. Sharon would resurrect his political career in 2000 when his Likud Party won enough votes in a national election to elevate him to the prime ministership. However, the stain of Sabra-Shatila was so great that it cost Israeli public support for an active role for Israel forces in Lebanon, although Prime Minister Ehud Barak did not withdraw all Israeli soldiers from southern Lebanon until May 2000. The decision did put Israel in compliance with UN Resolution 425, which called for the withdrawal of all foreign forces from Lebanon, and it also withdrew Syria's excuse for leaving its own forces in Lebanon, though those elements would remain in Lebanon for another four years.

THE AMERICAN DILEMMAS

The wake of the 1983 Israeli invasion had extensive consequences. As the PLO left, Amal and Druze militia fighters overran western Beirut, and the U.S. ability to shape events collapsed as the Lebanese Army proved to be powerless to prevent the takeover, dissolving as militia power rose.[37] The U.S. and the other multinational peacekeeping forces encamped outside of Beirut, while American leadership did not join France and Israel in carrying out retaliatory strikes against those believed responsible for the bombings against multilateral and Israeli forces (then-Secretary of Defense Caspar Weinberger vetoed the recommendation for retaliation). American planes did take to the skies over Syria, but while attacking Syrian antiaircraft batteries, two American Navy planes were downed by those very batteries. The surviving members of the aircrew were captured, and after a futile show of force by stationing the American battleship USS *New Jersey* off the Lebanese coast, Syria finally released the American aviators to the Reverend Jesse Jackson after the Reagan administration's prisoner release negotiations failed. After these setbacks, congressional patience with the peacekeeping operation wore thin, and in February 1984 the last American forces left Lebanon. Unfortunately for the United States, the withdrawal appeared to justify American weakness in the face of a difficult operation, and later Osama bin Laden would use the withdrawal as a sign of the lack of American backbone, particularly in the Middle East.

The only figure who appeared to be in charge in Lebanon in the mid-1980s was Prime Minister Rafiq Hariri, who managed to mediate with the warring militias after Syrian troops initially stopped militia fighting in February 1987. Hariri, who had become very wealthy from his vast construction business, treated Lebanese politics as a business, as this quote from the Lebanese ambassador to the United States indicates, "You want to operate in this country, you have to pay, otherwise you can't come in. You have to pay Berri, Jumblatt, the Lebanese forces, everybody. Hariri couldn't come to Lebanon without paying everyone."[38]

Hariri still had to face the limits of Lebanese politics and the outside forces, though, no matter what he "paid." The militia fighting continued until Syria again exercised its influence, prompting Amin Gemayel to appoint anti-Syrian general Michel Aoun to head a six-man military government, which then attempted to crush the Druze and Shi'a militia. The resulting conflict finally drew in Saudi Arabia, which was close to Hariri, to attempt a brokerage over the fighting. It, like many other efforts, ultimately failed. At the same time, another scourge for Lebanon was growing, the taking of foreign hostages for ransom and, sometimes, murder.

HOSTAGE TAKING

One of the first hostages taken was American Terry A. Anderson, a reporter for the Associated Press, seized by terrorists in March 1985. Thomas Sutherland, a faculty member at American University of Beirut, was also abducted. The hostage taking escalated when West German officials arrested Mohammed Ali Hamadei, suspected in the 1985 hijacking of an American airliner that resulted in the death of a U.S. military person. In retaliation for the arrest, Hamadei's colleagues in Beirut seized two German nationals there. Kidnappers also accosted British citizens, and when the representative of the Archbishop of Canterbury, Terry Waite, went to Beirut to negotiate their release, he instead joined their company. As the kidnappings gained more attention, other Lebanese militias joined the fray. The Fatah Revolutionary Council, headed by Sabry al-Banna (known by his *nom de guerre* Abu Nidal, killed in Iraq after the 2003 U.S. invasion) took two hostages, later releasing them to a Sunni Muslim leader. In the end, various militant groups abducted 96 hostages from many nations, but a majority of them were Americans.

Sometimes the kidnappers were more materialistic, demanding money, as did the "Islamic Holy War" group, grabbing a French hostage and then demanding $4.5 million for his safe release. Islamic Holy War was also implicated in several passenger plane hijackings, including that of a Kuwait Airways Boeing 747 in 1988, tying the release of its passengers to the release of 17 jailed terrorists in Kuwait.

The administration of President Ronald Reagan faced growing pressure to obtain the hostages' release. He was keenly aware of how a previous hostage situation in Iran had weakened his predecessor, Jimmy Carter, and believed that he had to respond decisively or risk a weakening of his presidency. Using the analogy of former President Richard M. Nixon's opening to China, presidential national security advisor Robert McFarlane suggested that the Reagan administration consider a swap with Iran for hostages in exchange for American-made arms.[39] While the hostage takers were ostensibly Lebanese, they reflected Iranian security motives more than Lebanese desires, with Gilles Kepel describing Hezbollah's own role in the kidnappings as little more than a contract operation for Iran. Moreover, as Kepel argues,

> Hostage-taking was the bitterest aspect of the confrontations between the Islamic Republic and its enemies in the mid-1980s. It was the means whereby Tehran loosened the stranglehold imposed by the war with Iraq and the hostility of the Arab and Western states; and it served as a dire warning that any initiative taken against Iran would be followed by terrorist retaliation.[40]

Reagan's desire to go directly to Tehran got support from Israel, which was increasingly worried about the consequences of an Iraqi victory in the increasingly bloody Iran-Iraq War. Israeli leaders were particularly worried about American efforts to tilt toward Iraq (Reagan sent special envoy Donald Rumsfeld, later twice the secretary of defense, to Baghdad to meet with Saddam Hussein to discuss intelligence sharing). Realizing that the Iran-Iraq War was bleeding Iran's limited military arsenal dry and that the country particularly needed antiaircraft missiles, Israelis both in and out of government began negotiating with an Iranian arms dealer. While hoping to improve Israeli-Iranian relations (which the Iranians had no interest in), Israeli officials persuaded Reagan officials to secretly enter into negotiations for a deal that would swap hostages for military weapons that Iran needed. Some of the weapons actually came from Israel, and although they were American made, they were not only the wrong missiles, but had Stars of David on them, infuriating the Iranians and almost closing the deal.[41] Ultimately a Beirut newspaper leaked the scheme, which became the Reagan administration's biggest embarrassment, though it did lead to the release of some, if not all, American hostages in Lebanon. It was a long and slow process, with the release of Terry Anderson, the first American taken, finally coming in December 1991. Some never came back; Malcolm Kerr, a noted scholar of the Middle East and president of American University of Beirut, lost his life to two gunmen outside of his office in January 1984. Later Islamic Jihad took responsibility, apparently uncaring or unaware that they had killed a scholar who truly understood and cared about the Arab world.

UN forces remained in Lebanon, losing members to land mines and other hazards. In February 1988, Hezbollah militiamen kidnapped an American Marine officer attached to the UN mission, and later two Scandinavians and a

German engineer also were abducted, apparently by a Palestinian group. While the Scandinavians and the German were later released, the Marine lieutenant colonel, William R. Higgins, was tortured and murdered by his Hezbollah captors. His capture and subsequent death caused friction between Amal, whose forces were largely responsible for security in the area where Higgins was abducted, near the city of Tyre, and Hezbollah (who signed their kidnapping manifesto the "Organization of the Oppressed on Earth"), and Amal dismissed its chief of security for the region as a consequence, while rounding up 45 Hezbollah members for questioning.

Lebanon's fragile political system weakened further as the violence continued. In September 1988, President Amin Gemayel, faced with a parliamentary logjam after firing Prime Minister Selim Hoss, appointed General Michel Aoun to the post, even though Aoun was a Maronite Christian filling a Sunni post.[42] Aoun named a military cabinet, selecting officers from the major religious groups, though not all agreed to serve. Aoun tried to cement his power by moving Lebanese military forces to take over ports under control of the Lebanese Forces, then allied with Syria. In March 1989, Aoun declared a war of liberation against Syria, putting him at odds with President Rene Muawad (who was assassinated in November of that year), and then with newly elected president Elias Hrawi, who dismissed Aoun, though the latter ignored the dismissal and moved into the presidential palace in Beirut.

THE TA'IF CONFERENCE AND AFTER

The civil war dragged on beyond anyone's expectation, inflicting horrendous casualties and damage, yet Lebanon's fragile political system seemed incapable of stemming it. Part of the problem was obvious: Lebanon's "civil war" had also become Syria's and Israel's civil war, and powerless Lebanon could not evict its neighbors or the groups they supported within the country. But the persistence of the conflict also had domestic explanations. As Hani A. Faris tells it, growing sectarian movements began to undermine Lebanon's power bases of local elites,

> The political elite was not suited to dealing with the issues that fueled the 1975 crisis. Traditionally, this elite had played a key role in settling differences. It had helped mitigate incipient conflicts by venting sectarian frustration and demands (without undermining the sectarian system), by providing services to citizens (bypassing bureaucratic rigidity), and by channeling government benefits to followers and regions . . . . By the late 1960s and early 1970s, however, a process of rapid social change in Lebanon was undermining the elite's role. As a nondoctrineaire group, its members were ill-equipped to counter the effects that spread in a dramatic fashion throughout the Arab world following the 1967 Arab defeat. The activities of these movements led to the maturation of a new, multireligious, secular, alienated, and activist counterelite, opposed to Lebanon's political arrangements, but debarred from participation in the formal system.[43]

In September 1989, Saudi Arabia brokered talks between the warring factions in Lebanon, who decided that it was too dangerous to meet in Lebanon, choosing instead to meet in the Saudi Arabian mountain city of Ta'if. Saudi Arabia had its own motives for organizing and hosting the Ta'if Conference: it had a reputation to preserve as internal peacemaker within the Arab League states, and it wanted to serve as a counterweight to Syrian influence, since Syria was an ideological rival to Saudi Arabia.[44] At Ta'if, Saudi Arabian King Fahd ibn Abdul-Aziz al-Saud managed to get the 62 delegates, half Christian and half Muslim, to agree on a formula to end the bloody civil war and to formulate a program to achieve a more stable political system following a cease-fire. The plan also called for the withdrawal of all foreign forces from Lebanon, thereby reducing one of the numerous sources of conflict (see Appendix C for the Ta'if Accord).

Ta'if had several long-lasting impacts for Lebanon. It brought an end to the seemingly irresolvable civil war, though it left many of its root causes in place. It readdressed the Christian-Muslim ratio in parliament from 6:5, making it even. Ta'if supposedly disarmed the militias, which were responsible for most of the violence, though there was an important exception. Hezbollah claimed that its arms served the defense of Lebanon against outsiders (specifically the Israelis) and refused to give up its weapons, which would be used not only against Israel in 2006 but also against rival militias in the spring of 2008. Ta'if also had its disappointments: neither Syria nor Israel agreed to withdraw forces from Lebanon, as Ta'if required, though the United States and other parties chose to look the other way instead of attempting to engineer an Israeli and Syrian departure. Thus Ta'if in a backwards way institutionalized the Syrian presence, seen by some as a U.S. reward for Syria's limited participation in the 1990–1991 war against Saddam Hussein after his invasion of Kuwait. The South Lebanon Army also refused orders to disband.

The leaders of the post-Ta'if period shaped political reconstruction to minimize the chances of civil war–era disunity reerupting. Thus the first two governments headed by Salim al-Hoss and Omar Karami (1989–1992) included only the representatives of groups that supported Ta'if, thus excluding those such as the followers of General Aoun who did not agree with Ta'if.[45] While helpful for domestic unity, the exclusion was a small measure that did not address the remaining issues that had fueled the civil war, including the Israeli presence and the Syrian support for Hezbollah.

Ta'if did not end all of Lebanon's political violence, though. In November, barely a month after Ta'if, assassins killed President-elect Rene Muawwad before he had a chance to take office, and Elias Hariri replaced him. Selim al-Hoss became prime minister and General Emile Lahoud replaced General Aoun as commander in chief of the army. The army itself, relegated to an almost observer status during the civil war, began to assert itself as an internal policing force. In July 1991, the Lebanese armed forces attacked Palestinian fighters guarding

PLO refugee camps near Sidon, committing 6,000 soldiers and 35 tanks to the operation. The Hariri government wanted to control the Palestinians in southern Lebanon to avoid further provocations and persuade Israel, with its own forces there, to withdraw. Israel compounded the problem by exiling Palestinians arrested in the first Palestinian uprising (*intifada*) in the Occupied Territories to south Lebanon. In some cases, despite the tensions between Palestinians and the Shi'a, Hezbollah indoctrinated some of the Palestinians in resistance tactics, in what some Lebanese referred to as "Hezbollah University." As Augustus Richard Norton noted, some of these Palestinians were eventually allowed to return to Israel, but the ties between them and Hezbollah continued, at Israel's considerable expense.[46]

Not only did the Israeli presence in Lebanon remain, but Israel raised the political temperature higher when its helicopter gunships assassinated Hezbollah Secretary-General Abbas al-Musawi in February 1992. A month later, unknown assailants bombed the Israeli embassy in Buenos Aires, Argentina, killing 29 people, with suspicion falling on Hezbollah. Syria suddenly had an opportunity fall its way when Saddam Hussein invaded Iraq, and both the United States and some prominent Arab countries called upon Syria to contribute forces. Though those forces did not engage in much combat against Iraqi forces, Syria's new relationship with the United States emboldened Syrian leadership, and Syrian air attacks drove Michel Aoun out of his palace and into exile in France in October 1990.

REBUILDING BEIRUT

The civil war badly damaged Beirut, once a significant center of commerce in the Middle East. The city's 1975 population of 3 million dropped to 300,000 by 1992 as Beirut's residents either fled to other parts of Lebanon or left the country altogether. The city had been an economic bridge between Europe and the Middle East, but its commercial elite moved their businesses either to Cyprus or to the Arab Gulf states, taking their capital and their overseas connections with them. Those who remained suffered from a lack of electricity, health care, sanitation, or communications, conditions that also destroyed Beirut's once-thriving tourist industry.[47] Many of Beirut's famous hotels had become formless piles of rubble, uncollected garbage provided breeding grounds for disease, and the education system was badly damaged, thus threatening to deprive the capital of a generation of educated citizens.

In October 1992, Rafiq al-Hariri became the prime minister. Hariri was a self-made business leader who had made a fortune in the construction industry; after assuming his office, he launched the rebuilding program that ultimately turned Beirut from piles of rubble to a modern city again, though the task was not completed by the time of his assassination. Hariri committed both his own funds along with funds he raised in other Arab countries (Saudi Arabia was a large investor), and Beirut began its rise from the ashes of war with new lime-stone buildings, broad streets, and rebuilt infrastructure.

HARIRI FACES ISRAEL

Hariri faced yet another challenge from Israel, which launched "Operation Accountability" in July 1993, following attacks carried out by both the Popular Front for the Liberation of Palestine and Hezbollah. Israel specifically targeted villages in the largely Shi'a area, hoping to turn the citizens against Hezbollah, but the villagers fled the aerial and naval bombardment and the United States brokered a fragile cease-fire. The attacks continued from both sides of the border, and ultimately Israeli forces launched another cross-border operation, labeled "Operation Grapes of Wrath," in April 1996. The timing of the operations coincided with an Israeli election in which acting Prime Minister Shimon Peres (replacing Yitzak Rabin, assassinated by a right-wing Israeli in November 1995), faced a serious challenge from Likud Party head Benjamin Netanyahu. "Grapes of Wrath" went terribly awry, though, and Israeli fire targeted a UN refugee camp, killing hundreds (the number is disputed) of Lebanese civilians. Once again, a delicate cease-fire went into place, though both sides violated it.

In November 1998, Emile Lahoud, commander of the Lebanese Army, became president, succeeding Elias al-Hrawi. This placed two strong rivals in critical political positions. As Talal Nizameddin noted, "Hariri as Prime Minister and Lahoud as President spent the four years from 2000 to 2004 in a state of perpetual conflict, leading to a failure to formulate significant economic and social policies or undertake urgently needed reforms."[48] While Hariri would pour billions of his own money into reconstruction, the political logjam between the prime minister and the president prevented any of the reform efforts envisioned at Ta'if.

ISRAEL WITHDRAWS FROM SOUTH LEBANON

In the spring of 1996, Israel held elections after the apparent backfire of "Operation Peace for Galilee" and the consequences of four Palestinian-inflicted suicide bombings in Israel that March. Benjamin Netanyahu's Likud Party won the election, though it got fewer seats in the Knesset than did the Labor Party (this was the result of an Israeli experiment with direct elections of the prime minister, since abandoned). The new prime minister formed a narrow coalition of rightist parties to take control of the government.

The new prime minister continued the confrontation in south Lebanon, with repeated Israeli raids on suspected Hezbollah targets. Netanyahu also had to consider a Lebanon withdrawal plan left by Rabin, and endorsed by the United States and France, and an offer by Hezbollah leader Hassan Nasrallah to avoid targeting Galilee from south Lebanon. But Netanyahu and his cabinet apparently worried that Syria, still seen as Israel's most significant opponent, might arm other enemies of Israel to operate against the Jewish state. Netanyahu also dismissed Hizbollah's promise of a pacific border:

> I think the great majority of Israelis feel, as I do and as most of the ministers in my government do, that a unilateral withdrawal from Lebanon would simply bring the *Hizbullah* terrorists right up to the Israeli-Lebanese fence, right up to the border, from which they'll simply attack deeper into Israel. And that is where we were actually not 10 years ago but closer to 20 years ago.[49]

As Israeli casualties mounted and as even the hawkish Ariel Sharon argued that Israel should evacuate south Lebanon, the words "Israel's Vietnam" got currency beyond Israel's political left. Lebanon's defense minister issued reassurances that Lebanon's army would police the border if Israel pulled out. Israeli casualties mounted in the area, with seven IDF soldiers killed in a two-week period in February 2000 by Hezbollah gunners, who seemed undeterred by punishing Israeli air strikes on villages where the gunfire originated. The Likud Party was split on the issue of Lebanese withdrawal and thus was unable to articulate a party position. A movement known as "Four Mothers," whose members had lost sons in Lebanon, began to mobilize for an Israeli withdrawal. And, according to a Hezbollah official interview in 2009, that organization stepped up its attacks on Israeli positions, striking and destroying the village of Aramta in April 1999, thus hastening Israel's withdrawal by several months while inflicting a humiliating defeat on Israel's forces.[50]

Pressure for a pullout mounted until Prime Minister Barak removed Israeli forces in May 2000 after setting July of that year as the deadline. The Foreign Ministry tried to put the best face on the decision:

> The withdrawal was the result of our recognition that the "security zone" concept was no longer effective or necessary, and that other means may now be available to secure Israel's northern border. We would have preferred to carry out the withdrawal in agreement with Lebanon. However, this option was not available, due to pressure brought to bear against Lebanon by external parties. We therefore chose to carry out the withdrawal unilaterally. By withdrawing from Lebanon, Israel removes any alleged "legitimacy" for continued terrorist attacks against the "occupier's" soldiers and civilians, strengthening Israel's position in its efforts to bring peace to its northern border. Israel is in essence regaining the initiative and redefining the parameters of its actions. No longer can terrorists wreak havoc and spread violence under the doubtful banner of "Lebanese liberation."[51]

The Israeli military disagreed with the withdrawal from south Lebanon, fearing that it would only embolden both the PLO and Hezbollah. IDF Chief of Staff Shaul Mofaz had earlier persuaded Netanyahu to remain in Lebanon after the prime minister had first proposed withdrawal, but Barak issued the withdrawal command anyway. Mofaz simply stated that the IDF "does not choose its own missions," and while the military argued that its obedience proved that the IDF complied with political leadership, others in the military argued that the withdrawal would allow the Israeli armed forces to blame that very same political leadership if anything went wrong in Lebanon.[52]

As Israeli forces departed south Lebanon, they took most of the SLA members with them. An Israeli Foreign Ministry official statement read as follows:

- Israel is morally and politically committed to the safety and security of the soldiers of the South Lebanon Army (SLA) and the civil administration officials who worked alongside Israel for many years to protect the southern Lebanese population from the encroachment of terrorist organizations. This commitment forms an integral part of the Israeli government's March 5 decision to withdraw from Lebanon.
- In this context, Israel is prepared to absorb any SLA soldiers or civil officials who choose to relocate to Israel, together with their families.[53]

Around 6,500 SLA fighters and some of their families moved into northern Israel, but some gradually drifted back to Lebanon. Eight years after the withdrawal, only 2,700 remained, perhaps fearful that they would face an uncertain welcome in Lebanon. Reports surfaced that some returning SLA members faced retribution for their deeds while collaborating with Israel, and others feared that Hezbollah, which gained power in the areas where the SLA members came from, would punish them should they return, though Hezbollah claimed to have forgiven them.[54]

In 2004, the United Nations Security Council resolved, through the passage of UN Resolution 1559 in September, that all of Lebanon's militias should disarm, to avoid the specter of another bloody internal conflict. However, Hezbollah argued that its stock of arms was intended to protect Lebanon from Israel, an unsurprising argument given that Hezbollah took credit for the removal of Israeli forces from southern Lebanon in 2000. But Hezbollah not only retained its weapons, supplies flowed from Iran into Syria and then into Lebanon to restock it, so that by 2006, Hezbollah had a considerable supply of weapons. Resolution 1559 also called for the withdrawal of all foreign forces from Lebanon, a measure clearly aimed at both Syria and Israel. Syria reacted in both direct and, some suspect, indirect ways to continue its influence. The direct method was to continue the presence of Syrian troops and intelligence agents in Lebanon. Indirectly, Syria decided to extend the presidential term of Emile Lahoud, which served to unite most of the anti-Syrian forces, including most Christian, Sunni, and Druze political actors. Walid Jumblatt took his Druze parliamentary bloc into the camp of the opposition, and Christian opposition formed the *Qornet Shahwan* Gathering. Lebanon's fractious political structure continued unabated.

Palestinian Cleavages

Lebanon's Palestinian communities largely kept allegiance to the Palestinian Liberation Organization's story line of nationalist emancipation, but the growing influence of Islamist identity for liberation movements arose in the 1990s in Lebanon's Palestinian camps. The Salifiyyist vision would ultimately clash in deadly struggles inside the Palestinian camps, as occurred in May 2003 when Fatah militants and members of *Usbar al-Ansar* set the seeds for a Palestinian civil war that Bernard Rougier notes, "Since the civil war ended, we can no longer speak of 'Palestinian society' in Lebanon, so deep are the rifts at both the national level and the local level of families and clans."[55] It was further evidence that Lebanon's fractured society had infected the Palestinians, one of the few groups to have once united under the banner of Palestinian nationalism.

Asad Dies

Prime Minister Hariri found himself in another quandary when Hafiz al-Asad died in June 2000. While Hariri had ties to the Syrian regime, they went through Hikmat Shihabi, the chief of staff of the Syrian military, and Vice President Abdul Halim Khaddam.[56] Shihabi retired from the military, possibly under political pressure, and moved to the United States, while the relationship between Khaddam and Bashar al-Asad, who became president after his father's death, became increasingly strained; Khaddam ultimately left Syria for Paris. Hariri had also built constructive relations with Ghazi Kanaan, Syria's intelligence director in Lebanon, whom Hariri reportedly paid a "salary" to avoid problems with Syrian politics. However, in December 2002, Bashar al-Asad relieved Kanaan, replacing him with his deputy, Rustum Ghazale.[57] Without his Syrian patrons, Hariri found it increasingly difficult to maintain his relatively good relations with Syria.[58] Bashar al-Asad also decided that his priorities should involve Syria more than Lebanon, focusing initially on some limited political and economic reform, and his interest in Lebanon lessened. Still, as rivalry grew between Lahoud and Hariri, Syrian support for Lahoud increased, and in 2002 Syria backed Saudi-born Walid ibn Talal for prime minister.[59] Hariri's rift with Syria and Lahoud grew, though Hariri bolstered his position by using his friendship with French President Jacques Chirac to draw around $4.3 billion from the November 2002 Paris II Conference in financial support for Lebanon. Syria manipulated a two-year extension of Lahoud's presidential term, a move that would trigger such anger in the opposition camps that it contributed to the massive political demonstrations that ousted the Syrian military after Hariri's assassination in 2005.

THE ASSASSINATION OF RAFIQ HARIRI

One of Lebanon's continuing political tragedies was the brutal pattern of political assassination, often by car bombing. One major figure after another from all across Lebanon's social spectrum perished in a flash of flame and smoke as a bomb detonated either in the car or placed strategically where the target was sure to pass. Hariri was aware of the danger he faced as he accumulated enemies. He constantly varied his routes to and from his office, and his limousine carried sophisticated equipment to jam radio signals to remotely controlled bombs. His concern for his own safety only grew after an assassin made an attempt on the life of Druze economic minister Marwan Hamadé in October 2004, and then a phone call warning that murderers lay in waiting for Hariri came from Khaddam on February 13. He was riding in a convoy through a Beirut neighborhood when a powerful bomb shattered Hariri's heavily protected Mercedes limousine on February 14, 2005, killing him instantly, along with 21 others, including several of his bodyguards.

The investigation that followed was clumsy, with the bomb crater flooded by broken pipes, and filled the next day, the vehicles involved taken away, and investigators trampling the site, obscuring any possible evidence.[60] These actions ignited anger in those communities that had supported Hariri, and the result was a series of spontaneous demonstrations that seemed to grow with time. Hariri was admired by Christians and Sunni Muslims alike, and his popularity, coupled with a growing anger at Syrian influence in Lebanon, finally broke the back of the government, which resigned as the Syrian forces announced a pull-back to the Beqaa Valley. Hezbollah, fearful of losing Syrian support (though Hezbollah had and would continue to also quarrel with Syria), launched counterdemonstrations, bussing in Shi'a from south Lebanon to attend. The largest Hezbollah demonstration occurred on March 8, when around one-half million people carrying both Hezbollah symbols and the cedar symbol of Lebanon massed in Beirut. The opposition topped the Hezbollah demonstration a few days later, when 1.5 million Lebanese gathered under the cedar flag on March 14, which gave rise to the term "Cedar Revolution," though the term was actually coined by U.S. Department of State official Paula Dobriansky, who may not have realized that while the cedar tree on the Lebanese flag is the national symbol, it is also the icon of Lebanon's Maronite community. The more important names came from the demonstration dates, the Hariri supporters became the "March 14 Movement," while the Hezbollah supporters took the name "March 8 Movement."

Political assassinations were common in Lebanon, but Hariri was such a high-profile victim that the United Nations became involved in the investigation, noting that virtually none of the political assassins had been indentified or arrested. In October 2005 the UN investigators, after completing their inquiries, released a report implying that Syrian officials had ordered the Hariri assassination (the executive summary of the report, known as the FitzGerald Report, is in Appendix C). The UN report specifically targeted Asef Shawkat, the brother-in-law of Bashar al-Asad, and Asad's brother Maher, suggesting that the evidence pointed to Shawkat and Maher al-Asad's meeting in December 2004 where they decided to order the Hariri killing. The report also implicated Lahoud in the assassination, but curiously did not mention Ghazi Kanaan, Hariri's one-time Syrian connection, who mysteriously committed "suicide" in Damascus on October 12, just before the publication of the UN report.[61] Yet other theories calculated that the assassination was aimed as much at Bashar al-Asad as it was Hariri. Argues David W. Lesch, "It (the assassination) also may have been a message sent to someone else: Bashar al-Asad," further arguing that Asad was the message recipient of elements in the Syrian and Lebanese security forces who did carry out the assassination, who feared that Asad was preparing to remove Syrian troops after the embarrassment of the bungled LaHood affair.[62] As of 2009, the investigation was continuing, though there was little reason to believe that the Hariri assassination, like almost all political murders before it, would end with a guilty verdict, or even solid evidence of the culprit or culprits.

The assassinations continued with the murder of Lebanese Communist Party former secretary general George Hawi in the typical fashion: a bomb blasted his Mercedes into pieces as he left his home in June 2005. The murder of Hawi, a professed atheist, indicated that even those with no religion were not immune from assassination if they opposed Syrian influence in Lebanon (though Hawi's son claimed that Israel was responsible for his father's death, according to Syrian news sources).[63]

THE 2005 ELECTIONS

The massive demonstrations that swept the government of Prime Minister Karami out of power and the Syrian military out of the country also paved the road for parliamentary elections in the summer of 2005. The elections were a partial victory for the Future Movement, Hariri's party, now led by his son Saad, which won 72 of the 128 parliamentary seats. The Druze Progressive Socialist Party of Walid Jumblatt, which had joined the anti-Syrian opposition, won 16 seats, while the opposition Resistance, Liberation and Development Party won 35 seats. The Shi'a-Hezbollah coalition gained 29 seats (15 for Amal and 14 for Hezbollah), and the Free Patriotic Stream Party, formed by Michel Aoun after his return from exile, got 14 seats.[64] The results were a fairly clear Lebanese rejection of Syrian power over their country, though Syria still had its supporters, as the election success of both Hezbollah and Aoun attested.

JUSTICE FOR HARIRI?

In August 2005, Lebanese authorities arrested four Lebanese general officers suspected in the Hariri murder, including former presidential guard chief General Mustafa Hamdan, the former head of the General Security department General Jamil Sayyed, the former head of the Internal Security Forces General Ali Hajj, and the former chief of army intelligence General Raymond Azar. If the authorities had hoped that these arrests would curb the assassination of anti-Syrian Lebanese politicians, they were mistaken: Gibran Tueni, former editor of *An-Nahar* and a member of parliament, died instantly when his armored Renault SUV was blown off the road in December. Tueni had been a bitter critic of Syria, going so far as to claim the discovery of a mass grave near Syrian intelligence headquarters in Anjar (the accusations proved to be false). Almost four years later, a Lebanese judge held that the prosecutor lacked enough evidence to charge the four Hariri suspects and ordered them to be released. The decision revealed just how deep the political divisions in Lebanon remained: in Hezbollah neighborhoods, celebratory gunfire punctuated the night, and former President LaHood sent an escort to retrieve General Hamdan, his former bodyguard, from prison. Samir Frangieh, an ally of Saad Hariri, said, "Everyone knows who these men were and what they did," and Saad Hariri himself plaintively stated, "Some Lebanese are not relieved by this decision."[65]

THE 2006 WAR WITH ISRAEL

In the spring of 2005, Hezbollah activity increased along the Israeli border, though Israeli officials traveling through the area seemed strangely dismissive of the Hezbollah threat, focusing instead on Palestinian militancy.[66] Israel also appeared to ignore the growing stridency of Hezbollah demands for the release of Hezbollah prisoners held in Israeli jails. Thus Israeli leaders were surprised when Hezbollah operatives ambushed an Israeli patrol on July 12, 2006, abducted two Israeli soldiers, and quickly defeated an Israeli patrol sent to rescue the hostages. A massive Israeli operation into Lebanon followed, with Israeli planes bombing the Beirut-Rafiq Hariri International Airport, effectively closing it, along with Hezbollah's *Al Manar* radio station, and the large housing complexes in Beirut and elsewhere believed to house Hezbollah supporters. Israeli troops streamed across the border to find Hezbollah rocket sites, as Hezbollah missiles streamed into Israel, killing dozens of Israelis in a number of towns and cities. Hezbollah rockets hit a neighborhood in Haifa, the deepest penetration of any rocket attack. Israel also launched a complete blockade against Lebanon, with Israeli naval units deployed off Lebanon's coast, while Hezbollah targeted one Israeli naval vessel with a radar-guided antiship missile, disabling it. Israel seemed surprised by Hezbollah's rocket capacity, though it had known that the organization had long-range missiles capable of striking Haifa since 2000.[67] Hizbollah rockets caused numerous forest fires in Israel, destroying over 16,000 acres of trees, while an Israeli attack on a Lebanese oil refinery caused one of the largest oil spills in Mediterranean history.

The escalation that followed the initial attack seemed to surprise both Israel and Hezbollah. William M. Arkin captures the reaction:

> Probably everything that there is to be said about the Israeli-Hezbollah war of 2006 can be traced to these first 48 hours: each side firmly believing that they were taking the action that was necessary for their security and standing; each convinced that they could control their actions, their opponent's reactions, and the effects; believing as well that they could precisely signal their intentions. The two sides implemented their "plans," suggesting deliberation and a thorough understanding of their objectives and of the enemy. Yet neither side really could anticipate how the conflict would unfold, nor did they properly assess the capabilities or actions of the other. Neither side really believed that there was ultimately a "military" solution that they could pursue to achieve victory over the other, yet they succumbed to the inexorable drag of war.[68]

What Arkin describes is exactly the "inexorable drag of war," common in so many wars, with neither side understanding the motives or fears of the other side, with both persuaded that they can dominate the escalation process to the point where the enemy throws in the war towel. Each side also appeared to believe that outside pressure would ultimately intervene to aid in its victory.

The external reaction was decidedly mixed. U.S. President George W. Bush declared the conflict to be a part of the "war on terror," saying, "Hizballah and its Iranian and Syrian sponsors have brought an unwanted war to the people of Lebanon and Israel, and millions have suffered as a result."[69] Secretary of State Condoleezza Rice described the situation thusly: "What we're seeing here, in a sense, is the growing—the birth pangs of a new Middle East,"[70] a statement that seemed highly insensitive to both the large-scale destruction and loss of life on both sides and to the global pressure on the United States to attempt a cease-fire. The Arab world was split, with the Arab League, Egypt, and Jordan condemning Hezbollah for initiating the conflict, while Yemen, Iran, and Syria denounced Israel. Saudi Arabia and the Gulf Arab states also found Hezbollah culpable, with Saudi Arabia placing a considerable portion of the blame on the Shi'a group. The negative Arab response surprised Nasrallah, who claimed that he had not anticipated the strong Israeli response to the initial soldier abduction, but he also subtly blamed the muted Arab reaction to his actions for the intensity of the Israeli military actions: "The Israeli reaction to the capture could have been harsh but limited, if it were not for the international and Arab cover."[71] He also admitted that had he known of the nature of Israel's response, "we would not have captured those soldiers."[72]

In the United Nations, Lebanon's representative pleaded for a cease-fire, but the United States, the United Kingdom, and several Arab countries delayed the vote on a cessation of violence, apparently hoping that Israeli forces could significantly weaken Hezbollah or that Lebanese casualties would turn the bulk of Lebanon's population against Hezbollah. As Hezbollah's attacks against Israel continued, and as Lebanon's public appeared to blame Israel more than Hezbollah, it became clear that this was not "the birth pangs of the modern Middle East" in Secretary

Rice's hopes. On August 11, the UN approved UN Security Council Resolution 1701, offering terms for the end of hostilities, which all parties ultimately accepted (see Appendix C for the text of UN Resolution 1701)

The cost of the 2006 war was high for Lebanon: reconstruction costs exceeded $4 billion, and 1,109 civilians are known to have died, though the number could be higher. Israel claimed to have killed between 650 and 750 Hezbollah fighters, and, again, according to Israeli sources, 43 civilians, a third of them Israeli Arabs, died from Hezbollah rockets and mortars, with almost 1,000 suffering wounds, along with considerable damage to infrastructure.[73]

The 2006 war left the political situation in Lebanon in a state of confusion and disorder. In November 2006, President Emile Lahoud's presidential term expired after the legislature extended his term for three additional years under Syrian pressure. The cabinet had to assume temporary presidential powers, but there was no single individual in charge as chief of state. The assassinations continued as well. In November 2006, assassins killed another member of the Gemayel family in the streets of Beirut. Pierre Gemayel, the minister of the interior, was a key supporter of the Fuad Siniora government, and his death was widely blamed on Syrian influences that remained in Lebanon after the 2004 withdrawal of the Syrian military.[74]

By December, rival groups had taken politics to the streets of Beirut, partly to express their dissatisfaction with the gridlock in the capital. General Aoun and his erstwhile ally, Amal, launched sit-down strikes in Beirut, hoping to embarrass the government into selecting a president. But the regime's leaders also hunkered down, barricading themselves in their offices. The Arab League attempted to intervene, but received no attention in Lebanon. The opposition groups suggested forming a parallel regime, but Moody's Corporation, an international investment rating group, implied that such a step would bankrupt the country.[75]

Another consequence of the political vacuum was the arrival of militant fighters from outside Lebanon. Insurgents arrived from Europe, Saudi Arabia, Yemen, Algeria, Syria, and elsewhere, forming radical groups such as Fatah al-Islam, Al Qaeda in Bilad al-Sham, and others, sometimes tying their groups to the larger al-Qaeda. The fighters were often Sunni and joined the mostly Sunni Palestinians in their refugee camps. Often the influx of foreign fighters ended in violence, as was the case in Tripoli in July 2007, when the Lebanese Army stormed a Fatah al-Islam stronghold, killing 12 militants and provoking a counterattack the next day in which 23 soldiers died. The bombers continued their deadly work as anti-Syrian Phalangist Party member Antoine Ghanem and six others died when an explosive turned their car into a smoldering hulk in September 2007, making him the eighth anti-Syrian leader to die in three years. As usual, Syria denied responsibility. The assassination raised fears that Syria and its allies in Lebanon were trying to reduce by murder the seats held by the anti-Syrian majority, prompting Fouad Siniora to declare, "This is a clear message to silence the voices of freedom and the revolution of independence, but the Lebanese people will not back off, and they will have a new president elected by parliament members no matter how big the conspiracy gets."[76]

Fearing that the political stalemate might rekindle a civil war, both Iran and Saudi Arabia worked behind the scene to get the Lebanese political factions back to the negotiating table. While Saudi Arabia and Iran had many issues separating them, both countries understood that a renewed conflagration in Lebanon would only spread. The agreement by both countries to seek conciliation in Lebanon surprised the United States, which worked to limit Iranian influence in Lebanon. But with Saudi Arabia and Iran working together, the United States could only sit on the sidelines.[77]

As the deadlock moved into the spring, the United States dispatched the Navy destroyer USS *Cole* toward Lebanon, along with two other ships, as the White House claimed that the move was "a show of support for regional stability," and Hezbollah denounced the action.[78] Regional tensions increased even more with the assassination of Imad Mugniyah, a senior Hezbollah official, in Damascus in February 2008. While Hezbollah accused Israel of the attack, others remembered that Mugniyah was accused of masterminding the 1982 bombing of the U.S. Marine barracks noted above. While Israel denied complicity in the Mugniyah assassination, Hezbollah still threatened to retaliate against Israeli targets, which prompted point-counterpoint charges that flew between Israel and Lebanon. Ahmad Murad warned Hezbollah, "The revenge will be rattling, and big surprises can be expected. Israel and its generals will not enjoy stability." Israel responded with vague threats to punish Lebanon for any Hezbollah acts against Israeli citizens, and Lebanese President Siniora sent a formal complaint to the UN Security Council about the Israeli threats.[79]

In early May 2008, the government overplayed its weak hand when it shut down Hezbollah's private communications network, including al-Manar television, and curbed Hezbollah's control over the Beirut-Rafiq International Airport. On May 7, Hezbollah quickly responded, sending its militia into the streets of Beirut, seizing almost all of the western part of the capital. The Lebanese Army tried to curb the violence, but was largely unsuccessful, as roadblocks sprung up to divide the city, and the fighting spread out of Beirut to the Beqaa Valley. The Sunni militia supposedly loyal to Saad Harari's "Future Movement" was withdrawn after it became clear that it was no match for Hezbollah's forces. After street violence claimed at least 29 deaths, the Lebanese Army offered to broker the conflict between Hezbollah and the government, proposing to investigate the closing of Hezbollah's communications and reinstating the Hezbollah head of the airport. The military was unable to start negotiations, distrusted by Hezbollah as an agent for the very government it was fighting, and thus the violence continued with over 80 Lebanese dying in the melee. Some Christians, still despairing of Aoun's alliance with Hezbollah, gave him credit for organizing aid for thousands of Shi'a victims of the war and of patching to a degree the historic divide between Christians and the Shi'a of Lebanon.[80]

As was the case in previous wars and disputes, Lebanon required outside assistance to broker an end to the conflict. The State of Qatar hosted the Lebanese National Dialogue Conference in Doha in mid-May 2008, achieving a consensus on how to end the national deadlock. The Doha Agreement that resulted set the following benchmarks for national reconciliation:

- The parties have agreed on having the Lebanese parliament speaker, based on the rules in effect, invite the parliament to convene within 24 hours to elect consensus candidate General Michel Suleiman, knowing that this is the best constitutional method to elect the president under these exceptional circumstances.

- The parties have agreed to form a national unity government composed of 30 ministers distributed among the majority (16 ministers), the opposition (11 ministers) and the president (3 ministers), and by virtue of this agreement, all parties commit not to resign or obstruct the government's actions.

- The parties agreed to readopt the caza as an electoral constituency in conformity with the 1960 law, whereby the cazas of Marjayoun-Hasbaya, Baalbek-Hermel and West Beqaa-Rachaya remain as a single electoral constituency.[81]

- They agreed to divide Beirut into districts, consisting of:
  1. The first district: Achrafieh, Rmeil, and Saifi
  2. The second district: Bachoura, Medawar, and the Port
  3. The third district: Minet al-Hosn, Ain al-Mreisseh, Al-Mazraa, Mousseitbeh, Ras Beirut, and Zoqaq al-Blat

- The parties agreed to refer the reform clauses mentioned in the draft law prepared by the National Commission on Electoral Law Reform to the parliament for discussion.

- The parties agreed to continue the provisions of the Beirut Agreement, especially Paragraphs 4 and 5:
  1. Paragraph 4: The parties commit to abstain from having recourse or resuming the use of weapons and violence in order to record political gains.
  2. Paragraph 5: Initiate a dialogue on promoting the Lebanese state's authority over all Lebanese territory and their relationship with the various groups on the Lebanese stage in order to ensure the state's and the citizens' security.[82]

The army remained neutral in the 2008 conflict, a role that enhanced the prestige of General Michel Suleiman, thus helping his election as the successor to President Lahoud. On May 25, 118 members of the 127-member parliament voted for General Suleiman as president, finally ending the long deadlock. Attending his inauguration was, among other dignitaries, Sheikh Hamad bin Khalifa Al-Thani, the emir of Qatar, who had helped to negotiate the selection. Once again, Lebanon's fragile and divisive political system proved to be incapable of resolving its own crises. And Hezbollah had once again demonstrated that it was the strongest party within Lebanese society, although it once again spurred anger among many non-Shi'a Lebanese, this time for breaking its promise of 2004 not to use its large weapons cache against its fellow Lebanese. The fighting had also changed the dynamics of conflict in Lebanon. Usually the roots of sectarian violence was the Sunni-Christian divide, but the dispossessed Shi'a, taking some Christians as allies, now threatened the Sunni dominance of Islamic politics in Lebanon in unpredictable ways.

Hezbollah, the most visible and powerful Shi'a organization in Lebanon, viewed the Doha Agreement as a victory for Hezbollah. Hezbollah Deputy Secretary General Naim Qasim argued that "the liberation of prisoners was a direct defeat for Israel while the Doha Agreement was a direct defeat for the United States because Israel waged the battle under the headline of prisoners but was defeated militarily and this defeat was crowned with the liberation of prisoners."[83]

In July 2008, another breakthrough in the political stalemate occurred when Lebanon finally named a cabinet. The decision, which awarded 11 of the 30 cabinet posts to the opposition, came when Saad Hariri, the leader of the majority, offered a concession to Hezbollah, acceding to the nomination of Ali Kanso, the former head of the Syrian Social Nationalist Party, to be the minister of state.[84]

The Doha Agreement also enhanced the status of Christian parties, according to the International Crisis Group. The new district map, particularly in Beirut, allows for more predominately Christian districts, thus reducing the requirement for most Christian parties to enter into coalitions with Muslim parties. As a consequence, the new district electoral results, coupled with the increased power of the presidential office, will allow for administrative reform (reducing the power of ministries that were often led by Muslims) and reduce pressures to grant Palestinian refugees Lebanese citizenship.[85]

As they had for so much of Lebanon's modern history, UN peace-keepers took positions in southern Lebanon to monitor compliance with UN Resolution 1701. But the very nature of 1701 was certain to cause confusion and disappointment. While Lebanese criticized the peace-keepers for not driving the Israelis from the village of Ghajar, Israel criticized them for not disarming Hezbollah and stopping its flow of arms. Said a French peace-keeper, "I don't believe Hezbollah's weapons figure in Resolution 1701. So we monitor that, but disarming an armed militia is not in 1701."[86] The UN peace-keepers, consisting largely of European military contingents, patrolled jointly with Lebanese armed forces and engaged in a number of civil actions that were intended to assist the rural populations in the areas they patrolled.

THE INTERNAL VIOLENCE CONTINUES

The cease-fire may have ended the violence at least temporarily between Israel and Hezbollah, but Lebanon's internal agonies continued. The assassinations continued in the usual manner despite the cease-fire. Saleh Aridi, a senior member of the Lebanese Democratic Party, died instantly when a bomb under his car exploded in September 2008. Aridi was allied with pro-Syrian Druze leader and

Youth and Sports Minister Talal Arslan, a rival to Druze anti-Syrian leader Walid Jumblatt. Jumblatt immediately denounced the attack as an effort to discredit the temporary alliance he had made with Arslan.[87] Violence also grew in the northern city of Tripoli in the summer of 2007 when the Lebanese Army launched an attack on Fatah al-Islam in Palestinian refugee camps, and particularly in the Nahr al-Bared camp. Fatah al-Islam, a Sunni jihadist group reportedly inspired by, if not linked to, al-Qaeda, was linked to a series of bank robberies and bombings, and after the suspect Fatah al-Islam members retreated to Nahr al-Bared, the Lebanese military followed them in and attacked their bases. In reported acts of revenge, bombs in Tripoli killed over 20 persons, many of them soldiers. A car bomb killed Lebanese Army Major General François al-Hajj and his bodyguard in December of that year. While revenge seemed to be the motive, other intentions for the bombings may also have been at play—some suggested that they reflected an escalation of Lebanon's sectarian schisms. Tripoli, in northern Lebanon, is largely Sunni, and there is resentment there against both Hezbollah and Syria, accelerated by Hezbollah's brief takeover of Beirut in May. Denying that the attacks were directed against the soldiers, one Sunni religious leader said, "We don't want anyone to attack the army; they are our brothers. What Fatah al Islam did was criminal and wrong."[88] Instead, religious quarrels emerged as the motive, with one journalist arguing that the violence stemmed from young out-of-work Sunnis: "Some of them don't even know how to pray, but they like the idea of fighting the Alawites and Hezbollah."[89] The reputed leader of Fatah al-Islam, Shaker al-Absi, reportedly fled to Syria, where he reportedly was killed by Syrian security agents in December 2008.[90] All this turmoil was a reminder of how difficult it has been for the Lebanese to forge ahead of the legacy left by centuries of sectarian strife. And, for some analysts, more difficulties are likely to follow. Those signs continued in March 2009 as a bomb placed under a manhole cover blew a car into an orchard south of Sidon, instantly killing Kamal Medhat, deputy head of the Palestine Liberation Organization in Lebanon. While the killing of a Fatah member would normally result in accusations against Israel, Medhat had been involved in power struggles within Fatah and was driving back from an effort to resolve a family dispute in the Mieh refugee camp.[91]

For some observers of Lebanon, the events of 2008 only shifted the crisis from the streets to the government.[92] Perhaps the good news for Lebanon was that collectively there was no more stomach for the spasmodic violence that wracked the country between 1975 and the Ta'if Accord. But it has also been the case that governmental paralysis has subsequently shifted conflict from the capital buildings in Beirut to the streets, and since the old methods of conflict resolution by the established families and factions have not been restored since the 1970s, more protracted mayhem is possible. Moreover, the outside forces that have often fueled Lebanon's troubles remain poised; the danger to Lebanon is perhaps as great as right before the civil war. Israeli activities are likely to escalate in

Lebanon, particularly in the Beqaa Valley, because Hezbollah is probably stronger than it was in 2006, and Hezbollah itself will continue its strategy of resistance, while both Syria and Iran will continue their support of both Hezbollah and Hamas in Lebanon.[93]

Lebanon's history is a record of turmoil for a country that should have had more opportunity for peace, given its fertile soil and rich cultural history. Tragically, conflict and a lack of opportunity have driven out some of Lebanon's most promising citizens, who have taken their talents to other parts of the world. Too many of those left behind are too poor to leave, though there are others who stay on because they believe that Lebanon will someday return to peace and prosperity. Lebanon's tragic history may belie their hopes, but it is only those who have hope for Lebanon who may eventually restore its dreams.

The structural problems forged in Lebanon's long and contorted history remain today: the confessional political and social system, the persistence of Syrian power and influence, the relative poverty of the Shi'a and the Palestinians, the continuation of the *za'im* traditional power bases, and the persistent reminders that Lebanon is a small country surrounded by determined and sometimes destructive rivals who too frequently inflict their deadly quarrels on Lebanon.

NOTES

1. This book uses the term "BCE" to denote "before the common era," and "CE" refers to "common era," replacing "BC" and "AD."

2. One of the best histories of early Lebanon is Philip K. Hitti, *A Short History of Lebanon* (New York: St. Martin's Press, 1965).

3. Christopher Tyerman, *God's War: A New History of the Crusades* (Cambridge, MA: Harvard University Press, 2006), 179.

4. Karen Barkey, *Empire of Difference: The Ottomans in Comparative Perspective* (Cambridge: Cambridge University Press, 2008).

5. Ussama Makdisi, *The Culture of Sectarianism: Community, History, and Violence in Nineteenth-Century Lebanon* (Berkeley: University of California Press, 2000), 35.

6. William R. Polk, *The Opening of South Lebanon, 1788–1840* (Cambridge, MA: Harvard University Press, 1963), 18.

7. Rodger Shanahan, *The Shi'a of Lebanon: Clans, Parties, and Clerics* (London: Tauris Academic Press, 2005), 20–21.

8. Hitti, *A Short History of Lebanon*, 176–177.

9. Maroun Kisirwani, "Foreign Interference and Religious Animosity in Lebanon," *Journal of Contemporary History* 15 (October 1980): 690.

10. Farid el Khazen, *The Breakdown of the State in Lebanon, 1967–1976* (Cambridge, MA: Harvard University Press, 2000), 34–36.

11. Ibid, 685–700. Ibrahim Pasha was the son of Egypt's ruler of the time, Muhammad Ali, and served as governor of Syria after his campaign there in 1832.

12. See Leila Tarazi Fawaz, *Occasion for War: Civil Conflict in Lebanon and Damascus in 1860* (Berkeley: University of California Press, 1994).

13. Ussama Makdisi, *Artillery of Heaven: American Missionaries and the Failed Conversion of the Middle East* (Ithaca, NY: Cornell University Press, 2008), 183–184.

14. Samir Khalaf, *Civil and Uncivil Violence in Lebanon: A History of the Internationalization of Violence* (New York: Columbia University Press, 2002), 151–153.

15. Philip S. Khoury, *Syria and the French Mandate: The Politics of Arab Nationalism, 1920–1945* (Princeton, NJ: Princeton University Press, 1987), 57–58.

16. See Patrick Seale, *The Struggle for Syria: A Study of Post-War Arab Politics, 1945–1958* (New Haven, CT: Yale University Press, 1965), 71; James L. Gelvin, *Divided Loyalties: Nationalism and Mass Politics in Syria at the Close of Empire* (Berkeley: University of California Press, 1998), 279–280.

17. Rania Maktabi, "The Lebanese Census of 1932 Revisited: Who Are the Lebanese?" *British Journal of Middle East Studies* 26 (November 1999): 219–241.

18. For a discussion of the debate in Lebanon, see Matthew Hughes, "Lebanon's Armed Forces and the Arab-Israeli War, 1948–49," *Journal of Palestine Studies* 34 (Winter 2005): 24–41. The Arab Liberation Army, established by the Arab League, comprising volunteer fighters from Arab countries. Fawzi al-Qawuqji, a Lebanese nationalist, led the ALA.

19. Benny Morris, *1948: A History of the First Arab-Israeli War* (New Haven, CT: Yale University Press, 2008), 159–160.

20. Michael C. Hudson, "Democracy and Social Mobilization in Lebanese Politics," *Comparative Politics* 1 (January 1969): 250.

21. Khalaf, *Civil and Uncivil Violence in Lebanon*, 107–108.

22. Khazen, *The Breakdown of the State in Lebanon, 1967–1976*, 177.

23. Khalaf, *Civil and Uncivil Violence in Lebanon*, 34.

24. Farid el Khazen, "Political Parties in Postwar Lebanon: Parties in Search of Partisans," *Middle East Journal* 57 (Autumn 2003): 606.

25. Ibid., 611.

26. See Naomi Weinberger, "How PeaceKeeping Becomes Intervention: Lessons from the Lebanese Experience," in *International Organizations and Ethnic Conflict*, ed. Milton J. Esman and Shibley Telhami (Ithaca, NY: Cornell University Press, 1995), 239.

27. "Amal" has two meanings. In Arabic it means "hope," but it is also an acronym for *Afwaj al-Muqawmat al-Lubnaniyya*, or "Lebanese Resistance Detachments."

28. Augustus Richard Norton, *Amal and the Shi'a: Struggle for the Soul of Lebanon* (Austin: University of Texas Press, 1987), 60.

29. For a good discussion of UNFIL, see Bjørn Skogmo, *UNFIL: International Peacekeeping in Lebanon, 1978–1988* (Boulder, CO: Lynne Rienner Publishers, 1989).

30. Kenneth M. Pollack, *Arabs at War: Military Effectiveness, 1948–1991* (Lincoln: University of Nebraska Press, 2002), 514–516; Charles D. Smith, *Palestine and the Arab-Israeli Conflict* (New York: St. Martin's Press, 1988), 250.

31. David Hirst, "South Lebanon: The War That Never Ends?" *Journal of Palestinian Studies* 28 (Spring 1999): 9.

32. Evidence shows that the attack was the work of the Popular Front for the Liberation of Palestine, which was not tied to the PLO. However, once Israel entered Lebanon, its primary target was the PLO.

33. According to Maoz, the head of Israeli intelligence informed Prime Minister Menachim Begin that the attack was the work of Abu Nidal and not the PLO. Begin stated

that "they are all PLO" and recommended a large-scale air attack against the PLO head-quarters in Beirut. Zeev Maoz, *Defending the Holy Land: A Critical Analysis of Israel's Security and Foreign Policy* (Ann Arbor: University of Michigan Press, 2006), 189.

34. Ibid., 174.

35. The person arrested for the bombing was an anti-Phalange Christian Lebanese who was alleged to have Syrian connections, at least according to Dilip Hiro, *Lebanon: Fire and Embers* (New York: St. Martin's Press, 1992), 92. The Phalange was a Lebanese Christian party that dated to the 1930s.

36. "104 Report of the Commission of Inquiry into the Events at the Refugee Camps in Beirut- 8 February 1983." Vol. 8, 1982–1983. Israeli Ministry of Foreign Affairs, http://www.mfa.gov.il/MFA/Foreign%20Relations/Israels%20Foreign%20Relations%20since%201947/1982-1984/104%20Report%20of%20the%20Commission%20of%20Inquiry%20into%20the%20e.

37. Nicholas Blanford, *Killing Mr Lebanon* (London: I. B. Tauris, 2006), 26.

38. Quoted in Blanford, 32.

39. Christopher Hemmer, *Which Lessons Matter? American Foreign Policy Decision Making in the Middle East, 1979–1987* (Albany: State University of New York Press, 2000), 95–97.

40. Gilles Kepel, *Jihad: The Trail of Political Islam* (Cambridge, MA: Harvard University Press, 2002), 129.

41. Trita Parsi, *Treacherous Alliance: The Secret Dealings of Israel, Iran, and the United States* (New Haven, CT: Yale University Press, 2007), 113–123.

42. "Military Cabinet Named in Lebanon," *New York Times*, September 23, 1988.

43. Hani A. Faris, "The Failure of Peacemaking in Lebanon, 1975–1989," in *Peace for Lebanon? From War to Reconstruction*, ed. Deirdre Collings (Boulder, CO: Lynne Rienner Publishers, 1994), 19.

44. Joseph Malia, "The Ta'if Accord: An Evaluation," in *Peace for Lebanon? From War to Reconstruction*, ed. Deirdre Collings (Boulder, CO: Lynne Rienner Publishers, 1994), 31–44.

45. Samir Makdisi, *The Lessons of Lebanon: The Economics of War and Development* (London: I. B. Tauris, 2004), 92–93.

46. Augustus Richard Norton, *Hezbollah: A Short History* (Princeton, NJ: Princeton University Press, 2007), 82.

47. Dona J. Stewart, "Economic Recovery and Reconstruction in Postwar Beirut," *Geographical Review* 86 (October 1996): 494–496.

48. Talal Nizameddin, "The Political Economy of Lebanon under Rafiq Hariri: An Interpretation," *The Middle East Journal* 60 (Winter 2006): 97.

49. Interview with Prime Minister Netanyahu on NBC's *Today*, February 14, 1997, Israeli Ministry of Foreign Affairs.

50. "Hizbullah Details How Israel Quit South in 2000," *Beirut Daily Star*, May 25, 2009. Hezbollah used this opportunity to not only burnish its credentials as a worthy Israeli opponent, but also to justify its claim that it, and not the national military, was the true defender of Lebanon. The unnamed Hezbollah commander said to the *Daily Star* reporter that Hezbollah had to take to the Aramta battlefield "after the state failed to shoulder its responsibilities in fighting the Israeli occupation."

51. Eytan Bentsur, "Op-ed Article on Israel's Withdrawal from Lebanon," Israeli Ministry of Foreign Affairs, May 25, 2000.

52. Yoram Peri, *Generals in the Cabinet Room: How the Military Shapes Israeli Policy* (Washington, DC: United States Institute of Peace Press, 2006), 94–95. For more discussion

on the role of the IDF in Israeli security policy, see Avraham Sela, "Civil Society, the Military, and National Security: The Case of Israel's Security Zone in South Lebanon," *Israel Studies* 12 (Spring 2007); Maoz, *Defending the Holy Land*; Yehuda Ben Meir, *Civil-Military Relations in Israel* (New York: Columbia University Press, 1995).

53. "The Israeli Withdrawal from South Lebanon: Background Points," Israeli Ministry of Foreign Affairs, May 24, 2000, http://www.mfa.gov.il/MFA/Peace+Process/Guide+to+the +Peace+Process/The+Israeli+Withdrawal+from+Southern+Lebanon-+Back.htm.

54. "Former SLA Fighters Face Uncertain Return to Lebanon," *Beirut Daily Star*, November 14, 2008.

55. Bernard Rougier, *Everyday Jihad: The Rise of Militant Islam among Palestinians in Lebanon* (Cambridge, MA: Harvard University Press, 2007), 148.

56. Shihabi once described himself as the "second-most powerful man in Syria." Author's interview, Damascus, Syria, March 1995.

57. William Harris, "Crisis in the Levant: Lebanon at Risk," *Mediterranean Quarterly* 18 (Spring 2007): 41.

58. Blanford, *Killing Mr Lebanon*, 42.

59. Ibid., 85.

60. Ibid., 149.

61. "A Damning Finger Points at Syria," *The Economist*, October 26, 2005, p. 1. Shawkat and Maher al-Asad had a strange history, though. Shawkat wanted to marry Hafiz al-Asad's daughter, Bushra, but Hafiz al-Asad and oldest brother Basil forbade the marriage. After Basil's death in a car crash in 1993, Shawkat and Bushra eloped, apparently enraging Maher, who reportedly stabbed Shawkat in the stomach with a knife. Later, though, Shawkat was made chief of Syrian intelligence, apparently having demonstrated his bravery by flaunting the wishes of the most powerful man in Syria.

62. David W. Lesch, *The New Lion of Damascus: Bashar al-Asad and Modern Syria* (New Haven, CT: Yale University Press, 2005), 129–130.

63. "George Hawi's Son Accuses Israel of Being Behind the Assassination of His Father," Syrian Arab News Agency, November 2, 2007.

64. Oussama Safa, "Lebanon Springs Forward," *Journal of Democracy* 17 (January 2006): 23.

65. "Suspects in Hariri's Death Released," *New York Times*, April 30, 2009.

66. Author's observations, northern Israel and Tel Aviv, March 2005.

67. "Hizbullahs New Katyusha Can Hit Haifa," *Jerusalem Post*, March 17, 2000.

68. William M. Arkin, *Divining Victory: Airpower in the 2006 Israel-Hezbollah War* (Maxwell Air Force Base, AL: Air University Press, 2007), 16.

69. "Bush Urges World Leaders on Middle East," *Washington Post*, August 13, 2006.

70. The quote was originally contained in Secretary of State Rice, "Special Briefing on Travel to the Middle East and Europe," U.S. Department of State, July 21, 2006, http:// www.state.gov/secretary/rm/2006/69331.Htm, but the Department of State has since disabled that link. The full quote, citing the same source, is Jeremy Pressman, "The United States and the Hezbollah War," Brandeis University Crown Center for Middle East Studies, No. 13, November 2006, http://www.brandeis.edu/crown/publications/meb/MEB13.pdf.

71. Quoted in Augustus Richard Norton, *Hezbollah: A Short History*, 137.

72. Ibid., 154.

73. Arkin, *Divining Victory*, 60, 74.

74. "Pierre Gemayel Was a Rising Star in Lebanese Politics," *International Herald Tribune*, November 26, 2006.

75. "Chaotic Lebanon Risks Becoming Militant Haven," *New York Times*, July 7, 2007.

76. "Anti-Syrian Lawmaker Killed in Beirut Blast," *Washington Post*, September 20, 2007.

77. "U.S. Ally and Foe Are Trying to Avert War in Lebanon," *New York Times*, January 30, 2007.

78. "Hezbollah Scolds U.S. for Sending Ships towards Lebanon," *New York Times*, March 1, 2008. The *Cole* was the same ship that terrorists bombed in Aden harbor, Yemen, in October 2000.

79. "Lebanon Lodges UN Complaint over Perceived 'Israeli Threats,' " *Haaretz*, August 22, 2008.

80. "Iran's Tool Fights America's Stooge," *The Economist*, May 17, 2008, 35.

81. The term "caza" approximates "county." Lebanon is divided into five administrative districts, or *Mohafazat*, which are divided into 29 cazas.

82. "The Doha Agreement," NOW Lebanon, May 21, 2008.

83. "Shaykh Qasim: The Liberation of Prisoners Is a Defeat for Israel and the Doha Agreement Is a Defeat for the United States; We Want a Strong, Capable, and Just State, and Lebanon's Problem Can Be Solved Only through Accord," Lebanese National News Agency (in Arabic). OpenSource Center, July 22, 2008.

84. "Lebanon Announces Unity Cabinet," *Al Jazeera*, July 11, 2008.

85. "The New Lebanese Equation: The Christian's Central Role," International Crisis Group, July 15, 2008, http://www.crisisgroup.org/home/index.cfm?id=5573&l=1.

86. "UN Troops Calm Lebanon, but Tensions Remain," *New York Times*, August 25, 2008.

87. "Lebanese Parties Vow to Work beyond Aridi Murder," *Beirut Daily Star*, September 12, 2008.

88. "Up North, Hothouse of Tension in Lebanon," *New York Times*, October 16, 2008.

89. Ibid.

90. "Leader of Sunni Jihadist Group Missing in Syria," *New York Times*, December 10, 2008.

91. "Senior Fatah Official Killed in Lebanese Bomb Attack," *International Herald Tribune*, March 23, 2009.

92. Author's interview with government agency, Cairo, Egypt, March 2009.

93. Ibid.

FURTHER READING

Blanford, Nicholas. *Killing Mr Lebanon*. London: I. B. Tauris, 2006.

El Khazen, Farid. *The Breakdown of the State in Lebanon, 1967–1976*. Cambridge, MA: Harvard University Press, 2000.

Hitti, Philip K. *A Short History of Lebanon*. New York: St. Martin's Press, 1965.

Makdisi, Ussama. *The Culture of Sectarianism: Community, History, and Violence in Nineteenth-Century Lebanon*. Berkeley: University of California Press, 2000.

———. *Artillery of Heaven: American Missionaries and the Failed Conversion of the Middle East*. Ithaca, NY: Cornell University Press, 2008.

Picard, Elizabeth. *Lebanon: A Shattered Country*. London: Holmes & Meier, 1996.

Salibi, Kamal. *A House of Many Mansions: The History of Lebanon Reconsidered*. Berkeley: University of California Press, 1988.

CHAPTER 2

The Demographics of Lebanon

Lebanon's most distinctive physical feature is its mountains, still snowcapped in March. The mountains provide Lebanon with its identity, but also serve as hiding places for displaced minorities, who seek safety in their remoteness. Thus, to understand Lebanon's mixed population of minorities, one must understand the attractiveness of isolated hiding places. This is why the Kurds, a linguistic minority, live in the mountains of Turkey, Iran, and Iraq. It is why the Druze, a religious minority, live in the mountains of Syria and Lebanon. It is why Lebanon, a land of heights, has attracted so many minorities over its long history. This chapter examines Lebanon's major population groups and their dynamics.

LEBANESE POPULATION DYNAMICS

Lebanon is officially an Arab country, as around 95 percent of its population speaks that language, with 4 percent Armenian, and 1 percent identified as "other."[1] Lebanon's religious identity is more difficult to ascertain, as there has been no census since 1932. The Central Intelligence Agency's (CIA) *The World FactBook* breaks down the religious composition of Lebanon's population as follows:

- Muslim 59.7% (Shi'a, Sunni, Druze, Isma'ilite, Alawite or Nusayri),
- Christian 39% (Maronite Catholic, Greek Orthodox, Melkite Greek Catholic, Armenian Orthodox, Syriac Catholic, Armenian Catholic, Syriac Orthodox, Roman Catholic, Chaldean, Assyrian, Copt, and Protestant), other 1.3%
- *Note:* 17 religious sects recognized (there are actually 18 official religious sects, because the Ta'if Accords added the Alawite (Nusayri) to the list of recognized religions).

The "Muslim" category lumps the Sunni and Shi'a together and includes the Druze and Alawite, whom are recognized as Muslims by most of the larger Muslim community. It is commonly believed that Lebanon's Shi'a population is the largest of the varied Muslim groupings, at around 40 percent of the total population, with the Sunni and Druze at around 20 percent. This estimate does not include much of the Palestinian population, which do not have the citizenship rights granted to other groups, but may number around 400,000 persons, most of them Sunni. Lebanese Christians are mostly Maronite, with a sprinkling of Greek and Armenian Orthodox, Catholic, and other smaller sects. While Arabic is the predominate language of Lebanon, and most Christians speak it, many Christians do not identify themselves as Arabs, but rather refer to themselves as Phoenicians, or Canaanites. Many speak French instead of Arabic as their language of choice. Lebanon's Armenian community generally speaks Armenian, preferring their old historical tongue to Arabic.

Accurate numbers are difficult to obtain, so any change over time must be treated with caution. Still, "official" statistics for 1956 suggest a considerable increase in the Shi'a population in particular. According to these figures, the two largest Christian groups, the Maronite (30 percent) and the Greek Orthodox (10 percent) are similar to the Christian percent for 2009, but in 1956 the Shi'a population was just 18 percent, with the Druze at 6 percent and the Sunni at 20 percent.[2] If these estimates are close to the actual numbers, then Lebanon's Shi'a population more than doubled since 1956, while the other groups (particularly Christians) have virtually not changed. The Armenian community in Lebanon is thought to number around 160,000.

THE MARONITE CHRISTIANS

The name "Maronite" comes from St. Maron, a fifth century Syriac monk, who lived as a hermit near Antioch, now located in modern Turkey. They are now Lebanon's largest Christian group. The date of their actual founding as a sect is 680 CE; thus they are around as old as the Islamic faith.

The Maronites, like some other early Christian sects, were involved in the dispute over the nature of Christ that ultimately split the Church. The issue involved the question as to whether Christ was one entity, both divine and human, or was Christ both completely divine and completely human. The Council of Chalcedon, held in Turkey in 451, concluded that Christ had a dual nature, both wholly divine and wholly human, while the opposition argued for a single person, godly and human. Those Christians who held the second view, particularly the Nestorian Church, were known as Monophysites. The doctrine of Monophysitism spawned an offshoot, known as Monothelitism, which argued that while Christ had two natures, both divine and human, he had but one will. The Maronite Church may have started as a Monothelite church in the seventh century, but abandoned the doctrine in the twelfth century when it constructed ties to the Catholic Church, though retaining its own liturgy and priesthood.[3] Yet the charge against the Maronites of holding both Monothelite and Monophysite views remains, though the church officially abandoned the latter position when Maronite leadership recognized Catholic papal authority in 1182.

The Maronite community as a whole increasingly rejected the Arab world, instead leaning more toward ancient roots of places such as Phoenicia, and to early languages, initially Aramaic and later Syriac. Even in the current era, many Maronites favor English or French over Arabic, though Arabic is the official language of Lebanon. Lebanon's Maronite community supported the Crusaders when they arrived in the region in 1099 (unlike Egypt's Christian Copts, who did not), which originated the Maronite ties to the Catholic Church.[4] They refused the notion of being *Dhimmi* under the protection of the larger regional Muslim community. In this sense, some Maronites felt a kinship with the Jewish population of the Middle East, and the establishment of Israel in 1948 drew significant Maronite support, though there were others in the Maronite community who believed that ties to a Jewish group would only bring condemnation from the Arab majority.[5] Maronite support for Israel, though, was often assumed by Israeli policy makers without understanding its foundations. Thus, when Israeli forces invaded Lebanon in 1982, they assumed that the Maronite groups would support them, but that assumption proved to be false, resulting in, among other things, high Israeli casualties. As Kirsten E. Schulze put it,

> Israeli-Maronite relations, however, had less to do with friendship than with expediency —a fact that was often disregarded by Israeli decisionmakers, many of whom considered the existence of the relationship itself as proof of Maronite reliability. This view was supported by the Mossad, which was responsible for establishing these relations. Such a perception was most likely due to the over-identification of Mossad Weld agents with their hosts' plight. Thus, when the invasion was implemented, it came as a surprise when the Maronites refused to cooperate and Israeli forces got bogged down in Lebanon's confessional war, resulting in a high number of Israeli casualties.[6]

In 1932 the Maronites were a majority in Lebanon, but they have a lower birth rate than do the Shi'a, Sunni, and Druze. That, coupled with Maronite emigration from Lebanon to other parts of the world, has dropped the relative percentage of Lebanese Maronites to around 30–35 percent of the total population, though the numbers are imprecise. Fearing a loss of the political bargains set when the Maronites were the majority, including the designation of the presidency and the 6:5 ratio of seats that favored the Maronites in parliament, the Maronites have blocked efforts to update the 1932 census.

Like most other religious bodies, the Maronite Church has engaged in debate over both church and political reform. One consequence of the Vatican II Council of 1962–1965 was the emergence of reform movements within the Maronite Church to increase the spiritual life of the church and to bring it closer to its parishioners.[7] From these wellsprings came the Church for Our World, founded in 1965, and the *Mouvement Social*, that found political ground after the 1967 War, supporting the Palestine Liberation Organization (PLO).[8] That position conflicted with the larger Maronite communities' fear of the growing PLO power in Lebanon, though, and the *Mouvement Social*'s concerns over the suffering of the Palestinians died in the flames of the coming civil war.

Like other Christians who live in the Middle East, Lebanon's Maronites have seen their numbers, and thus their influence, decline in both Lebanon and in the greater Middle East. In Turkey, where there were millions of Christians a hundred years ago, now there are around 150,000, Jerusalem has seen its Christian population drop from 20 to 2 percent between 1948 and 2009, and a Lebanese Christian journalist feared for members of his faith in his country, said Sarkis Naoum: "Unless there is a turn toward secularism in the Arab world, I don't think there is a future for Christians here."[9] At least one Muslim writer argued that the decline of alternative religious identity would have negative consequences for all faiths: "Here in Lebanon, Muslims will often tell you Lebanon is no good without the Christians, and they mean it. The mix of religions and cultures that makes this place so tolerant would disappear."[10]

THE SHI'A

The Prophet Muhammad died in 632 CE without leaving a designated successor to him as spiritual and political leader of the Muslim community. Some in his community believed that his cousin and son-in-law Ali ibn Abu Talib should have become his successor (or "caliph"), while others in the Muslim group believed that the successor should be chosen by the Prophet's companions. The latter group held sway, and three caliphs (Abu Bakr, 573–634, Umar ibn al-Khattab, 581–644, and Uthman ibn Affan, 580–656) took turns as successor. Only after the murder of Uthman in 656 did the community appoint Ali as caliph, but he demurred the selection, causing a loss of faith in some of his followers, one of whom assassinated him in Kufa in 661. Ali's eldest son Hassan would gain the mantle of his followers, known as *Shi'at Ali*, or "partisans of Ali," but Hassan refused the position, which befell to another of Ali's sons, Hussein. Hussein picked up the Shi'a mantle and, attempting to build a base in modern-day Iraq, left Medina in October 680, but he was ambushed at the city of Karbala by a Sunni army under Caliph Yazid who massacred Hussein and his followers, ending the Shi'a caliphate.[11]

Since that fateful day in Karbala, the Shi'a have lived in the shadow of that event, mourning the loss of Ali and Hussein, fates that reinforced their perception of martyrdom and oppressed minority. As Ajami noted, "Kerbala cast a long shadow; for the faithful it annulled time and distance. Succeeding generations had told and embellished the tale, giving it their sense of separateness and political dispossession."[12]

Most of the succession of Shi'a *imams* (the descendents of Muhammad and Ali) died mysteriously, and the Shi'a believed that the Sunni rulers in Baghdad poisoned them. The twelfth successor, a young boy, went into hiding in 873, possibly to protect himself from the fate of his ancestors. The largest body of the Shi'a, the "*Imamiyya*" or "Twelver" group, believes that the 12th imam, Muhammad Mahdi, actually went into "occultation," disappeared but not dead, someday to return to the Muslim community and usher in a thousand years of peace and justice. While there are some (including former Israeli Prime Minister Binyamin Netanyahu) who claim that Iranian Shi'a in particular are infected with the cult of the Mahdi, who wish to hasten the return of the "Hidden Imam" by violence against non-Shi'a, as Ze'ev Maghen shows, "[G]enuine chiliastic messianism or mahdism has never been a potent force in within Shi'iam, and therefore is not today."[13] The "twelvers" are now the majority of the Shi'a world-wide, and the majority of Shi'a in Lebanon.

The Shi'a have had challenging relations with the majority Sunni community, repressed by the Umayyad Caliph of 691–750 (reinforcing the power of messianism) and betrayed by the Abbasids (750–1250) who the Shi'a believed duped the Shi'a into supporting their revolution against the Umayyad.[14] They faced continual threats from Sunni Salifiyyists who regarded the Shi'a as apostates, as when Unitarian "Wahabbist" soldiers from Arabia attacked Shi'a holy sites in Iraq in the early nineteenth century to the menace from al-Qaeda that persuaded Iran to support the United States in its attack on Taliban Afghanistan in 2001.

The Shi'a practice Islam in its fundamental manifestations, though elements of that practice differ slightly (the Shi'a hold their hands beside themselves during prayer while the Sunni hold their hands in front of them, for example). The Shi'a do differ from the majority Sunni in the praxis of leadership, though. The Sunni have reduced the importance of religious leadership, noting early warnings from the Prophet Muhammad that religious leaders undermined Christianity and Judaism because they took the mantle of religion to justify political power and thus opened the door to the possibility of tyrannical rule. Thus the Sunni may elevate a person respected for religious knowledge to the status of *imam*, or prayer leader, but the role of the imam is generally restricted to granting religious advice. Sometimes a Sunni reaches a particular pinnacle that may allow him to comment on political decisions (the rector of Al-Azhar University in Cairo, or the Grand Mufti of Saudi Arabia, for example), but such figures are rare in the Sunni corpus. The Shi'a, however, have given more status to those with religious knowledge, and there is a particular hierarchy based on religious knowledge and education to determine relative status:

- Grand *Ayatollah* (*Ayatollah 'uzma*) or "Great Sign of God"
- *Ayatollah* ("Sign of God")
- *Hojat al-Islam* ("Authority on Islam")

- *Mubellegh a- Risala* ("Carrier of the Message")
- *Mujtahid* (a graduate of a religious seminary)
- *Talib ilm* (a religious student)[15]

This ranking matters more in post-1979 Iran than it does in other Shi'a communities, though religious education still provides particular authority. What also matters for authority in Shi'a communities is descendance from the family of the Prophet Muhammad. The Shi'a believe that those who have such bloodlines bear a part of the special knowledge that God granted to Muhammad and thus have a heightened understanding of God's will. They bear the title "Sayyid" and are distinguished by their black turbans.

In Iran, the Ayatollah Ruhollah Khomeini developed the praxis of clerical rule, or *Vilayat-i Faqih*, or literally "guardianship of the supreme jurist." The treatise conflicts with a more standard Shi'a understanding that true rule belonged only to the Mahdi, and all other temporal rule is thus illegitimate until the Mahdi returns at the end of time. As Mohammed Ayoob notes, such doctrine is anathema to most Shi'a theologians both inside and outside of Iran.[16] It is for this reason that most Shi'a outside of Iran dismiss the logic and veracity of *Vilayat-i Faqih*.

The Lebanese Shi'a

It is unclear when the first Shi'a arrived in modern Lebanon, but it was apparently during the seventh century or the eighth century CE, possibly exiled there from Yemen by the Sunni caliphate in Damascus.[17] The Sunni Mamlukes ruled Lebanon, then a part of Syria, and both they and their Ottoman successors oppressed the Shi'a, attacking their towns and villages, forcing them deeper into mountain recesses and into hiding their Shi'a identity.[18] They turned to agriculture, cultivating fruits, grains, cotton, and silkworms to sustain themselves in what had become a feudal society dominated by clans. They faced persecution from the Sunni Mamlukes, forcing them into remote regions of Lebanon such as the Beqaa Valley, but even in these secluded areas, the Shi'a found themselves practicing the art of *taqiyya*, or "hiddenness," imitating the Sunni to escape further discrimination. The assumption of Ottoman power after 1517 left the Shi'a in this position, as Ottoman rulers identified the Shi'a as Sunni, thus requiring them to perform particular Shi'a ceremonies (such as the *Ashura* commemoration) in secret.[19]

The confessional government system created after Lebanese independence only exacerbated tensions between Lebanon's Muslim communities. The Shi'a complained that the Sunni got the largest share of political positions reserved under the confessional system for Muslims.[20] That was partly because of the population patterns; the Sunni were more likely to live in populated areas, with more representation and influence, while the Shi'a remained in rural areas. As a consequence, the rural areas largely populated by the Shi'a got progressively fewer resources, which tended to flow to urban areas such as Beirut and the large coastal cities. Thus the percentage of Shi'a who worked in agriculture, one backbone of Shi'a life and identity in Lebanon, declined from 38 percent of the total Shi'a population to 11 percent between 1960 and 1980, driven into Beirut and other cities by stagnate prices for tobacco and other cash crops.[21]

The Shi'a situation in Lebanon grew worse as a crackdown on the Palestinian PLO in Jordan in 1970 sent streams of PLO members and their families into Lebanon. Many settled in south Lebanon and used their location north of the Israeli border to launch attacks into Israel, resulting in Israeli retaliation that too frequently targeted both Palestinian and Shi'a populations. One consequence was a growing Shi'a migration to Lebanon's cities, and large Shi'a slums filled with impoverished Shi'a grew, particularly in south Beirut. This growth of the Shi'a urban areas put the Shi'a and Sunni city communities into closer proximities, thus exacerbating the probability of conflict should Lebanon's climate grow violent, as it did during the civil war of 1976–1988. Another consequence was that many Shi'a initially welcomed the Israeli invasions of south Lebanon in 1976 and 1983, believing that they would weaken the hold of the Palestinians who had gained so much power in that area.

THE SUNNI

The Sunni, literally as-Sunnah, or "path," are the largest of the Muslim groups, constituting around 85 percent of the Muslim world. Their foundation is the argument that the consensus of the Muslim community of the time should determine the successor to the Prophet Muhammad. The first four caliphs, Abu Bakr (caliph from 632 to 634), Umar ibn al-Khattab (634–644), Uthman ibn Affan (644–656), and, finally, Ali ibn Talib (656–661), were selected this way, even though Ali's followers argued that his selection should have been automatic, given his bloodline. After Ali's death, the caliphate moved to Damascus with Mu'awiyah ibn Abi Sufyan (602–680) as the first Umayyad caliph. From Mu'awiyah's time on, the Sunni would rule as caliph until the end of that office, often dated to 1922, when Turkish president Kemal Atatürk abolished the caliph. The most powerful and influential Islamic periods were Sunni, including the Umayyad (661–750), the Abbasid (750–1258), and the Mamlukes (1250–1517). The Sunni became dominant with the Turkish-based Ottoman Empire, which controlled the entire Arab world with the exception of Morocco.

When Sunni Islam came into contact with the West through Western expansion, some of its adherents argued that the West had become powerful at the expense of the Islamic world because Muslims had lost their theological bearings and needed to return to a more pious world of the time of the Prophet and his companions. The adherents of this form of Islam argued that the Islamic community could not regain its relative strength until it once again emulated the "pious ancestors" or *salaf* of Muhammad's era. They thus became known as *salafists* and while many eschewed violence, others argued that only violent struggle against both Muslim rulers who had departed from traditional Islam and the foreign enemies they had courted was the only way to preserve the Muslim world.[22] While many Muslim scholars and journalists rejected the application of *jihad* to resistance,[23] or argued that it was inapplicable to enemies outside of the Muslim world,[24] the violent jihadists gained particular traction in poor communities, and in particular, refugee camps such as those for Palestinian Sunni Muslims in Lebanon.

The Lebanese Sunni

In Lebanon, the Sunni families were less powerful than were the dominate Christian and Druze families, but they had enough political weight to gain the prime minister post under the National Compact. Some of that influence came from the privileged positions that leading Sunni families held during the Ottoman period, and some of that influence carried over into the French Mandate period. The French created a Supreme Islamic Council, headed by a Grand Mufti. They also crafted a Directorate of Waqfs, or religious trusts, to manage funds for religious activities. As the Sunnis were then the majority Muslim group, they managed to control these positions. Moreover, most Lebanese Sunni lived in cities—more than two-thirds of them lived in Beirut, Sidon, and Baalbek—unlike the Shi'a, who were largely rural, and thus the Sunni were closer to the seats of power in Lebanon.

One factor that differentiated the Lebanese Sunni from other religious groupings was the lack of powerful Sunni parties. As Farid el Khazen notes, no major Sunni leader rose to political prominence through a political party.[25] They apparently learned late that they needed some political vehicle in order to compete with the more powerful Shi'a and Maronite parties. Thus the "Future Movement," affiliated with Saad Harari, son of assassinated former Prime Minister Rafiq Harari, emerged after Rafiq Hariri's assassination. Apparently fearing the rise of Hezbollah, the Future Movement organized its own Sunni militia, but in May 2008, the Future militia disintegrated after a brief battle with Hezbollah, leaving one disappointed militiaman to complain, "Where do we get ammunition and weapons from? We are blocked. The roads are blocked. Even Saad Hariri has left us to face our fate alone."[26] For the Sunni, the defeat was symbolic of its larger problem, the rise of the Shi'a Hezbollah as the most powerful group in Lebanon, eclipsing the traditional role of the Sunni. Their most recent fate had to be a disappointment to the United States, the European Union, and some Arabian Gulf countries that pledged $6.7 billion in January 2008 to strengthen the Sunni Siniora government. However, given the complex nature of Lebanese politics, it was not clear who was being strengthened. The Sunni of Lebanon have also been more attracted to Salafist movements, and some of those movements appeared to gravitate toward Hariri, the most powerful Sunni group. Said one Salafist leader, Daii al-Islam al-Shahal, "There's a relationship between ourselves and Sheik Saad when it's needed. The biggest Sunni political power is Hariri. The biggest Sunni religious power are the Salafis. So it's natural." Hariri denied connections with Salafist groups, saying, "We sponsor culture and education, not terrorism . . . we never had blood on our hands and we never will."[27] That may be true for Lebanese Sunni, but the Palestinian refugees, almost entirely Sunni, have not been so quick to abandon violent struggle, and there are growing *Salifist* movements in their ranks, as noted in the Palestinian section.

THE DRUZE

The origins of the Druze lie in the Fatimid Imamate, which started in Tunisia in 912 and moved to Cairo in 973, ruling until 1174 when Salah al-Din (Saladin) overthrew it. One of the most famous and notorious Fatimid caliphs was al-Hakim bi'Amr Allah,[28] whose followers included Muhammad al-Darazi. Although Darazi was assassinated in 1019, two years before al-Hakim himself, his interpretation of some of al-Hakim's own theology, derived from the Ismailia branch of Shi'a Islam, was to form some roots of early Druze beliefs, though contemporary Druze regard those beliefs as apostasy. Following the death of al-Hakim, the Druze (the name is believed to be a derivation of Darazi) fled to Lebanon, which has the largest Druze population in the Middle East. The Druze are secretive about their core beliefs, but they refer to themselves as "al-Mowahidden" which roughly translates into "monotheism."[29]

The Druze vary considerably from mainstream Islam (even from Shi'a Islam) in their belief systems. They do not accept converts and have not since 1043, they believe in the transmigration of souls (thus when one Druze dies, another is born), they do not believe in predestination, and they reject polygamous marriage, or temporary marriage. They do not perform the *hajj*, nor observe Ramadan and their religious writ, including the *Kitab al-hikma*, contains both Quranic and non-Quranic text passages, thus leading mainstream Muslims to regard the Druze as not true Muslims. Thus the Druze in Lebanon have had a tense relationship with the Sunni and Shi'a populations, though they have also clashed with Lebanon's Christians.

The Lebanese Druze

Today the Druze population in Lebanon is around 250,000, though precise numbers do not exist. They live mostly in Mount Lebanon, the Chouf area, Beqaa Valley, and southern Lebanon. The Druze communities are divided on Lebanese political identity, with one prominent Druze faction, the Druze

Progressive Socialist Party—which boasts of the majority of Druze supporters and is led by Walid Jumblatt. The Progressive Socialist Party is officially nonsectarian, emphasizing social and economic issues rather than religious stances. Opposing that faction is Talal Arslan, head of the Druze Democratic Party, which is allied with Shi'a opposition groups Hezbollah and Amal, along with the Christian Free Patriotic Movement.[30]

THE PALESTINIANS

The term "Palestinian" is fraught with ambiguity. It refers roughly to peoples whose original homeland lies in the eastern Mediterranean, south of historic Lebanon and north of Gaza. The land contains the Valley of Jezreel, a major route for both invaders and traders. Its largest and most historical city is Jerusalem, but it also has old trading ports along its coasts. Its soil is mostly fertile, except in the southern part. Its borders, like most of the traditional Middle East, have been fluid over time, sometimes including not only modern Israel but also modern Jordan and Syria. The Palestinian borders of modernity came from British mapmakers who divided the Ottoman Empire into zones of influence after the Ottoman defeat in 1918. Palestine became a part of the British mandate, which contained land that ultimately became Israel and Jordan, but never a state called "Palestine." The pain of no Palestinian state for the Palestinians only compounded the negativity of their narrative of occupation and powerlessness. Their occupiers included the Ottomans, the British, and now, for most Palestinians, the Israelis.[31]

The Lebanese Palestinians

The 1948 Arab-Israeli War drove over 700,000 Palestinians into neighboring Arab countries. Those who lived in the Galilee area fled north to Lebanon, quickly prompting that country to restrict Palestinian immigration. Over 100,000 Palestinians, around 14 percent of the total refugee population, crossed over to Lebanon, where they filled 12 refugee camps, which remain today.

Lebanon's Palestinian population swelled after the September 1970 conflict in Jordan, where Jordanian forces ousted Palestinian militants who threatened to turn Jordan into a radical Palestinian state. Lebanon's Palestinian issues became much more complex, partly because Yasser Arafat's PLO, now located in Lebanon, rapidly organized the Palestinian refugees into a parastate. Resources flowed into Palestinian camps, including funding for health clinics, broadcasting, and infrastructure. The largesse benefited Fatah, the militant wing of the PLO, which took over the provision of most PLO services, and extended its influence from the rural camps to urban areas such as Sidon and Tyre.[32]

By 1975 the Palestinian population had grown to over 200,000. By the early 2000s, the number of Palestinian refugees living in Lebanon was estimated at

370,000, according to Bernard Rougier.[33] But, according to the United Nations Relief and Works Agency (UNRWA), 409,714 Palestinians lived in these camps in 2006, the last year that the UNRWA conducted a census. The largest camps are at Ein el-Hilweh, outside of Saida, with 45,967 Palestinians, Nahr el-Bared (31,303) outside of Tripoli, and Rashidieh, south of Tyre, with 29,361.[34]

Palestinian refugees live under varying restrictions in their host countries. Jordan grants Palestinians citizenship, and relative freedom, though their voting power is diluted by the Jordanian district electoral map that favors the "East-Bankers," the old Bedouin descendants, over the Palestinian Jordanians. Egypt also allows Palestinians citizenship, but the process is complex, often taking years. Lebanon, however, denies citizenship to its Palestinian refugees, fearful of altering the balance between factious populations by adding mostly Sunni Palestinians to the mix. Lebanon also denies Palestinian refugees the right to own property or to work in middle income positions, or to return to Lebanon if they leave for more than six months.[35]

There are over 200,000 registered Palestinian refugees in the various Lebanese camps, distributed according to Table 2.1[36]

Lebanon's polyglot population has had a mixed relationship with its Palestinian population. On one hand, there was considerable sympathy for the original Palestinian plight among Lebanese of all religious stripes; the Palestinians were,

Table 2.1 Location and Population of Palestinian Refugee Camps in Lebanon

Camp	Number of Registered Refugees
Mar Elias	616
Burj el-Barajneh	15,718
Dbayeh	4,025
Shatila	8,370
Ein el-Hilweh	45,967
Mieh Mieh	4,569
El-Buss	9,508
Rashidieh	29,361
Burj el-Shemali	19,074
Nahr el-Bared	31,303
Beddawi	15,947
Wavel	7,668
Dikwaneh & Nabatieh (destroyed camps)	16,518
Total	**215,890**

after all, Arabs, and their defeat in 1948 was marked by many Lebanese as a defeat for all Arabs, no matter what religion. Later, as Palestinian activism grew, there was quite a show of solidarity for attacks against Israel, and the death of one Palestinian militant, Kyhalil al-Jamal, in April 1968 brought about the closing of Lebanon for a day of mourning and a funeral attended by, among other dignitaries, Christian president and Phalange leader Pierre Gemayel.[37] Afterwards Israeli retaliation for Palestinian raids began to hurt Lebanon itself, starting with a December 1968 Israeli commando raid that destroyed 13 Lebanese civil airliners in Beirut. The Lebanese state security apparatus decided to limit Palestinian activities aimed at Israel, beginning a long period of declining Palestinian-Lebanese relations.

The Palestinians in Gaza, the occupied West Bank, and elsewhere are cleaved by different loyalties, principally to the more moderate Fatah (the original organization of Yasser Arafat), and the more militant Hamas, and such cleavages also exist in Lebanon's Palestinian community. While Fatah stressed the tale of Palestinian (and, to a lesser extent, Arab) nationalism, Hamas pushed Islamist identity as the path of struggle. The backbone of the Palestinian resistance was the PLO, which carried its nationalist message into Lebanon originally, but competing narratives followed the Palestinians, one from Shi'a Iran and one from Sunni Saudi Arabia; each vision gained Palestinian adherents at the expense of the Palestinian identity-based position. The 1982 Israeli invasion of Lebanon helped to radicalize the Palestinians as it radicalized the Shi'a, with religious figures such as Sheik Ibraham Ghunaym and his student Hisham Abdallah Sharaydi establishing the "Partisan's League," or *Usbat al-Ansar*, in 1985, marking the beginning of the establishment of a variety of Salifiyyist groups that emerged to challenge the Fatah emphasis on Palestinian identity.[38] Their challenge was the Shi'a Hezbollah, as Rougier describes that relationship: "For the Islamists, their goal, then, was to separate strategy from religion: they sought to associate themselves with Hezbollah's campaign against regional peace, while further developing a sectarian orientation that testified to their powerful distrust of Shi'ite Islam and their constant vigilance against its presumed proselytizing."[39]

For most non-Palestinian Lebanese, the Palestinians have been and remain unwelcome. For centuries, the various factions of Lebanon had worked out their uneasy but necessary compromises. Sometimes those compromises broke down, with devastating consequences, but after such failures, the confessional communities learned that such conflicts produced few winners and many losers and resolved informally to try and prevent them in the future. The National Pact solidified these informal agreements with power-sharing arrangements. However, the Palestinians were not a part of the National Pact and thus had no role in Lebanese governance. Thus they remained on the sidelines, not valued by any of the confessional groups because Palestinians had little to offer.

Moreover, as the various national Lebanese factions tried to mend the rifts that had propelled them into the civil war of 1975–1990, they sought to transfer blame to "outsiders."

The Palestinians also represented an avenue to conflict with Israel that many Lebanese resented. As noted earlier, Lebanon managed to avoid the Arab-Israeli wars of the past, but when the Palestinians arrived in large numbers after the 1967 War and the 1970 exodus from Jordan, they brought their war with Israel with them. They increased the number of cross-border raids into Israel, incurring Israeli retaliation in return. The Israelis conducted retaliation with the principle of asymmetric force: an action would be met with a disproportionate reaction to punish severely not only those who had attacked Israel, but also their neighbors. The hoped-for result for Israel was to have the local population turn against those who attacked Israel and either drive them out or at least isolate them; thus non-Palestinian Lebanese paid the price for Palestinian operations against Israel. Israeli warplanes bombed Lebanese villages, and Israeli troops swarmed through areas of Lebanon, causing destruction and often provoking the flight of hundreds of thousands of refugees. While the non-Palestinian population vented its anger against Israel for such actions, it often also blamed the Palestinians for instigating Israeli reprisals. As Michael C. Hudson remarked,

> [T]he issue of the 300,000–350,000 Palestinians resident in Lebanon remains highly contentious. Without movement on permanent status issues (including refugees) between Israel and the Palestinians, it is difficult to envision a solution to this problem. Most Lebanese resent having had their country drawn in as a proxy battleground between Israel and the PLO from the 1960s to the 1980s; and so the idea of tawtin (permanent resettlement and even naturalization) of Palestinians in Lebanon is anathema.[40]

Even Mahmoud Abbas, the president of the Palestinian Authority in the West Bank, made it clear that the right of Palestinian return to the land of Palestine (however that may evolve) was paramount for the Palestinians in exile (over 4.6 million worldwide) and that permanent settlement outside of Palestine for these refugees would defeat that position. On Lebanon's Palestinians, Abbas was clear, "We are against the resettlement of Palestinians in Lebanon," adding, "We are with the decision of the Lebanese government in terms of Palestinian weapons . . . In Lebanon, we are under the law and not above it," referring to the Lebanese government's decision to disarm militias[41] (except Hezbollah). The reality might be different, however. Israel had stridently opposed the return of Palestinians displaced by the 1948 Arab-Israeli War because if all or even most did return, the majority of Israel's population would shift from Jewish to Muslim, clearly challenging Israel's identity as a Jewish state.

The first month of 2009 brought about a small measure of hope for Lebanon's beleaguered population, which was beginning to recover from the bloody summer of 2006. Hezbollah seemed unwilling to continue the armed struggle against Israel and seemed ready to become more of a political force. But Lebanon's hopes for peace have often been dashed by the realities of its neighborhood. In late December 2008 the simmering conflict between Israel and Hamas in Gaza boiled over, and as Hamas rockets reached ever deeper into Israel (a blunt reminder of Hezbollah's rockets in 2006), Israeli aircraft and troops launched an offensive into Gaza. In January 2009, a small rocket barrage landed in Israel from Lebanon, kindling fears that Lebanon would once again be caught in regional wars. Hezbollah denied responsibility, which was later attributed to a Palestinian group. Hezbollah did hold a rally in support of the Gazan Palestinians, and one member expressed his willingness for the conflict to escalate: "This demonstration is to show our support for Gaza and the Palestinian resistance. I would even sacrifice my son," he claimed, but others genuinely seemed exhausted by the long years of battle, as Tareq Mitri, the information minister, said that there was a nationwide "sense that we do not want to be drawn in" to a new war. Expressing solidarity with Gaza does not mean wanting to provoke an Israeli attack on Lebanon, or giving any pretext for that."[42]

OTHER MINORITIES

While Maronites, Sunni, Shi'a, and Druze compose the majority of Lebanon's population, there are other minority groups. They include the Syriac (or Syrian) Catholics, a ancient faith that traditionally uses a variety of "Eastern" liturgies, the Syriac Orthodox Church (which rejects the findings of the Council of Chalcedon discussed earlier in the chapter), and uses Syriac as its liturgical language, the Armenian Orthodox, which has a body of doctrine and language similar to the Syriac Orthodox Church, the Alawi, an offshoot of Shi'a Islam, who consider Ali ibn Talib as close to a deity, the Melkite Greek Catholic Church, and a variety of other religions groups. Lebanon recognizes 17 different religions in all.

As Elizabeth Picard notes, the Syriac-speaking Christian communities are relative newcomers to Lebanon, having moved there from Turkey in the early twentieth century, fleeing Turkey, Iraq, and northern Syria.[43] They have limited rights, and only half have citizenship. The restricted representation that the Lebanese Syriacs do get comes through the Syriac Union Party, headed by Ibrahim Mrad.

Lebanon's Armenian community is another minority that clings with determination to its linguistic identity, retaining its own language (with its unique alphabet), and its own political character. Like many other ethnic groups in Lebanon, there is a leading Armenian party, Tashnaq, which is actually a branch of the global Tashnaq that operates in 35 countries. Lebanese Armenians did not take sides in the civil war, preferring to blend in between Lebanese Maronites and Lebanese Muslims. Said one Lebanese Armenian, "I remember when I used to get stopped at a checkpoint, they would ask, 'Are you Christian or Muslim?' I would say 'Armenian,' and it was like a third category. They didn't know what to do."[44]

THE REGIONS OF LEBANON

It is impossible to understand Lebanon without understanding its regional heritage, its localized politics, and the interplay among its sections. They range from cosmopolitan Beirut to the often desolate poverty of the south. While there is no exact agreement on the regions and their borders, they are, in general, the following:

- North Lebanon
- The Beqaa Valley
- Beirut
- Mount Lebanon
- South Lebanon

North Lebanon

This is a mountainous region that borders southern Syria. It was probably the place of origin for much of the Maronite legacy and has significant Maronite sites. The largest city is historic Tripoli. The population was once largely Maronite, but the region between the border and Tripoli extending eastward is now largely Sunni Muslim, reflecting the influx of Palestinian refugees who have moved there. The population of Shi'a extends northward from the Beqaa Valley into North Lebanon. There is also a large Palestinian refugee population, including the large Nahr al-Bared outside of Tripoli, which was the site of large-scale fighting between Palestinian Islamist groups and the Lebanese military. The Baddawi Palestinian Refugee Camp is also located near Tripoli.

The Beqaa Valley

This fertile region lies between the Lebanon and anti-Lebanon mountain ranges and is actually a part of the Great Rift, a depression stretching from Turkey to East Africa. It is an area of small villages with no dominant city, though the historical shadows of Baalbek, one of the world's great historical sites (and the location of a major Lebanese cultural festival) remain as a reminder of the Beqaa Valley's value on a major trade route. The main economic activity in the Beqaa Valley is agriculture, which includes both food crops and illicit drug production. As in North Lebanon, the population of the Beqaa Valley is largely Shi'a, though there are areas of mixed population as well.

Beirut

The Beirut area includes not only Lebanon's capital city but also an urban area surrounding it that ranges from opulent housing to squalid slums and refugee camps. It is an ancient city with a history dating back for more than 5,000 years, passing through the Phoenicians, Greeks, Romans, and the Ottomans. It declined to a sleepy backwater until the mid-nineteenth century, when it began a revival as a significant trading center for the eastern Mediterranean. Lebanese Maronite Christians dominated the commercial part of the city, benefiting from ties to France in particular, and French funds came into the city to support the construction of a modern harbor in the late nineteenth century, along with railroads linking the capital to the rest of the country. The city grew, becoming one of the Middle East's most important cities, with major universities, newspapers, shopping districts, and a cultural life that fused European and Middle Eastern traditions (the American University of Beirut was founded in Beirut in 1866). The city was badly damaged by the civil war and was later rebuilt, though some of the new buildings were destroyed or damaged again in the 2006 Hezbollah-Israel War.

The pulverization of much of Beirut during the civil war necessitated massive reconstruction, which revitalized much of the old ruins, though some argued that the scale of rebuilding erased much memory of the old city. The old souks, the heart of any Arab or Ottoman city, were bulldozed under, replaced by a new "souk" with Burger Kings, KFC's, and Pizza Huts,

> The demolition crews, and the powerful financial interests behind them, have produced a irreversible fait accompli. In retrospect, from at least 1983 there has been a concerted effort to wipe clean the surface of central Beirut, to purify it of all historical associations in the form of its buildings; to render it pure space, pure commodity, pure real estate.[45]

Of course such commentary could apply to any city under urban development; memories are the first casualties, but one side benefit for historians was that the reconstruction of the capital was so extensive that it uncovered much of Beirut's long-lost past in the process.

Mount Lebanon

This area is one of Lebanon's two mountain ranges, with peaks rising sharply from Lebanon's coast. On the north, Mount Lebanon is separated from the Nusayriyah Mountains of Syria by the river Nahr al Kabir, and on the south it is bounded by Al Qasimiyah River, giving it a length of 105 miles, or 169 kilometers.

South Lebanon

The south is a region of productive agriculture, with olives, cherries, citrus, tobacco, and many other crops growing along the hillsides. It comprises around 10 percent of the country's population, and while it is predominantly Shi'a, there are also populations of Maronite, Sunni, Druze, and other minorities living in south Lebanon.

As Samir Khalaf observes, the south was often the locus of progressive and radical movements. In the 1940s, the Lebanese Communist Party gained a foothold, and Arab nationalism and Arab socialism gained traction in small villages and in the urban areas of Sidon and Sour.[46] Later Shi'a resistance movements grew in response to provocations by Israel and by renegade elements of the Lebanese military. Unsurprisingly, south Lebanon has borne the brunt of Lebanon's wars, a situation that has not only filled local cemeteries, but also stimulated an exodus from the area. Typical is the Greek Orthodox town of Marja'uyun, with a registered population of 35,000 residents in 1999 but only around 600 people actually living there.[47]

PROMINENT REGIONAL FAMILIES

Lebanon's National Pact institutionalized the old elite groups that dominated regional Lebanese affairs for centuries. In Lebanon's regions, political leaders were more than just decision makers: they also controlled patronage, doling it out to supporters and withholding it from opponents. The power of regional families was especially important. They included the following:

- The Gemayel family is located in the Mount Lebanon region north of Beirut. This Maronite family has produced presidents, members of the House of Deputies, and cabinet members. Pierre Gemayel founded the Kataeb party, or Phalange party, in 1936 as a paramilitary formation, and it later grew into a powerful political party.
- The Jumblatt family is a Druze family that moved into the central Lebanese mountains from Syria in the fifteenth century. Currently Walid Jumblatt serves as speaker of Lebanon's parliament.
- The Yazbeki family, another prominent Druze family, is a traditional enemy of the Jumblatt family.
- The Hawayek family is a Maronite family from the coastal Mount Lebanon area.
- The Chamoun family, another noteworthy Maronite family, is from the Chouf region. Camille Chamoun served as Lebanon's president between 1952 and 1958, and his son Dany headed the powerful National Liberal Party until his assassination in October 1990.

Lebanon's demographic quilt forms the basis for its political system, and, to a less obvious but important way, its economic system. Lebanon's challenge is to build and maintain a political arrangement that can deliver decisions on resources and power while at the same time refereeing the needs of Lebanon's varied community structure. The systems and process that attempt this goal are the subject of the next chapter.

NOTES

1. The demographic data are from the CIA's *The World FactBook*.
2. From *An-Nahar*, No. 6249, April 26, 1956, as quoted in Ralph E. Crow, "Religious Sectarianism in the Lebanese Political System," *Journal of Politics* 24 (August 1962): 491.

3. See Leila Tarazi Fawaz, *Occasion for War: Civil Conflict in Lebanon and Damascus in 1860* (Berkeley: University of California Press, 1994), 10–11.

4. Kamal Salibi, *A House of Many Mansions: The History of Lebanon Reconsidered* (Berkeley: University of California Press, 1988), 92–96.

5. Kirsten E. Schulze, *Israel's Covert Diplomacy in Lebanon* (New York: St. Martin's Press, 1998), 14–15.

6. Ibid; "Israeli Crisis Decision-Making in the Lebanon War: Group Madness or Individual Ambition?" *Israel Studies* 3 (Fall 1998): 221.

7. Farid el Khazen, *The Breakdown of the State in Lebanon, 1967–1976* (Cambridge, MA: Harvard University Press, 2000), 78–79.

8. Ibid, 79.

9. "Mideast's Christians Declining in Influence," *New York Times*, May 13, 2009.

10. Ibid.

11. For sources on the Shi'a, see Heinz Halm, *Shi'ism* (2nd ed.) (New York: Columbia University Press, 2004); Moojan Momem, *An Introduction to Shi'a Islam* (New Haven, CT: Yale University Press, 1985).

12. Fouad Ajami, *The Vanished Imam: Musa al Sadr and the Shia of Lebanon* (Ithaca, NY: Cornell University Press, 1986), 138.

13. Ze'ev Maghen, "Occultation *in Perpetuum*: Shi'ite Messianism and the Policies of the Islamic Republic," *Middle East Journal* 62 (Spring 2008): 232–257, esp. 251–252, 256.

14. Patricia Crone, *God's Rule: Government and Islam: Six Centuries of Medieval Islamic Political Thought* (New York: Columbia University Press, 2004), Chap. 8.

15. Adapted from W. Andrew Terrill, *The United States and Iraq's Shi'ite Clergy: Partners or Adversaries?* (Carlisle, PA Strategic Studies Institute, 2004), 5.

16. Mohammed Ayoob, *The Many Faces of Political Islam: Religion and Politics in the Muslim World* (Ann Arbor: University of Michigan Press, 2008), 55.

17. Majed Halawi, *A Lebanon Defied: Musa al-Sadr and the Shi'a Community* (Boulder, CO: Westview Press, 1992), 29–30; Roschanack Shaery-Eisenlohr, *Shi'ite Lebanon: Transnational Religion and the Making of National Identities* (New York: Columbia University Press, 2008), 126.

18. See Karen Barkey, *Empire of Difference: The Ottomans in Comparative Perspective* (Cambridge: Cambridge University Press, 2008), Chap. 5 and esp. 176–177 for a treatment of the Shi'a under Ottoman rule.

19. Amal Saad-Ghorayeb, "Factors Conducive to the Politicization of the Lebanese Shi'a and the Emergence of Hizbullah," *Journal of Islamic Studies* 14, no. 3 (2003): 293.

20. Hawali, *A Lebanon Defied*, 42.

21. Augustus Richard Norton, *Amal and the Shi'a: Struggle for the Soul of Lebanon* (Austin: University of Texas Press, 1987), 22.

22. See John L. Esposito, *Unholy War* (New York: Oxford University Press, 2002); Michael Bonner, *Jihad in Islamic History* (Princeton, NJ: Princeton University Press, 2006); David Cook, *Understanding Jihad* (Berkeley: University of California Press, 2005); David Cook, *Martyrdom in Islam* (Cambridge, Cambridge University Press, 2007).

23. Raymond William Baker, *Islam without Fear* (Cambridge, MA: Harvard University Press, 2003).

24. Fawaz A. Gerges, *The Far Enemy* (Cambridge: Cambridge University Press, 2005).

25. El Khazen, *The Breakdown of the State in Lebanon*, 54.

26. Lebanon's Sunni Bloc Built Militia, Officials Say," *Los Angeles Times*, May 12, 2008.

27. "Radical Group Pulls in Sunnis as Lebanon's Muslims Polarize," *Washington Post*, June 17, 2007.

28. Al-Hakim was probably clinically insane, and his bizarre behavior included walling up women in bathing houses, sending his troops to destroy the Church of the Holy Sepulcher in 1009, ordering the execution of anyone who harmed a donkey, an attempt to steal the body of the Prophet Muhammad from Medina and rebury it in Cairo, and the banning of popular foods. He was apparently murdered in 1021, when he rode out of town on a donkey and disappeared. The next day searchers found the donkey's severed feet and al-Hakim's bloody robe. Suspicion focused on his sister, whom he had accused of adultery. After his disappearance, some of his followers held that he was not dead, but had "disappeared" in the same manner as had earlier Shi'a imams, or that he had really moved to eastern Persia. Some early Christian historians maintained that he had actually converted to Christianity.

29. One of the most informative books on the Druze is Robert Benton Betts, *The Druze* (New Haven, CT: Yale University Press, 1988), from which much of this section is drawn.

30. Mona Alami, "Lebanon: Clash with Hezbollah Unifies Druze Community," Global Information Network, May 22, 2008. The Christian Free Patriotic Movement has a Christian majority, but it is not officially a "Christian" party.

31. For more on the Palestinian narrative, see Baruch Kimmerling and Joel S. Migdal, *The Palestinians* (Cambridge, MA: Harvard University Press, 1994); James L. Gelvin, *The Israeli-Palestinian Conflict* (Cambridge: Cambridge University Press, 2007).

32. Kimmerling and Migdal, *The Palestinians*, 230–233.

33. Bernard Rougier, *Everyday Jihad: The Rise of Militant Islam among Palestinians in Lebanon* (Cambridge, MA: Harvard University Press, 2007).

34. For a full list of Palestinian refugee camps in Lebanon, see the UNRWA page on Lebanon at http://www.un.org/unrwa/refugees/lebanon.html.

35. "The Wandering Palestinian," *The Economist*, May 10, 2008, 58.

36. See UNRWA at http://www.un.org/unrwa/refugees/lebanon.html.

37. el Khazen, *The Breakdown of the State in Lebanon, 1967–1976*, 136–137.

38. Rougier, *Everyday Jihad*, 46–51.

39. Ibid, 55.

40. Michael C. Hudson, "Lebanon after Ta'if: Another Reform Opportunity Lost?" *Arab Studies Quarterly* (Winter 1999), http://findarticles.com/p/articles/mi_m2501/is_1_21/ai_55541669/pg_9?tag=artBody;col1.

41. "Abbas Firmly Opposes Any Plan to Resettle Palestinians in Lebanon," *Daily Star* (Beirut), August 29, 2008.

42. "Lebanese Fear Being Drawn into Battle," *Financial Times* (London), January 9, 2009.

43. Elizabeth Picard, *Lebanon: A Shattered Country* (New York: Holmes & Meier, 1996), 11.

44. "In Lebanon's Patchwork, A Focus on Armenians' Political Might," *New York Times*, May 26, 2009.

45. Saree Makdisi, "Reconstructing History in Central Beirut," *Middle East Report* 203 (Spring 1997): 25.

46. Samir Khalaf, *Civil and Uncivil Violence in Lebanon* (New York: Columbia University Press, 2002), 213–214.

47. David Hirst, "South Lebanon: The War That Never Ends?" *Journal of Palestine Studies* 28 (Spring 1999): 13.

FURTHER READING

Ajami, Fouad. *The Vanished Imam: Musa al Sadr and the Shia of Lebanon.* Ithaca: Cornell University Press, 1986.

Ayoob, Mohammed. *The Many Faces of Political Islam: Religion and Politics in the Muslim World.* Ann Arbor: University of Michigan Press, 2008.

Betts, Robert Benton. *The Druze.* New Haven, CT: Yale University Press, 1988.

Halawi, Majed. *A Lebanon Defied: Musa al-Sadr and the Shi'a Community.* Boulder, CO: Westview Press, 1992.

Khalaf, Samir. *Civil and Uncivil Violence in Lebanon.* New York: Columbia University Press, 2002.

Kimmerling, Baruch, and Joel S. Migdal. *Palestinians: The Making of a People.* Cambridge, MA: Harvard University Press, 1994.

Norton, Augustus Richard. *Amal and the Shi'a: Struggle for the Soul of Lebanon.* Austin: University of Texas Press, 1987.

———. *Hezbollah: A Short History.* Princeton, NJ: Princeton University Press, 2007.

Rougier, Bernard. *Everyday Jihad: The Rise of Militant Islam among Palestinians in Lebanon.* Cambridge, MA: Harvard University Press, 2007.

Salibi, Kamal. *A House of Many Mansions: The History of Lebanon Reconsidered.* Berkeley: University of California Press, 1988.

CHAPTER 3

Political and Economic Development in Lebanon

Modern Lebanon has one of the most confusing and disorderly political systems in the world. Known as a "confessional" system, it is one of the few political structures based on power apportionment by religious identity. As Chapter 2 indicated, Lebanon has no majority population, a situation with both positive and negative political costs. The advantages are that there is no majority to dominate or control the minorities, something absent in most countries. The negatives include a system that divides power among minorities so that none has a final say in political decisions—majority rule does have advantages. It is not surprising that Lebanon has rarely enjoyed decisive governance, though it has also avoided the worst of "decisive governance," a totalitarian regime that rules by fiat. It is also handicapped by the fact that its political communities are based on faith, instead of language or region. While language or other forms of ethnicity can certainly infuse emotion into a political milieu, religion has a particular potential to infuse politics with a passion that often makes compromises almost impossible.

Lebanon's national political system, created by the National Pact of 1946, as noted in Chapter 1, divided power across the national political institutions by religious identity. Thus by agreement, the president is a Maronite Christian, the prime minister is a Sunni Muslim, and the speaker of the National Assembly is a Shi'a Muslim. The president appoints the prime minister and deputy prime minister in consultation with the National Assembly.

Like most modern governments, Lebanon's system has formal participants, systematized initially by the unwritten National Pact. And, also like other national polities, Lebanon has an informal political system, which is very important because institutional paralysis limits what outputs the formal system produces.

The formal institutions include a president, a parliament, a prime minister and a cabinet, and a judicial system. However, it is necessary to look beyond the institutions to really understand Lebanese politics. This is partly because the 1946 system created a political logjam since each institution is dominated by a particular faction (the Maronites normally have the presidency, the Sunni the prime ministership, the Druze the speaker of parliament, and the Shi'a the head of the judicial system. However, since no population has a majority in Lebanon, there cannot be majority rule. The power of institutions is thus compromised by the very division of power into factions. Thus, power has defaulted to those powerful families and their heads, and they really run Lebanon. Elizabeth Picard puts it well:

> [I]t is wrong to talk of a Lebanese "democracy by consensus" comparable to the Dutch and Swiss systems, for the Lebanese populations were clearly not consulted and the system that was adopted had the effect of keeping them in the communal framework under the thumb of the traditional notables, heads of families, landowners, and clerical authorities.[1]

Thus the National Pact, despite the unity implied in its name, really helped to institutionalize the fractious nature of Lebanon as a nation of communities where loyalties to the locale are more important in many ways than loyalties to the nation of Lebanon.

THE INFLUENCE OF THE ZU'AMA

The term "*zu'ama*" (singular is *za'im*) is commonly used in Lebanon to denote the "bosses," or "the big men" (for almost all of Lebanon's powerful individuals are men). The *zu'ama*, through family connections, or guile, or sometimes by fortune, have risen to positions where they can control enough of Lebanon's resources to buy and maintain power. Some *zu'ama* lean on their past to claim their position: the Shi'a Hamadi family claims its *zu'ama* status through the claim that an ancestor fought on Imam Hussein's side at the Battle of Karbala, while the al-Fadl family alleges that Salah al-Din (the Kurdish Muslim leader during the Crusader wars) was a forbearer.[2] Sometimes they use their own resources (Rafiq Hariri was a billionaire who spent his own money buying influence, for example), but he is not the only one. Other *zu'ama* use private collection systems to gather resources. Antoine Lahad, the Lebanese Christian leader of the South Lebanon Army, quickly adapted the role of a *za'im* when he replaced Saad Haddad, taking control of the economy in south Lebanon, creating a virtual monopoly for Israeli goods there (see Chapter 5).

The *zu'ama* are usually accountable first to themselves, or to their families, or to their list of clients, rather than to the state of Lebanon. Thus they may engage in bargaining outside of Lebanon's borders if they believe it is in their interests to do so. So many *zu'ama* found themselves seeking support from Syria, or getting offers of Syrian support. Rafiq Hariri, Selim Hoss, Nabhi Berri, and many others relied on Syrian power to keep them in power, even though such influence usually benefited Syria more than it did Lebanon. Others such as Amin Gemayel reached out to Israel in the 1980s in his effort to keep power in his family.

The *za'im* tradition has a dramatic impact on Lebanese politics. Most of Lebanon's presidents are from notable families, as are many members of the cabinet and of the parliament. Michael C. Hudson notes the significance of notability within the structure of the confessional system:

> An important supporting institution for confessionalism in the parliamentary elections is the list system. Voters in each district are obliged to elect several deputies, usually including some of a confession different from their own. This requirement has led to the formation of powerful lists under the patronage of the most powerful notables of the district. Aspirants for the minority seats will often pay handsomely to join the list—and therefore the coattails—of a major notable from a majority sect.[3]

THE INSTITUTIONAL PARTICIPANTS IN LEBANESE POLITICS

Lebanon has a parliamentary system, though there is no exact model for the relative power of the systemic parts. Often in a parliamentary process, the president serves as head of state, with little internal power, but in Lebanon the president has more power than does the president of Israel, for comparative example.

The President

The Lebanese legislature elects the president. The Lebanese constitution gives the office of president considerable powers, including the role of commander in chief of the Lebanese military, the power to appoint and dismiss the prime minister, the administration of laws passed by the parliament, the power to issue emergency decrees, the authority to dismiss the Chamber of Deputies, and great influence within the Lebanese bureaucracy. Prior to the Ta'if Accord, the president had considerable power, but the compromises at Ta'if reduced this power to the benefit of the office of prime minister, whose powers Ta'if increased.

The Prime Minister

The president, with the concurrence of the Chamber of Deputies, selects the prime minister, who technically oversees the administration of the government. The constitution also gives the president the power to dismiss the prime minister, though that is an action that can cause instability when a Christian president dismisses a Muslim prime minister. The post of prime minister is the highest position allocated to a Muslim by Lebanon's constitution, so the office has considerable symbolic importance, though it is trumped in power by the president.

The Cabinet

The cabinet has the power to approve legislation from the parliament. With a parliamentary system, Lebanon's cabinet is all-important. Positions on the cabinet represent considerable power, and its composition is the subject of highly charged political wrangling. There is often compromise, though, between some of the more extreme party positions and the necessity to provide Lebanon with a cabinet that at least functions with a semblance of stability. An example of such a compromise came about in early July 2008 when Lebanon formed a new government after long months of stalemate without a cabinet. Fouad Siniora, reinstated as Lebanon's prime minister, announced the new cabinet, in which the opposition gained 11 of the 30 seats. Other members included

- Mohammad Chatah, a close adviser to Siniora, finance minister
- Mohammad Fneish, a Hezbollah official, labor minister
- Fawzi Salloukh, a lawyer and diplomat, foreign minister

The upshot of these and other appointments was that the parties, frustrated after a long period of inaction, worked to largely select members with moderate credentials.[4] The cabinet may not have the usual firebrands of the past, but it also might have an opportunity to accomplish some of Lebanon's unfinished public business after decades of paralysis.

Reform of the cabinet continued in 2008, when Lebanese factions met in Doha, Qatar, to effect yet more change. The Doha Agreement changed the cabinet to 16 seats for the majority, 11 seats for the opposition, and 3 to be nominated by the president, allowing the opposition to veto cabinet decisions, something that previous governing coalitions had refused to accept.

The Parliament

Lebanon's parliament consists of a single chamber National Assembly or *Majlis Alnuwab*. It has 128 seats, with members chosen by popular election, with results apportioned by religious identity. Each district is divided into seats by district, and then into towns. Seats are apportioned as shown in Table 3.1.

The Ta'if Accord altered the number of seats accorded to both groups, raising Christian seats from 54 to 64 and Muslim seats from 45 to 64, thus unofficially acknowledging the growth in Muslim population relative to the Christian population. With a tie in seats, the formation of parliamentary coalitions is almost mandatory to get anything through, and so Christian and Muslim parties are constantly attempting to woo members of the other faith to their positions.

The last parliamentary election was held in June 2005, with the next election scheduled for 2009. Members of the legislature elect the presiding officer, the

Table 3.1 Confession Group and Parliamentary Seats

Confession	Seats
Christian	
Maronite	34
Greek Orthodox	14
Greek Catholic	8
Armenian Orthodox	5
Armenian Catholic	1
Protestant	1
Total Christian	*64*
Muslim	
Sunni	27
Shi'a	27
Druze	8
Total Muslim	*64*

speaker, and the deputy in the opening session. By custom, the speaker is a Shi'a, and Nabhi Berri, formerly the head of the Amal militia, currently holds the position. Lebanese laws originate in parliament, though a cabinet majority must approve draft laws for them to become legal.

The results for the 2005 election, by party and number of parliamentary seats, were as follows:

- Future Movement Bloc 36
- Democratic Gathering 15
- Development and Resistance Bloc 15
- Free Patriotic Movement 15
- Loyalty to the Resistance 14
- Qornet Shehwan 6
- Lebanese Forces 5
- Popular Bloc 4
- Tripoli Independent Bloc 3
- Kataeb Reform Movement 2
- Syrian National Socialist Party 2
- Tashnaq 2
- Syrian Ba'th Party 1
- Democratic Left Movement 1
- Democratic Renewal Movement 1
- Kataeb Party 1

- Nasserite Popular Movement 1
- Independent 4

For a period of two years after an election, the Chamber of Deputies may vote only once to withdraw confidence in either the speaker or deputy speaker. A passing vote requires a two-thirds majority following the introduction of a no-confidence petition signed by a minimum of 10 members. Should that vote pass, the Chamber must then meet immediately to replace the ousted member. This mechanism was designed at Ta'if to create more stability in the Chamber. As noted above, Ta'if also changed religious membership in the Chamber, with the 128 seats from subdistricts drawn from districts and split equally between Christians and Muslims. There are five such districts: Beirut, Beqaa, Mount Lebanon, north Lebanon, and south Lebanon.[5]

Like most legislatures, the Chamber of Deputies is divided into committees: 13 in all, including Budget and Finance, Foreign Affairs and Emigrants, Public Works, Defense and Security, and Planning and Development. The Chamber of Deputies also approves the presidential nomination of the prime minister, who is required by law to be a Sunni Muslim.

The Ta'if Accord strengthened the Chamber of Deputies in four ways. First, it involved the Chamber in the selection of the prime minister. Second, it gave parliament the sole authority to remove the prime minister. Third, it limits the power of the president to declare a bill "urgent." Fourth, the speaker's role has been strengthened.[6] Given the increased representation of the non-Maronite in the Chamber, the net impact of the Ta'if-inspired constitution is to increase the power of the majority groups in Lebanon. However, certain minorities such as Hizbollah also gained influence. The network of services that Hizbollah provided in impoverished south Lebanon has helped it to become one of the stronger political parties in Lebanon.

Political Parties

Lebanon has a rich multiparty tradition, reflecting Lebanon's social makeup. While most parties are affiliated with a religious grouping, some parties are more closely tied to family rather than to a faith. That reality is hardly surprising, given the power of the *zu'ama*, and thus parliamentary blocs representing the interests of powerful families held sway during much of the postwar period. There was, for example, the Constitutional Bloc of Bashar al-Khoury, the National Bloc of the Eddé family, and the National Liberal Party of the Chamoun family, which not only represented family interests, but called for an independent Christian Lebanon (where powerful Maronite families might gain even more power).[7] Ralph E. Crow suggests that parties may be supplementing if not replacing the blocs, but the parties themselves remained sectarian and often headed by a *za'im*, as was the Progressive Socialists, affiliated with the Druze Jumblatt family.[8] Still, as Farid el Khazen notes,

> Lebanon does not have a party system, as in the case of two-party or multi-party systems in functioning democracies. The political process is centered on party-based politics as well as on non-partisan "independent" politicians. Although no party in Lebanon reached power and ruled as parties do in parliamentary systems, parties have shaped parliamentary debates and participated in government, and party leaders, particularly those of established parties, are influential political figures.[9]

The traditional role for political parties is to contest elections, though not all of Lebanon's parties exist for this purpose. As Michael W. Suleiman noted some years ago, some parties exist more as a vehicle for political activity outside of the electoral sphere: "Lebanese parties are not the main electoral organization, but ideological groupings, primarily interested in gaining converts to their cause. They do not really compete for power in the Western sense."[10] That notion remains true today, while some parties do compete for parliamentary and local seats, and others that were once closer to Suleiman's description now contest in elections, notably Hezbollah. But Lebanon's political landscape is still marked by parties in a looser sense, such as "March 8" and "March 14," and Hezbollah, which performs a number of functions including its role as a parliamentary party.

Popular Participation

Political participation can be measured in a number of ways, from electoral turnout to membership in public organizations to public service to participation in political demonstrations. While large impassioned demonstrations and counterdemonstrations marked the aftermath of the Hariri assassination, such political passions are lower for the more traditional practice of voting. Turnout depends on situational factors, such as the ability for some groups to muster their supporters at the polls, as happened in the June 2005 elections when an alliance between Amal and Hezbollah excited Shi'a voters while disappointing Christian voters, whose numbers in that election declined significantly from previous contests.[11] In some Christian districts, voter turnout did not exceed 5–10 percent.[12] In the 1996 elections, the largely Maronite area of Mount Lebanon gave a 45 percent turnout, which, according to Graham Usher, is a high turnout by Lebanese standards.[13] This seems to be a part of traditional Lebanese politics, and institutional efforts to increase turnout (in March 2009, the Lebanese parliament passed legislature that lowered Lebanon's voting age from 21 to 18 years of age) may not work. Hudson offers one possible reason for low electoral turnout as he argues, "In short, the state is accepted for certain limited purposes by most of the important groups most of the time, but it commands little inherent respect, and the idea of public interest is but poorly developed."[14] With such attitudes, it is hard to argue a reason for large-scale participation.

Moreover, Hudson also notes that there are so many parties that even the domi-nant parties get few seats in parliament, with the Kataeb (Phalange) Party getting only 4 seats out of 99 in its most successful year, the 1960 elections.[15] More recently, despite the excitement and headlines it generates, Hezbollah has only 4 seats in the Lebanese parliament.

Too often the road to voter participation is paved with corruption. Election laws are vague at best, and creative candidates and parties find numerous ways to sidestep them. Outright vote-buying is common, and often when a voter gets a payment for a vote, the payee offers a color-coded ballot for his particular party, so he knows that the payoff resulted in a vote. For poor Lebanese, in particular, the elections represent not simply a chance for political participation, but, more importantly, an opportunity to rake in significant cash. Said one unemployed young male in south Beirut, "Whoever pays the most will get my vote. I won't accept less than $800."[16]

THE POLITICS OF DIVISION

Lebanon may have one of the most divided governmental structures in the world, and its weaknesses are legendary. Samir Khalaf expresses it well:

> Confessional loyalties . . . undermine civic consciousness and commitment to Lebanon as a nation-state. Expressed more poignantly, the forces that motivate and sustain har-mony, balance, and prosperity are also the very forces that on occasion pull the society apart and contribute to conflict, tension, and civil disorder. The ties that bind, in other words, also unbind.[17]

Lebanese political factions go beyond religions or family groupings, produc-ing a collection of odd-coupe coalitions that often transform themselves over-night to something else. Since all individual groupings are too small to individually gain in the Lebanese system, coalitions are normal, but they fre-quently cross religious lines. The most recent set of coalitions included the "March 14 Alliance" and its opposition, the "March 8 Coalition," with each bloc consisting as shown in Table 3.2.[18]

The coalition membership was composed partly of groups of convenience, united by a common interest or a common enemy (or both). In other cases, revenge was a probable motive. The Free Patriotic Movement led by General Michel Aoun was a case of the latter, as General Aoun as prime minister between 1988 and 1990 had led a struggle against Syrian influence in Lebanon at the close of the civil war and was ousted from the country for his efforts. He returned to Lebanon in May 2005 with aspirations to replace President Emile Lahoud, and, after Lahoud's term expired, expected the job himself. But the March 14 Alliance refused to give him support, and thus he joined the opposition, paring with Hezbollah, and supported by Syria, even though he had once opposed Syrian influence in Lebanon. In yet another indicator of how quixotic Lebanese

Table 3.2 Members of Major Lebanese Political Coalitions

March 14 Alliance:		
Group	Religious Groupings	Leader
Future Movement	Mostly Sunni	Saad Harari
Progressive Socialist Party	Druze	Walid Jumblatt
Lebanese Forces	Maronite	Samir Geagea
Kataab Party	Maronite	Amin Gemayel

March 8 Coalition:		
Group	Religious Groups	Leader
Hezbollah	Shi'a	Hassan Nasrallah
Amal	Shi'a	Nabih Berri
Free Patriotic Movement	Mostly Christian	Michel Aoun
Syrian Social Nationalist Party	Mostly Orthodox Christian	Ali Qanshu

politics can be, Syria invited Aoun, its old enemy, to visit Damascus in December 2008. Said Aoun proudly as he came under fire from the March 14 coalition for his visit, "They are welcoming me with admiration and respect . . . I was a rival and the rivalry has ended and I may become a friend."[19]

In an ironic way, this comment by Aoun seemed to put him in league with some Lebanese Shi'a who decried the "splittist" tendencies of the March 14 Alliance:

> There was a group in Lebanon that had stated its clear options, carrying out the American agenda with Condoleezza Rice and the neo-cons. This group is known. They called themselves March 14. They are a US group, not March 14. God rest the soul of martyr Rafiq al-Hariri. He had nothing to do with this option that they are trying to impose on him. There is an option of a US group that was carrying out a conspiracy, on the eve of 2005 and July war, targeting the weapons of this resistance, trying to besiege it and drown it in the sectarian struggle between Sunnites and Shiites, isolating it to undermine its internal partisans.[20]

The Shi'a, despite their status as a plurality in Lebanon, hold a constitutionally mandated 27 seats out of the 128 total parliamentary seats. Graham E. Fuller argues, though, that because of Hezbollah's status, national power is gradually shifting to the Shi'a in parliament despite their limited number of seats.[21] The Shi'a have reached out to form coalitions not only with Aoun's movement, but also with Lebanon's Armenian community and their Tashnaq Party. Tashnaq had aligned with Syrian interests during the civil war (though the Armenian community tried to remain neutral during that conflict), but in the spring of

2009, Saad Hariri tried to woo Armenian votes for his political movement. In typical Lebanese fashion, the number of parliamentary seats was the deciding issue, and in the end Hezbollah offered Tashnaq more control over the seats in heavily Armenian districts, which Hariri did not do, according to Armenian leaders.[22] In the end, political interests trumped ideology and religious identity, as they commonly do in the cement mixer of Lebanese politics.

The Consequences of Division: Lebanon's Informal Government

The achievement of agreement on almost any salient issue within the formal governmental structure is almost impossible. The confessional system has built-in paralysis, driving many Lebanese political actors to seek alternative means of doing political business. The consequence is a dizzying array of organizations, militias, social clubs, and other groupings that offer an alternative route to political action.

The Lebanese armed forces are one such group. Historically the army was dominated by Maronite officers, but the military lost power and control during the civil war. In an effort to reconstruct the army and to unify Maronite forces at the same time, leading Maronite families created the Lebanese Front (originally the Front for Freedom and Man in Lebanon). Its initial purpose was to produce a response to the threat to Maronite power in Beirut in April 1975 during the civil war, and ultimately to provide a mandate for the Lebanese armed forces to enforce. Its founders included Camille Chamoun, Pierre Gemayel, Suleiman Frangieh, Charles Malek, Father Sharbal Qassis (head of the Maronite Order), Fouad Shamali, leader of the Tanzim militia, Sa'id Aql, leader of the Guardians of the Cedar, and Marun al-Khouri, head of the Lebanese Youth Movement. Later, the Lebanese Front limited its membership to civilian leaders, with militia leaders attending only when the Front discussed militia matters.

Militias are another vital part of the Lebanese political landscape. During the Lebanese Civil War (1975–1990), the divided civilian government was virtually unable to provide most government services, and thus militias, often with *za'im* leadership, moved in to fill the government vacuum. The Lebanese Front, as an example, assumed a caretaker role. That group, a coalition of right-wing Christian parties, provided communications to mobilize the civilian population in the time of crisis (which was almost perpetual during the civil war), to plan for the reconstruction of infrastructure after the war (including electricity, finance, water, and other essential provisions), civilian transportation, traffic management, consumer protection, public order (including crime control), and public welfare.[23] The Lebanese Forces organized Popular Committees, which connected them to the public and connected needs to military provision, in areas such as health, education, finance, environment, civil defense, planning, and social affairs. The Popular Committees were organized at the district level and staffed with a combination of military officers and local officials, and managed to bypass the old established systems of patronage to accomplish goals. The popular committees had regular inspections to root out corruption, and though this alone increased their popularity, they were most effective in Maronite communities, and less so in Muslim areas, a difference that stemmed from the reality that the Lebanese Front was made up of Maronites.[24]

The Lebanese Front later underwent considerable infighting as the Gemayel family and other prominent Maronite families began violent conflict with each other over a number of issues, including accusations of Syrian influence. Assassination after assassination followed, and ultimately the Lebanese Front devolved into a political party, which now holds 5 of the 128 seats in parliament.

All in the Families?

Most polities have powerful political families that contribute leaders out of proportion to their percent of the population. The Saud family in Saudi Arabia, the Sabah family of Kuwait, and the Bush and Adams families in the United States are examples of powerful families that have contributed more than one family member to a top national post. Few countries, though, have as many dynasties as has Lebanon, including, the Edde, Chamoun, Karamah, Lahoud, Frangieh, Jumblatt, Hariri, and Gemayel families. While Lebanese politicians have risen to top positions who come from outside these powerful families (Michel Suleiman and Rafiq Hariri, for example), they continue to exercise considerable sway over Lebanese politics.

There is clearly a debate over the merits of family dominance. Some might argue that these families have often had to coexist for centuries in Lebanon and have arranged enough compromise measures over time to have set "rules of the road" for getting along. It may also be argued that dynasties maintain continuity and stability, as has generally been the case in Saudi Arabia. On the other hand, dynasties can lead to stagnation because they may prevent the introduction of new blood and new ideas (significantly, one of Lebanon's most dynamic leaders, Rafiq Hariri, did not come from an elite family). It is also the case, as one commentator noted, that rule through influential families is a connection to the past that needs to be broken for Lebanon to move from the shadows of its often-tragic past. Rabih Haddid writes, "Lebanon has, however, reached a peculiar crossroads of its history, where many are asking if the current status quo regarding our political system is necessarily the best way forward. Is Lebanon's best possible future through the same political families that have dominated its past?"[25]

The 1989 Ta'if Accord partially addressed this question by reducing the power of some traditional Maronite families in the Lebanese parliament while at the same time increasing the number of parliamentarians with party, as opposed to family, ties. As Hudson observed,

Some 47 percent of the new deputies were affiliated with a political party or movement (as opposed to a traditional grouping or independent status), compared with 31 percent in the 1972 parliament. Some of the parties showed continuity—for example, the Ba'th, Walid Junblat's [Jumblatt] Progressive Socialist Party, and the Armenian Dashnak. More striking was the disappearance of many traditional Maronite actors—personalities like the Shamuns, [Chamouns] Gemayels, and Eddes, and parties like the Phalanges.[26]

In some ways, the 2005 parliamentary elections reified the importance of family power and the traditional role of the *za'im*. Thus while Hezbollah and Amal won in the south with a combined list, families dominated the rest of the regional outcomes. Saad Hariri, the son of Rafiq Hariri, won almost without challenge in Beirut and the Sunni areas of eastern Lebanon, and in the north, where he won 28 seats, while former general Michel Aoun, recently returned from exile in France, swept the Mount Lebanon region, with his party taking 21 total parliamentary seats.[27]

CIVIL SOCIETY IN LEBANON

Like most other Middle Eastern countries, Lebanon has civil society elements. What makes civil society in Lebanon distinct from other Middle Eastern countries is the reality that a weak-by-design government empowers the purpose of civil society in ways not found in states with more viable state centers. In Lebanon, most civil society organizations have a religious base, but others emphasize a particular cause, such as the environment or women's issues.

Hezbollah functions as a part of civil society, even though it now participates in the Lebanese political system. While widely known as a terrorist group, the origins of Hizbollah date to the Israeli invasion of Lebanon in 1982.[28] Guided spiritually by the charismatic cleric Sa'id Muhammad Hussein Fadlallah, Hizbollah gained ground in Lebanese politics after Israeli actions drove Shi'a Muslims to Beirut from south Lebanon.[29]

Hezbollah is more than a militia organization, though. Augustus Richard Norton has described it as "arguably the most effective and efficient political party in the country."[30] In many of the poor Shi'a areas of Lebanon, Hezbollah provides education, medical facilities, community centers, food distribution systems, and other services not provided by the government.[31] There is also evidence that Hezbollah is gradually turning from violence to accommodation with the realities of both Lebanese politics and the Israeli presence to the south. Since the Shi'a population is a minority (so, for that matter, is every religious group), it may be wise for an organization drawing support from at least some of Lebanon's Shi'a to draw closer to the Lebanese political system.[32] Still, Hezbollah did not miss the opportunity to add to its credibility among (and beyond) Lebanon's Shi'a population by its actions against Israel in 2006, which also allowed it to take on even more civil society functions as the rebuilder of the parts of Lebanon destroyed in the fighting. That may have a negative impact on the idea of Lebanese nationhood, though, as one critical essay noted: "[T]heir (Hezbollah's) efforts constitute not a boon for the country but rather a serious challenge, and drive Lebanese citizens' attention and loyalties even further away from the national state and healthy democratic politics."[33] That being said, the question remains as to whether the failing state or Hezbollah is responsible for such devolution of public fealty to Lebanon.

Other Lebanese civil society groups include those interested in preserving and improving the environment (the "Green Forum" and Green Peace, for example), who fill in for the largely inefficient Ministry of the Environment.[34] Other groups focus on women's issues, where they have become a voice in the issues noted below. They include Hezbollah's own women's group, Al-Hay'at al-Nisa'iyya, fi Hizbullah (Women's Association of Hezbollah), Jam'iyyat Taqadum al-Mar'a (Women's Charitable Organization), and Al-Majmu'a al-Jam'iyya al-Lubnaniyya lil-Tanmiya (Lebanese Association for Development, or LAD). LAD, founded in 1994, is a microfinance nongovernmental organization that initially focused on empowering women to enter Lebanon's economic space. It has since expanded its activities to include all eligible Lebanese, though there remains a women's focus element. The new direction for LAD is postconflict reconstruction and addressing the dire economic circumstances of Palestinian refugees, with 25 percent of its financial recipients living below the poverty line in 2007.[35]

There are a variety of religious organizations that constitute a religious element within the larger context of civil society. They include *Jama'ah Islamiyya*, or Association of Muslims, which bears the same name as violent Islamist groups in Egypt and Indonesia, among other places. The movement, founded in 1948 by Muhammad Umar al-Dauk, focused on educating those Lebanese Muslims that al-Dauk believed had strayed from Islamic roots, but it has not taken hold in Lebanese Sunni society. Mneimneh may be correct to argue that the reason for *Jama'ah Islamiyya*'s lack of import among Lebanon's Sunni is the competition. Hassan Mneimneh argues that

> Islamization as a project and Islamism as an ideology have remained at the margins of Lebanese Muslim sociocultural mainstream. This resistance arises less from the much-touted pluralism and cosmopolitanism of Lebanese society—which are still factors—than from the surviving pattern of traditional dynastic paternalism that is the primary mode of leadership in all Lebanese communities.[36]

Perhaps, but then how does one explain the enormous attraction that Hezbollah has in the Lebanese Shi'a communities? Hezbollah is less than 30 years old, but currently exceeds the power of Lebanon's prominent Shi'a families. Hezbollah may have found the political space below the influence of traditional *za'im*, no matter what their faith, and it is possible that other social movements may follow Hezbollah's example.

THE LEBANESE JUDICIAL SYSTEM

The Lebanese court system is divided into four Courts of Cassation, three for civil and commercial cases and one for criminal matters. The system also contains special purpose courts such as the Higher Court, created in 1992, which tries senior officials and ministers, and is composed of seven members of parliament and eight judges. Other special courts include the Court of Audit, which is designed to curb corruption by public officials. The Court of Audit, nominally attached to the prime minister's office, is empowered to examine the expenditure of public funds to ensure that they are appropriated within the scope of what they were intended. The court can investigate both public officials accused of misspending public funds and the procedures to spend such monies. The Lebanese military also plays a significant role in the judicial system, holding military tribunals to try terrorist suspects.[37]

The court's discretion over capital crimes was reduced in 1994 by a law requiring judges to give the death penalty for all murder cases, premeditated or not, and limiting the power to commute such sentences to the president of Lebanon.[38] The court has also come under criticism for its failure to resolve some highly controversial cases, such as one involving a five-year-old girl who died after repeated sexual assaults, but with no resolution by the courts.[39]

The power of the judicial system remains unclear relative to other centers of national power. The police fall under the control of the Interior Ministry, which apparently tested its own sense of authority when it rounded up over 200 followers of Michel Aoun (see above). The action appeared to be an independent test of judicial power that drew condemnation and suggestions that the judicial agencies were working against the president.[40]

LEBANESE NEWS MEDIA

Lebanon has a vibrant news media, representing a variety of viewpoints, some with support from the state and many outlets from Lebanon's varied political, religious, and social groupings. Lebanon's major newspapers based in Beirut include the following:

- *Al Nahar*, a private Arab language daily
- *Al Anwar*, a private Arab language daily
- *Al Safir*, a private Arab language daily
- *14 March*, the outlet of the March 14 Coalition
- *Daily Star*, an English language daily

There are a few regional papers as well, such as *Al Bayan* and *Al Inshaaa* in Tripoli. The Lebanese National News Agency is the official voice of the government, operated by the Ministry of Information.

Many political factions also have their own television and radio stations, including Hezbollah, operating *Al Manar* television stations (often the targets of Israeli warplanes during the 2006 war), Future TV, the voice of the Hariri movement, the Lebanese Broadcasting Corporation, Lebanon's first private network, and numerous tabloids focusing on entertainment and celebrity gossip. Lebanon also features a number of other news outlets catering to local and regional tastes.

Some argue that the politicization of Lebanon's media into factions has contributed to the magnitude of Lebanon's violence during periods of crisis. One report held that during the relatively calm 1990s, most satellite stations in particular agreed to suspend partisan political broadcasting (except for Hezbollah's *Al-Manar*), but,

> [n]onetheless, in a short time, these satellite channels violated the decision, which organized the work of the Lebanese audio and visual media outlets. All of these satellite channels have become engaged in the domestic conflicts and reciprocal media campaigns, as a result of the development and escalation of these conflicts . . . The danger of these reciprocal psychological wars through the satellite channels may lie in the fact that they can adopt hated sectarian course and dimensions in order to contribute to breaking the national fabric or national unity of any country that is plagued with such situation.[41]

The question remaining is whether the media fanned the fires of conflict or if the media simply reported an increase in the heat of the conflict. Some politicians argued that it was the politicians rather than the media who were accelerating conflict. Information Minister Ghazi al-Aridi argued,

> I say and repeat now that the media are not responsible for what is taking place in the country. It is the politicians who are responsible. But does this mean that the media do not assume any part of the responsibility? Certainly not; we must assume some respon sibility, but the general climate in the country was not created by the Lebanese media, whether the written, visual, or audio. In the end, it reflects the current deep political dispute in the country.[42]

SALIENT POLITICAL ISSUES

The structure of the Lebanese government is only a part of the overall political picture. There are significant political issues that any government must manage, and conflicts to be addressed.

Reconstruction of Memory

Societies rest on structures of mythology, either real or imagined or, more likely, a combination of reality and images. Lebanon has generations of social myths, most founded on the turbulent past. However, the response of most Lebanese regimes has been to try and move forward after a period of conflict without noting it. Sune Haugbolle put it elegantly, "In general, none of the rounds of communal fighting in 1840, 1860, 1958, and most recently 1975–90 brought with them any profound change in the system of feudal and sectarian power sharing. Instead, in each postwar situation, a strategy of oblivion was imposed in order to let the social system in place prevail."[43] Consequently, memory is largely the province of clans, families, and regions within Lebanon. But since the 2004 Harari assassination, both portions of the government and civil society have reified the imagined lessons learned from the civil war, partly to improve their positions relative to other actors, and partly to attempt a pave-over of the cleavages that remained. As Oren Barak notes, leaders attempted to highlight both Lebanon's prewar conditions and its Phoenician past. Educational reforms included new curricula that emphasized national unity.[44] Whether such reforms might work is speculative. They may have helped to curb the spread of violence in the 2008 Hezbollah uprisings in Beirut and elsewhere, but as Barak himself notes, "Since 1943, Lebanese leaders have referred to 'political sectarianism' as an ill that needed to be abolished, while making the most out of its continued existence."[45] Others hope for the power to forget, perhaps realizing that when memories become too powerful, they become foundations for resurgence of hatred and blind revenge, or for perpetual mourning for a lost past. Said Kamal Salibi,

> Thankfully we are a very forgetful culture. Those who committed the worst crimes and atrocities have long been forgiven. Few people in Lebanon can afford to bear grudges for too long. Who remembers Sabra and Chatila? At the time it was terrible: who could ever forgive mass murder like that? But twelve years later even the unfortunate Palestinians have probably forgotten and forgiven.[46]

Samir Khalaf holds less hope for the erosion of memory, particularly recalls of the civil war:

> The demoralizing consequences of the war are also visible in symptoms of vulgarization and impoverishment of public life and erosion of civility. The routinization of violence, chaos, and fear only compounded the frayed fabrics of the social order. It drew seemingly nonviolent groups into the vortex of bellicose conflict and sowed a legacy of hate and bitterness. It is in this fundamental sense that Lebanon's pluralism, radicalization of its communities, and consequent collective violence have become pathological and uncivil. Rather than being a source of enrichment, variety, and cultural diversity, the modicum of pluralism that the country once enjoyed is now generating large residues of paranoia, hostility, and differential bonding.[47]

Reconstruction and emphasis of memory can be a dangerous practice where the fissures of conflict remain: recall the image of Slobodan Milošević waving the bloody shirt of the Battle of Kosovo (1389) as he dispatched Serb forces to massacre hundreds of thousands of Kosovars. The bombing of the al-Askari Mosque in Samarra, Iraq, by al-Qaeda was another act that rekindled centuries of memories of Shi'a repression in Iraq by Sunnis, triggering such violence that it almost led to national civil war before the spasm of violence ultimately helped to weaken the hold of al-Qaeda in Iraq. Yet at the same time, memory is the cement that helps communities to build identities and to learn to move forward from tragedy or other loss by learning lessons from those events. Drew Gilpin Faust makes this point about the toll of the American Civil War, over 620,000 military plus thousands more civilian deaths, a cost about equal to all other American wars between 1776 and 1953—a cost so terrible that it forced America to rediscover the art of political compromise that has since served the country well.[48] Private memory may be particularly important when state or collective memory either cannot or will not record memory. But private memory can either be a direction toward healing in divided societies if the lesson is that conflict is never worth the level that we recall, or it can be an accelerant to further violence if the lesson is that last time we did not do enough to win.

Other narratives come from those Lebanese who fled the country during the violent civil war and have now returned. Many who left with their families as children are now opening their voices from a perspective that those who remained during the unrest lacked: the vision of the relatively peaceful societies that they took refuge in. For Roseanne Saad Khalaf, those voices offer a kind of hope for a country whose inability to reshape its social and political milieu is legendary:

> Contrary to some expectations, particularly those who perceive exile and the diaspora as primary an unsettling and tension generating experience, returnee students opt not to position themselves as passive victims bereft of the language of resistance and deprived of any ability to act. They challenge power differentials and rigid mindsets, moving beyond individual texts to craft a collective narrative that transcends the prevailing culture of cynicism, impotence and exclusion. And in forming a space capable of being analyzed in articulation with others, it is only a matter of time before their views begin to circulate in the mainstream, to be heard and taken into account as they move closer to disrupting and discrediting those at the center.[49]

Perhaps for Khalaf, who departed Lebanon herself for almost 10 years, there is reason for optimism, though it will likely take more than the passions for change from those whose diaspora and return have fueled such hope for Lebanon's future.

GOVERNMENT EFFECTIVENESS

It is a primary job of government to administer the country, providing services, collecting resources, adjudicating disputes, and supplying infrastructure, among other myriad tasks. It must in some way balance its resources and its expenditures as it provides government allocations to the population. Governments are either the primary means of accomplishing societal functions, in a state-centric country, or they supplement the private sphere, undertaking those responsibilities that the private sector either cannot do (provision of national security) or will not do (mass public education).

Because public functions exist either outside the marketplace, or to supplement it, the normal marketplace measures of effectiveness (share price, profit margins, market shares, and so on) rarely apply. Thus other measurements of government effectiveness are required. The World Bank has measures of "government effectiveness," some of which it gets from other sources and some it develops itself. Compiling a multi-indicator index, including such measures as budget management, quality of bureaucracy, consensus building, government-citizen relations, and dozens of other statistics, the World Bank compiles a score for almost all countries in the world, ranging from 1.00 to 0. While some Nordic countries score very high on the index (Norway and Denmark scored .99), other countries drew extremely low scores (Turkmenistan got a .06 and North Korea and Somalia both got a perfect zero), the Arab countries ranged considerably. The United Arab Emirates was awarded a .79, while Yemen got .13 and Iraq came close to North Korea with a .02. Lebanon scored a .29, considerably below Algeria (.36), Oman (.67), and Egypt (.39).[50]

Lebanon's low scores are explainable by many factors, including the total lack of a functioning government for much of 2007 and into the summer of 2008. It was also hampered by a very high public debt, which in 2007 was 187 percent of the total gross domestic product (GDP), compared to the United States at around 61 percent, or Egypt at 105 percent (Japan's public debt to GDP ratio is 196 percent, though).

The Lebanese public does not hold much faith in either the state of its country or its national government. According to a Pew Charitable Trust survey of 47 countries, Lebanese attitudes on both the condition of Lebanon and support for the national government are quite low, as Table 3.3 illustrates.[51]

Here Americans, Canadians, and French citizens appear much more "satisfied" with their lives than is the case in the Middle East, with the notable exception of Israel. Yet there is less of a difference in the "state of the nation" question, with only 25 percent of Americans saying that the state of the nation was positive, compared with 83 percent for China. In the Middle East, the measure varied considerably, ranging from 5 percent positive in the Palestinian territories to 56 percent in Morocco and Jordan. The political chaos that marks Palestinian and Lebanese society is clearly reflected here. Support for the current national government also varied considerably, with about half of Americans showing support for the national government, while only 13 percent of Egyptians give positive support for their government. It is also noteworthy that Israel, the only country ranked "free" in the Middle East by Freedom House (a New York–based nongovernmental organization that ranks countries annually on a "freedom scale"), shows less support for the national government than all of the "not free" or "partly free" countries of the Middle East in the survey except Egypt. It is noteworthy that only 6 percent of Lebanese expressed

Table 3.3 **Comparative Levels of Government Satisfaction (2007 Data)**

Country	Satisfied with Life? (%)	State of Nation Good? (%)	Satisfied with National Government? (%)
United States	65	25	51
Canada	71	47	58
France	57	22	35
China	34	83	89
Turkey	26	39	61
Egypt	25	47	13
Jordan	28	56	45
Kuwait	46	52	45
Lebanon	**28**	**6**	**61**
Morocco	15	56	47
Palestinian terr.	24	5	52
Israel	68	18	23

satisfaction with the "state of the nation." Of course, "satisfaction with the nation" involves much more than governmental effectiveness, but, given the size of Lebanon's public sector, it is a reminder of how problematic public service is in Lebanon.

LEBANON'S SOCIAL MOSAIC

While the study of Lebanon necessarily focuses on the cleavages posed by religious groups, there are other contending elements of Lebanese society, including gender relations, and the gulf between economic groups.

The Status of Women in Lebanon

Women in Lebanon have not suffered from legally imposed restrictions, but at the same time Lebanese tend to be conservative socially and current conditions facing women there reflect this. Men are a majority of the workforce, except in low-paying jobs.

Women gained the right to vote in 1953, and Lebanon ratified the UN Convention on the Elimination of All Forms of Discrimination against Women in 1996. Suffrage differs in Lebanon by gender, however. While voting is mandatory for all males upon reaching age 21, it is authorized but not compulsory for women, and only if they have an elementary education.

There is resistance to change in the status of women in Lebanon, which is reflected in the personal-status codes that each religious group uses to influence the behavior of its followers. In a study of the 15 different personal status codes in Lebanon, Lamia Rustum Shehadeh finds that each of the personal-status codes has provisions that cause a woman to lose most of her legal rights relative to her spouse. This means that women received unequal treatment in such matters as divorce, child custody, postdivorce income, and the right of remarriage.[52] For example, women are entitled to custody of sons in divorce cases until the boy reaches seven years old, but often the trial is postponed until the son is over seven, so the mother never actually gets custody.[53]

While women are not prohibited from running for public office, tradition may impinge on the outcomes. Only in November 2004, for the first time in Lebanon's history, did two women enter the Lebanese cabinet, Layla Al-Solh, who was appointed as minister of industry, and Wafa Hamza became minister of state. However, that government resigned in February 2005, two weeks after the assassination of ex-prime minister Rafiq Hariri, and neither woman received reappointment to the new government.

As is the case in some other countries,[54] some of Lebanon's Islamist movements have opened doors for women, despite the impression that Islamist conservative social orthopraxy might shun social and political openings for women. The Sunni religious institute Murshid, an arm of the Palestinian Combatant Islamic Movement, has placed considerable emphasis on training women preachers, believing that women are the best way to reach men in Palestinian Lebanese society.[55] The Palestinian group Jama'a Islamiyya also encourages women's involvement in social activism and education.[56] Hezbollah, the Shi'a organization, voiced similar support. In 2008, Mohammad Hussein Fadlallah, the founding voice of Hezbollah, provided his perspective on the role of Lebanese women in politics, arguing against the position that women are weak and thus should not become involved in political life: "Some want women in the Middle East to remain ignorant ... Human beings are born physically weak but both men and women can grow strong if they work on themselves, and urged women to become more confident in such roles: Women should feel confident, because I fear women doubt their capacities."[57] As memtioned earlier in this chapter, Hezbollah has its own women's unit, Al-Hay'at al-Nisa'iyya fi Hizbullah (Women's Association of Hezbollah).

The road to full social and political participation for women in Lebanon is forked, as is the case in many societies. One road is through the substitution of traditional "women's roles" such as housewife, mother, or in "care giving" occupations such as nursing, which are valued by society but offer limited upward mobility. Some hold that in a traditional society, women may advance through traditional venues, to include motherhood. Zeina Zaatari makes the argument that Lebanon's social value structure (at least in south Lebanon, where she did research) emphasizes the family over the state, particularly when the state is relatively absent during war years. Moreover, the motherhood role, in particular, had value because mothers were the primary step in creating the moral foundations in offspring (but, for Zaatari, sons in particular[58]), valued not just by Muslims but also by Christians. The other road moves beyond tradition to private sector and governmental positions that not only raise the value of women to society symbolically and practically, but allow them to reach their full potential.

Political space is not the only sphere where Lebanese women find barriers, but also in the commercial world. The situation is better than it was in the 1970s when women's participation in the labor force was around 18 percent; it had risen to over 30 percent in the early 2000s.[59] Still, interviews with Lebanese women in the workforce reveal that there are widespread perceptions of discrimination and devaluation of working women, including a common belief that women are more committed to their families than to their occupations or professions and are more emotional than rational in decision making.[60] Moreover, there were few religious differences in beliefs about attitudes: 77 as opposed to 76 percent of Muslims as compared to Christian women believed that corporate culture favors men, and Muslims and Christian women tie at 70 percent who point to a lack of corporate support mechanisms for women.[61]

THE LEBANESE ECONOMY

Like most Middle Eastern countries, Lebanon's economy was historically divided between rural and urban elements, with agriculture dominant in rural areas, while trade and small manufacturing were the roots of urban commerce. The two sectors mutually supported each other, with produce coming into the city in exchange for consumer goods produced and purchased there. Beirut in particular became more Europeanized as Lebanon's Maronite community encouraged contacts with the Christian West, and those contacts brought Western-style banking and trade to Lebanon. As Islam had a prohibition on the charging of interest, Christians in Lebanon established banks that propelled Lebanon into a center of financial activities in the Middle East. Some of these banks serviced deposits from predominately Muslim Arab countries that used Lebanese banks to evade the interest prohibition in their own countries, allowing the Lebanese banking system to grow, particularly during times of rising oil prices.

The other tradition that carried over into independence was that of a market-oriented economy, inspired by the old traditional business class and its ties to Lebanese political leadership. This bred conservative fiscal and monetary policies, and an exchange system relatively free of controls or other restrictions. The state incubated a business-friendly environment, and one consequence was that Lebanon attracted capital from other countries that did not enjoy such business support from their own governments.[62] Lebanese liberalism also supported a free trade tradition, with few restrictions on current payments or capital transfers, along with a flexible exchange rate.[63]

War and the Economy

Economic issues are rarely the primary source of conflict, but they can be contributing factors, and there is evidence that in the Lebanese case, problems such as inflation and income disparities between confessional groups did contribute to the passion of the civil war. Inflation rose in the early 1970s, rising particularly in 1974 in response to oil price increases triggered by the October 1973 War, and income disparities grew as foreign capital flowed into Lebanon, enriching commercial sectors in Beirut while the agricultural sector waned in comparison.[64] These inequalities had the effect of driving poorer citizens from the rural areas into Beirut as they sought jobs in the commercial sector, ultimately forming some of the front ranks of the militias who fought in the civil war, though Khazen argues that "it was not a determining factor in the political crises and military confrontations linked to the PLO before and after the outbreak of war."[65]

War is generally bad for both economic stability and growth, and Lebanon is no exception. Lebanon managed to avoid the devastation of most of the region's wars, but suffered considerably from its own civil war and repeated Israeli invasions. The impact on Lebanon's economy of the civil war and the Israeli invasions that lasted from 1975 to 1990 was mixed, according to Samir Makdisi. On one hand, the violence, some of the worst in the region, did not change the fundamentals of Lebanon's economy. Trade did drop, but not in all sectors—the devaluation of the Lebanese pound increased industrial exports because they became more competitive on the international market, and construction rose,[66] as militias with mortars used against buildings paradoxically created a later construction boom. Real wages dropped, partly because many of Lebanon's skilled workers departed the country while unskilled construction workers migrated in.[67] Banking, a cornerstone of the Lebanese economy, initially remained stable, but began to suffer as the war dragged on. Still, according to Makdisi, "Despite almost sixteen years of political fragmentation and military conflict, the national economy, while deteriorating and suffering tremendous losses, did not collapse: no mass lay-offs and no voluntary mass closures of production units took place, and not until 1983 were huge transfers of capital abroad registered."[68]

Still, following Ta'if, much of Beirut lay in ruins, hundreds of thousands of refugees eked out a subsistence living at best, and the country's international credit rating plummeted. The tourists who used to flock to Lebanon in search of beaches and nightlife had gone elsewhere during the conflict and feared to return even after the violence ended. Many wealthy Lebanese fled the country during the conflict, taking their wealth with them, while those who remained still transferred their liquid assets offshore if they could. So Lebanon as a country faced a massive reconstruction effort while the resources needed to complete the task were simply too sparse.

The task of economic reconstruction thus fell to Prime Minister Rafiq Hariri. Hariri funded much of the reconstruction, particularly in Beirut, from his own fortune (estimated at between $2 billion and $16 billion), using his own construction companies, while he also implemented a value-added tax,[69] privatization of Lebanon's state-owned economy, and stabilized the Lebanese currency. Hariri hoped that privatization might draw in foreign capital and companies without competition from state funds and enterprises. Hariri also appreciated the inefficiency and favoritism associated with the state sector, and his wish was that his steps might also invigorate Lebanese confidence in a postwar economy.

However, Hariri's steps were unpopular, as privatization threatened state-guaranteed jobs and the power of the ministries. The value-added tax hit the poor especially hard, and currency stabilization meant cutting subsidies and holding the line on government spending, which was keeping many of Lebanon's poor from sinking even deeper into economic despair. The development of Beirut concentrated on the reinstatement of its status as an international business community, while it neglected the needs of others. Noted Dona J. Stewart, "Perhaps the greatest weakness in the reconstruction plan, with its external focus on the international business community, is its failure to address needs of the poor."[70] Hudson came to a similar conclusion about the impact of Hariri's economic policies,

> While the prime minister beguiled the international financial community with his show-case project—the reconstruction of Beirut's central business district—he eased the tax burden on the rich while increasing it on the poor, and permitted the debt burden to reach astronomical levels (with a gross domestic product of $13 billion in 1997 the total public debt was more than $15 billion). Middle-class Lebanese regularly lament the demise of the middle class in Lebanon and point to the growing ostentation of the super-rich while the poor seem to get both poorer and more numerous.[71]

Lebanon's economic reconstruction evolved through four phases, according to Makdisi. The first phase, from 1991 to 1994, saw growth rates of around 8 percent, fueled by increases in public spending and construction, while the second, from 1995 to 2000, saw government borrowing at high interest rates slow the growth rate. The third stage, from 2001 to 2004, saw higher growth rates return, reaching around 6 percent in 2004, accelerated by Arab capital that flowed once again into Beirut, along with tourist spending, though it would not last. The fourth phase, from 2005 to 2006, ushered in the massive destruction of Lebanese infrastructure in the Israeli-Hezbollah conflict, estimated at around $2.5 billion, and a resulting economic decline of 3 percent.[72]

The year 2007 witnessed a turnaround in Lebanon's economy as it grew at a 4 percent rate, and Moody's raised its rating of Lebanon from negative to stable, a testament to the strength of Lebanon's public finances in the face of political disorder. The Lebanese pound remained relatively constant partly due to the weakening of the U.S. dollar, to which Lebanon's currency is pegged.[73] Lebanon's banks also did surprisingly well, even though certain other economic sectors lagged. For 2007, the banking sector assets grew by 3.8 percent, customer deposits by 4 percent, lending by 8.9 percent, and profitability was up by 4.7 percent.[74]

The data for Lebanon's economy for 2009 follow:[75]

- GDP/capita (PPP): $11,100.
- Unemployment rate: 9.2 percent
- Inflation rate: 10 percent
- Budget:
    Revenue: $7 billion
    Expenditures: $10 billion
- Public debt: 164 percent of GDP
- Export partners: Syria, 25 percent; United Arab Emirates, 12 percent; Switzerland, 8 percent; Saudi Arabia, 6 percent
- Import partners: Syria, 12 percent; Italy, 9 percent; France, 8 percent; United States, 7 percent; China, 6 percent; Germany, 3 percent
- External debt: $34.7 billion

The figures give an interesting but partial picture of Lebanon's economic health. The wealth base is unequally distributed, a condition found in many middle developing countries, but exacerbated by confessional grouping. The Maronite Christian population tends to be wealthier than the Muslim population, and the Sunni and Druze groups do relatively better on the economic ladder than do the Shi'a. The overall index of inequality is known as the Gini Index, which measures the actual income distribution by percentile or decile in comparison to a perfect income distribution. The perfect Gini number would be zero, so the larger the number the larger the inequality. Lebanon's Gini Index number is .37, which, compared to some Latin American countries at .55 (or the United States at .45) is relatively low. This maldistribution is also demonstrated by consumption patterns: the bottom 20 percent account for only 7 percent of all consumption, while the richest 20 percent account for 43 percent of the total consumption, six times greater than the bottom 20 percent.[76]

Even this cross-section of the Lebanese economy does not give a picture of regional differences. There is much more extreme poverty in north Lebanon and in the Mount Lebanon area than in the rest of the country, as Table 3.4 shows.[77] A further breakdown of the results indicated that 28 percent of Lebanon's population was living in poverty (less than US$2 per day), while 8 percent lived in extreme poverty, less than US$1 per day. The cost of alleviating the conditions came in at US$48–50 million, but according to one authority, the cost was not the biggest barrier to poverty reduction. According to Kamal Hamdan, "With $48–50 million, we can neutralize the worst forms of poverty. The major problem is lack of targeting. We are not giving the money to the people who are subject to extreme poverty. It's managed by inefficient public entities where money is not being pushed in the right direction."[78] From these data, it is hardly surprising that there is more support for groups such as Hezbollah and Fatah al-Islam in these poorer areas than there is in places such as urban Beirut or in Nabatieh.

Lebanon and the Global Recession, 2008–2009

Some analysts expected that the global economic crisis of late 2008–2009 would have dire consequences for Lebanon. The crisis hit the Arabian Gulf oil-producing states hardest because they had put much of their oil revenues into the global financial market and real estate development to help diversify their economies. The booming economies in such states as the United Arab Emirates (UAE) and Qatar drew in many Lebanese seeking jobs that paid more than they could earn at home. By late 2008, over 400,000 Lebanese worked in the UAE, Qatar, Saudi Arabia, Bahrain, Oman, and Kuwait, remitting over $6 billion, or 25 percent of Lebanon's GDP per year.[79] The data indicated not only how vulnerable the Lebanese economy was to a slowdown where Lebanese workers had migrated, but also how dependent Lebanon's economy was on foreign work in general. Thus when the Lebanese labor migrants came back from the Gulf after the economic slowdown there, it only complicated Lebanon's economic problems.

Concerns about the impact of the global recession on Lebanon turned out to be well-founded. The annual report of the International Monetary Fund for

Table 3.4 Distribution of Poverty in Lebanon Across Governorates, 2004–2005

Governorate	Extremely Poor	Moderately Poor	Total Poor	Proportion of Total Population
Beirut	.9	2.6	2.1	10.4
Mt. Lebanon	18.9	30.5	27.3	39.9
North	46	34.9	38	20.7
Beqaa	17.2	11.4	13	12.7
South	15.4	15.6	15.6	10.5
Nabataea	1.6	4.9	4	5.9
Total	100	100	100	100

2009 minced few words for Lebanon's economic predicament: "Among the non-oil-producing countries, Lebanon is set to experience the steepest slowdown, as difficult external liquidity conditions raise the cost of debt servicing and the downturn in the Gulf reduces remittances."[80] While noting that Lebanon's economy grew at record rates in 2008, the report suggested that 2009 would be different:

> [T]he worsening international macroeconomic outlook will affect Lebanon in 2009. The authorities expect lower global liquidity and the world economic downturn, particularly in the Gulf, to affect remittances, tourism, foreign direct and portfolio investment, as well as deposit inflows. Thus, growth is likely to slow to 3 percent this year from over 8 percent in 2008, and deposit growth is expected to decline to 10 percent from 15 percent in 2008. Inflation will remain low, in line with international price trends. Lower oil prices will reduce the current account deficit, even though the capital account will likely weaken due to lower investment flows.[81]

However, not all the economic news on Lebanon was bad. Tourism, a key ingredient in Lebanon's historical economic success, had bounced back from the low points of the civil war and the 2006 Hezbollah-Israel conflict. For January 2009, tourism increased by almost 23 percent from the previous January, with 77,308 visitors coming to Lebanon, growing from 62,987 the previous year.[82] This time, unlike previous years, the big-spending tourists were from the Arabian Gulf instead of Europe. Other data also indicated that Lebanon might not have been harmed by the global recession of 2008–2009 as badly as earlier forecasts indicated. According to the Banque du Liban, Lebanon's GDP grew at 9 percent, not the 7.5 percent it had indicated earlier, new car sales also increased at 9 percent, and the value of bank deposits in Lebanon rose by 15 percent, to US$94 billion.[83] One reason for the performance is that Banque du Liban avoided investing in risky financial instruments that helped to sink many other international banks; another was the inflow of funds from countries such as Iran to assist in war damage rebuilding from the 2006 war.[84]

Syria and the Lebanese Economy

The Syrian presence in Lebanon was more than political; it also offered significant economic advantages for Syria. Syrian political influence allowed Syrian workers and merchants to gain a foothold in the Lebanese economy, often at the expense of Lebanese citizens. Syrian construction workers built buildings in the boom that followed the Ta'if Accord, and Syrian street vendors and mechanics and other workers left the stagnant Syrian economy for a more prosperous Lebanon, often encouraged by the Syrian government, which feared the instability from Syrian unemployment. By 2005, the Lebanese Ministry of Labor reported 54,000 laborers from outside the country, and while the report did not specify country of origin, most were Syrian. Unofficial reports put the number at over 1 million, and the real number was probably somewhere in between. After the "Cedar Revolution," many Syrian laborers and merchants followed the Syrian military back to Syria, and some who did not were attacked and, in some cases, murdered. Some Lebanese celebrated their departure, with one Lebanese street vendor stating, "[T]hey were bloodsuckers, and now that they are gone, we are relieved. Our selling record is increasing day after day."[85] It was also the case that Syrians sometimes did the jobs that most Lebanese refused to do.

Syrian influence ran deep into most of the debates on the Lebanese economy. A classic example is the debate on Lebanon's cell phone industry. Given that the civil war damaged Lebanon's landline phone system, the government chartered two new cell phone companies, LibanCell and Cellis in 1994. Both companies had important political connections: LibanCell's largest shareholders were the sons of former defense minister Mohsen Dalloul, seen by some as proxies for former Syrian vice president Abd al-Halim Khaddam, while Cellis was connected to the family of Najib Miqati, who in turn had associations with the Asad family.[86] Prime Minister Hariri and President Siniora wanted to continue their private status, while Lahoud believed that the contract was awarded unfairly and should be placed under state ownership. The debate resulted in policy paralysis, though Hariri kept the auction of the companies as official policy.[87] The issue continued to fester, caught between factions. In many ways, the cell phone issue demonstrated the effectiveness of the Syrian-backed elements in Lebanon in weakening the Hariri government.[88] In 2008, the new telecommunications minister Jabran Bassil called for privatization of the two cell phone firms, which became the position of the Free Patriotic Movement, but the overall dispute between the Free Patriotic Movement and the March 14 group again delayed a privatization decision, even though the "Paris III" donor conference decisions strongly urged privatization.[89] The cell phone issue might have ignited sparks even in the absence of Syrian influence, but it appears that Syrian pressure only made it more flammable.

Other Foreign Influences

Lebanon's economy has required outside assistance to cope with the dislocations of war. For example, in the 1990s, Saudi Arabia contributed over $3.4 billion to the Lebanese economy and announced another $1 billion in the aftermath of the 2006 Hezbollah-Israel conflict.[90] Lebanon also benefited from several international donors' conferences intended to restore the Lebanese economy after a period of conflict. In September 2006, just months after the summer 2006 war ended, Sweden hosted the "Conference for Supporting Lebanon and Reviving its Economy" in Stockholm, which allowed Lebanese political leaders to get much public attention from potential donors and the news media about the cost of the conflict to Lebanon's economy. The next January saw the opening of the "Paris III" conference, which called for a series of Lebanese economic reforms in exchange for donor assistance. With high-level attention from the UN general secretary, the acting president of the European Union, and the U.S. secretary of state, the Paris III conference was a significant indication that senior officials in the United States, Europe, and the United Nations understood Lebanon's fragile economy and its connection to the equally fragile political situation. Going into the conflict, Lebanon carried over $42 billion in public debt and faced a crisis because the economic devastation caused by the war made it almost impossible to keep paying it off. To assist, the European Commission pledged $519 million, and the United States an additional $770 million in grants, including $220 billion to rebuild the Lebanese military.[91]

Other outside assistance covers Lebanon's energy sector. Lebanon has no exploitable oil or gas and thus must import its energy to generate electricity. Lebanon has a large but inefficient electric generating and distributing system, run by the state, whose losses in 2008 topped $1.5 billion, adding to the already bulging public debt. In August 2008 Lebanon signed an agreement with Egypt that would allow Egyptian natural gas to power some of the Lebanese electric generation, possibly saving as much as $200 million a year. But despite the gas imports, Lebanon still had an inadequate power generating capacity, capable of producing only 1,600 megawatts, while the requirements stood at 2,300 megawatts.[92]

The global financial crisis of late 2008 challenged the economies of a large number of countries, particularly those whose large banks were capitalized with foreign assets. Many countries had to bail out their banks, to the tune of billions of national currency. However, the Lebanese banks found themselves in a position to bail out the state in a reversal of the common practice elsewhere. Lebanon's economy during much of its history was based on its banking system (earning it the sobriquet "Switzerland of the Middle East"), and a combination of experience in turmoil and prudent banking practices made Lebanon's banks an exception to the global banking meltdown. Lebanon's banks barred investments in derivatives and other securitized investments and instead based their assets on deposits, which accounted for around 83 percent of their holdings.[93] Given that stability, some conservative investors began to deposit funds in Lebanese banks, whose deposits for 2009 grew by 16 percent over 2007. As a consequence, funds in Lebanon's national banks exceeded the value of the entire Lebanese economy, holding over $100 billion to the national GDP of $25 billion. As one Lebanese analyst noted, "In this crisis, governments in the U.S., Europe, and elsewhere have been stepping in to rescue their banking sectors. Whereas in Lebanon the sector is so large it has been supporting the state for years."[94]

Despite problems posed for Lebanon by the global economic crisis, voices of optimism remained in Lebanon. Saad Hariri, son of the assassinated prime minister, claimed, "Lebanon has endured an Israeli war, assassinations, bombings and terrorist attacks over the past few years. But nevertheless, the economy remained relatively strong," and noting that Lebanon's GDP was hardly $2 billion after the civil war, he noted his own father's optimism: "But late Prime Minister Rafiq Hariri asked why Lebanon couldn't have a GDP of $20 billion. He managed to fulfill this promise."[95] Head of the Central Bank Riad Salameh also predicted higher economic growth for Lebanon, suggesting that it would grow from its current level of $24 billion to $29 billion at the end of 2009.[96] Moreover, Lebanon's public debt as a share of its GDP dropped by 18 percentage points, from 180 percent of GDP in 2006 to 162 percent in 2008.[97]

Lebanon has struggled with both political and economic stability, but despite a wrenching civil war, repeated high-visibility assassinations, and political logjams, the country has managed to produce periods of relative stability, with a return to elections and a preservation of a market economy. With its patchwork quilt population and a long history of tragedy, it is perhaps remarkable that the Lebanese political and economic systems have even survived.

NOTES

1. Elizabeth Picard, *Lebanon: A Shattered Country* (New York: Holmes & Meier, 1996), 71.

2. Majed Halawi, *A Lebanon Defied: Musa al-Sadr and the Shi'a Community* (Boulder, CO: Westview Press, 1992), 86.

3. Michael C. Hudson, "Democracy and Social Mobilization in Lebanese Politics," *Comparative Politics* 1 (January 1969): 252.

4. "Lebanon Announces Unity Cabinet," *Al Jazeera*, July 11, 2008.

5. The mix of Beirut was well reflected by its representatives: six were Sunni, three Armenian Orthodox, two Greek Orthodox, two Shi'ite, one Greek Catholic, one Armenian Catholic, one Protestant, one Druze, one "Christian Minority," and one Maronite.

6. Abdo Baakline. Guilain Denoeux, and Robert Springborg, *Legislative Politics and the Arab World* (Boulder, CO: Lynne Rienner Publishers, 1999), 95–96.

7. Ralph E. Crow, "Religious Sectarianism in the Lebanese Political System," *Journal of Politics* 24 (August 1962): 497.

8. Ibid., 497–498.

9. Farid el Khazen, "Political Parties in Postwar Lebanon: Parties in Search of Partisans," *Middle East Journal* 57 (Autumn 2003): 605.

10. Michael W. Suleiman, "The Role of Political Parties in a Confessional Democracy: The Lebanese Case," *Western Political Quarterly* 20 (September 1967): 683.

11. Bilal Al-Amine, "Lebanon Election Report: Resistance Sweeps the South," June 8, 2005, http://www.beirut.indymedia.org/ar/2005/06/2786.shtml.

12. "Sfeir Regrets the Low Turnout for the Lebanese Elections," *Arab News*, June 1, 2005.

13. Graham Usher, "Hizballah, Syria, and the Lebanese Elections," *Journal of Palestinian Studies* 26 (Winter 1997): 61.

14. Hudson, "Democracy and Social Mobilization in Lebanese Politics," 248.

15. Ibid., 57.

16. "Money from Abroad Floods into Lebanon to Buy Votes," *New York Times*, April 23, 2009.

17. Samir Khalaf, *Civil and Uncivil Violence in Lebanon: A History of the Internationalization of Communal Conflict* (New York: Columbia University Press, 2002), 27.

18. "Iran's Tool Fights America's Stooge," *The Economist*, May 15, 2008, 35. The name "March 14 Alliance" came from a large anti-Syrian rally held on that date.

19. "Lebanon's Aoun Visits Syria," *Al-Jazeera*, December 3, 2008.

20. Comment by Secretary General Rafi Madayan of George Hawi's Youths Rafi Mada, Talk of the Hour (*Hadith Al-Sa'ah*), OpenSource, GMP20081111689007 Beirut *Al-Manar Television* (in Arabic), October 24, 2008. Mayadan supposedly remained a Marxist, though his loyalties, like many Lebanese politicians, are switchable.

21. Graham E. Fuller, "The Hizballah-Iran Connection: Model for Sunni Resistance," *The Washington Quarterly* 30 (Winter 2006–2007): 144.

22. "In Lebanon's Patchwork, A Focus on Armenians' Political Might," *New York Times*, May 26, 2009.

23. Lewis W. Snider, "The Lebanese Forces: Their Origins and Role in Lebanon's Politics," *Middle East Journal* 38 (Winter 1984): 19–22.

24. Ibid., 24–28.

25. Rabih Haddad, "Lebanese Political Dynasties: Pro and Con," *Daily Star* (Beirut), August 1, 2008.

26. Michael C. Hudson, "Lebanon after Ta'af: Another Reform Opportunity Lost?" *Arab Studies Quarterly* (Winter 1999), http://findarticles.com/p/articles/mi_m2501/is_1_21/ai_55541669/pg_2?tag=artBody;col1.

27. Oussama Safa, "Lebanon Springs Forward," *Journal of Democracy* 17 (January 2006): 35–36.

28. For more on the origins of Hizbollah, see Hala Jaber, *Hizbollah: Born with a Vengeance* (New York: Columbia University Press, 1997).

29. See Martin Kramer, "The Oracle of Hizbollah: Sayyid Muhammad Husayn Fadlallah," in *Spokesmen for the Despised: Fundamentalist Leaders of the Middle East*, ed. R. Scott Appleby (Chicago: University of Chicago Press, 1996), 83–181.

30. Augustus Richard Norton, "Hizballah: From Radicalism to Pragmatism," *Middle East Policy* 5 (January 1998): 148.

31. "To U.S., A Terrorist Group; to Lebanese, a Social Agency," *New York Times*, December 28, 2001.

32. Norton, "Hizballah," 151–152.

33. "Hizbollah Is Rearing an Uncivil Society," *Financial Times* (London), September 1, 2006.

34. Paul Kingston, "Patrons, Clients, and Civil Society: A Case of Environmental Politics in Postwar Lebanon," *Arab Studies Quarterly* 23 (Winter 2001): 55–73.

35. Al-Majmoua Annual Report, 2007, 7, http://www.almajmoua.org/images/report07.pdf.

36. Hassan Mneimneh, "The Islamization of Arab Culture," *Current Trends in Islamist Ideology* 6 (2008), 59–60.

37. "Court Sentences 25 in Bombings," *Daily Star* (Beirut), December 21, 2003.

38. "Mixed Messages," *The Middle East*, August 1998, p. 14. The most common means of execution is public hanging, which has been carried out 14 times since the law was passed.

39. "Berri, Hrawi Agree on Constitutional Change, Speaker Takes More Moderate Approach to Amendments," *Daily Star* (Beirut), January 1, 1998.

40. "Baabda Faces New Crisis over Charges of 'Police State,' " *Daily Star* (Beirut), August 9, 2001.

41. Rida al-Sammak: "The Role of Satellite Channels in Agitating the Lebanese Crisis," *Akhbar Al-Khalij*, May 18, 2008, BBC Monitoring Middle East, May 21, 2008.

42. Lebanese National News Agency Web site, Beirut (in Arabic), April 11, 2008, BBC Monitoring Middle East, April 14, 2008.

43. Sune Haugbolle, "Public and Private Memory of the Lebanese Civil War," *Comparative Studies of South Asia, Africa, and the Middle East* 25, no. 1 (2005): 193.

44. Oren Barak, " 'Don't Mention the War' The Politics of Remembrance and Forgetfulness in Postwar Lebanon," *Middle East Journal* 61 (Winter 2007): 49–70.

45. Ibid., 65.

46. Quoted in Haugbolle, "Public and Private Memory of the Lebanese Civil War," 196.

47. Khalaf, *Civil and Uncivil Violence in Lebanon*, 233.

48. Drew Gilpin Faust, *The Republic of Suffering: Death and the American Civil War* (New York: Alfred A. Knopf, 2008).

49. Roseanne Saad Khalaf, "Youthful Voices in Post-War Lebanon," *Middle East Journal* 63 (Winter 2009): 65.

50. For the scores and methodology, see "Governance Matters, 2009," The World Bank Group, http://info.worldbank.org/governance/wgi/sc_chart.asp.

51. *Global Opinion Trends, 2002–2007: A Rising Tide Lifts Mood in the Developing World.* The Pew Global Attitudes Project, July 24, 2007, http://pewglobal.org/reports/pdf/257.pdf.

52. Lamia Rustum Shehadeh, "The Legal Status of Married Women in Lebanon," *International Journal of Middle East Studies* 30 (November 1998): 501–519.

53. "Divorce Rules 'Stack the Deck' against Women," *Daily Star* (Beirut), December 6, 1999.

54. Women have advanced in at least two Islamist parties, taking active roles in both Yemen's Islah Party and in Jordan's Islamic Action Front. Janine Astrid Clark and Jillian Schwedler, "Who Opened the Window? Women's Activism in Islamist Parties," *Comparative Politics* 35 (April 2003): 293–312.

55. Bernard Rougier, *Everyday Jihad* (Cambridge, MA: Harvard University Press, 2007), 61.

56. Ibid., 105.

57. "Fadlallah Urges Women to Enter Politics: 'Strength Means Responsibility,' " *Daily Star* (Beirut), September 11, 2008.

58. Zeina Zaatari, "The Culture of Motherhood: An Avenue for Women's Civil Participation in South Lebanon," *Journal of Middle East Women's Studies* 2 (Winter 2006): 33–64.

59. Dima Jamali, Yusuf Sidani, and Assem Safieddine, "Constraints Facing Working Women in Lebanon: An Insider View," *Women in Management Review* 20, nos. 7–8 (2005): 584–585.

60. Ibid., 588–589.

61. Ibid., 590.

62. Samir Makdisi, "Rebuilding without Resolution: The Lebanese Economy and State in the Post-Civil War Period," in *Rebuilding Devasted Economies in the Middle East*, ed. Leonard Binder (New York: Palgrave Macmillan, 2007), 99.

63. Samir Makdisi, *The Lessons of Lebanon: The Economics of War and Development* (London: I. B. Tauris, 2004), 13.

64. Farid el Khazen, *The Breakdown of the State in Lebanon, 1967–1976* (Cambridge, MA: Harvard University Press, 2000), 256–257.

65. Ibid, 258.

66. Makdisi, *The Lessons of Lebanon*, 47–48.

67. Ibid.

68. Ibid., 75.

69. "Value-added tax" is a consumption tax that taxes value added to a good or service at each production stage.

70. Dona J. Stewart, "Economic Recovery and Reconstruction in Postwar Beirut," *Geographical Journal* 86 (October 1996): 501.

71. Makdisi, "Rebuilding without Resolution," 99.

72. Ibid., 110–112.

73. "A President at Last?" *The Economist*, May 3, 2008, 58.

74. "Lebanon: Banks Ride High Despite Economic Slowdown," *Euromoney*, September 2007.

75. CIA World FactBook, 2009, https://www.cia.gov/library/publications/the-world-factbook/geos/le.html#Econ.

76. Heba Laithy, Khalid Abu-Ismail, and Kamal Hamdan, "Poverty, Growth, and Income Distribution in Lebanon," International Poverty Centre, Country Study 13, January 2008, 4.

77. Ibid., 10.

78. "Some 28 Percent of Lebanese Live Below Poverty Line—Study," *Daily Star* (Beirut), February 5, 2009.

79. "Recession in Gulf States Would Have Dire Consequences for Lebanon—Experts," *Daily Star* (Beirut), November 20, 2008.

80. *Global Financial Stability Report: Responding to the Financial Crisis and Measuring Systemic Risks.* International Monetary Fund, April 2009, 91–92.

81. Ibid., 8.

82. "Tourism Sector Bounces Back," *Middle East Economic Digest*, April 3–9, 2009, 31.

83. "Bucking the Trend," *The Economist*, April 25, 2009, 52.

84. Ibid.

85. "Many Lebanese Prosper with Syrians Gone," *Washington Post*, April 17, 2005.

86. "Talal Nizameddin, "The Political Economy of Lebanon under Rafiq Hariri: An Interpretation," *The Middle East Journal* 60 (Winter 2006): 105–107.

87. Ibid, 107.

88. Ibid. Hariri's phoenix-like rise in 2000 may have generated Syrian fears that the only way to keep him out of power in 2004 was to assassinate him.

89. "Bassil for Lebanese Privatization—at Right Price," *Daily Star* (Beirut), July 15, 2008.

90. "Saudi Foreign Minister Addresses Paris III Donor Conference on Lebanon," BBC Monitoring Middle East, January 25, 2007.

91. "Donors Gather to Help Lebanon's Government," *New York Times*, January 25, 2007.

92. "Egypt to Provide Lebanon with Electricity, Gas," *Daily Star* (Beirut), August 18, 2008.

93. "Armored against Turmoil, Lebanon Lures Investors," *New York Times*, October 29, 2008.

94. Ibid.

95. "Salameh Predicts Higher GDP, Lower Inflation, Stable Pound for Lebanon," *Daily Star* (Beirut), November 24, 2008.

96. Ibid.

97. "Barclays Warns Lebanon Still Facing Key Economic Risks," *Daily Star* (Beirut), April 16, 2009.

FURTHER READING

Halawi, Majed. *A Lebanon Defied: Musa al-Sadr and the Shi'a Community*. Boulder, CO: Westview Press, 1992.

Jaber, Hala. *Hizbollah: Born with a Vengeance*. New York: Columbia University Press, 1997.

el Khazen, Farid. *The Breakdown of the State in Lebanon, 1967–1976*. Cambridge, MA: Harvard University Press, 2000.

Makdisi, Samir. *The Lessons of Lebanon: The Economics of War and Development*. London: I. B. Tauris, 2004.

Picard, Elizabeth. *Lebanon: A Shattered Country*. New York: Holmes & Meier, 1996.

CHAPTER 4

Hezbollah in Lebanon

Lebanon's political culture reflects the roots of its founding, and the power of the then-Maronite Christian majority, which secured the presidency and a majority of parliamentary seats. The Sunni Muslim population got second place in the confessional government, in both parliamentary seats and with the post of prime minister. The Druze were the third power center, reflecting their centuries-long existence as a regional power in Lebanon. The Shi'a, by contrast, lacked access to political power compared to the other religious groupings, epitomized by their gaining the relatively powerless post of speaker of the Lebanese parliament. For the Shi'a, the alternatives were to either hope to gain access to more power as a function of their growing population or to find alternative routes to power. The birth and rise of Hezbollah must be understood in this context.

The Shi'a of Lebanon have lived there for many centuries, though their places of origin are unclear. Some of Yemeni descent may have migrated to Lebanon in the tenth century, and over the years other Shi'a from Sunni-majority countries settled in Lebanon. Yet others migrated back and forth from Iran, particularly after the Qajar Dynasty established the Shi'a religion as the official faith of Persia in the sixteenth century. As they were relative newcomers to Lebanon compared to the Maronites and the Sunnis, the Shi'a often moved into the more remote south and into the Beqaa Valley near the Syrian border. They faced repression by the majority Sunni rules during Lebanon's outside rule, as noted in Chapter 3. After independence, the Shi'a Lebanese labored chiefly in agriculture, which received a very small part of the national budget.

For centuries the Shi'a leaders followed Lebanese tradition, serving as local *zu'ama*, like the other leaders of religious groups in Lebanon, with largely local interests and clients.[1] They derived power from the strength of family relations and from their success in gaining land grants from the ruling dynasties, rather than through Shi'a piety.[2] However, Musa al-Sadr arrived in Lebanon in 1959 and became a local leader for the Shi'a living in Tyre. Al-Sadr was an Iranian, though his family had roots in Lebanon. Al-Sadr also broke down the community identity of most of Lebanon's Shi'a, giving them a more nationalist identity, although their communities are divided geographically across Lebanon, thus preventing closer integration. He was a powerful speaker who seemed particularly able to articulate the grievances of Lebanon's Shi'a population, though he urged his followers to eschew the idea of an Islamic republic and to instead work within the confessional system, and within Lebanon's democratic framework.[3] Unlike previous Shi'a leaders, Al-Sadr reached beyond his local community to Lebanon's Shi'ite population, thus coincidently weakening the regional power of the Shi'a *zu'aima*. After the disappearance of Musa al-Sadr on a visit to Libya in 1978, the loose movement that had followed him formed Amal, which is both an acronym for *Afwaj al-Muqawmat al-Lubnaniyya* and Arabic for "hope."

THE ROOTS OF HEZBOLLAH

In September 1970, the Hashemite monarchy of Jordan expelled members of the Palestinian Liberation Organization (PLO), which had taken over the Jordanian city of Irbil after bloody conflicts with the Jordanian military, and most of the PLO fighters were sent to Lebanon in 1971. After their arrival there, many PLO members moved into the Shi'a areas of Lebanon, particularly in the southern parts. From there they could launch cross-border attacks against Israel, drawing in turn Israeli responses, which did not always discriminate between Palestinian and Lebanese Shi'a. As the Israelis retaliated, either by shooting across the border or sending in troops (as they did in 1976, for example), the Shi'a caught the fire meant for the PLO, and relations between the Shi'a and the Palestinians deteriorated quickly. The Lebanese government seemed powerless to respond, and Israeli troops freely crossed the border again in 1982 and swept through the Shi'a areas on their way to Beirut. In 1982 some Amal members split from that group to create *Amal al-Islami*, the Islamic Amal, which demanded a closer relationship to Iran than Amal was willing to grant, and stronger resistance to the Israeli presence in south Lebanon.[4] But their resistance was minor, and thus other Amal members formed Hezbollah, literally "Party of God."[5] Hezbollah quickly found its voice in the person of Sayyid Muhammad Hussein Fadlallah, the scion of a famous Shi'a family from Najaf, Iraq, who reached out to Lebanon's young Shi'a in particular. Fadlallah established centers for Shi'a youth, emphasizing religious education and nuanced support for the Palestinians in Lebanon.[6] While he denies being the "founder" of Hezbollah, he was clearly a major source of its inspiration and doctrine.

Hezbollah began its resistance in south Lebanon, from where most of the original Maronite and Greek Orthodox population had fled northward, leaving the Shi'a, often too poor to move, as a majority in many parts of south Lebanon. There Hezbollah honed its organizational and military skills, attacking both Israeli and South Lebanon Army forces, concentrating mostly on soldiers, while avoiding civilian areas. As David Hirst notes, Hezbollah understood that if it kept civilian casualties to a minimum in south Lebanon, it would gain a psychological advantage over Israel, because the Israeli operations killed or wounded far more civilians, partly due to the larger weapons Israeli forces used.[7]

Hezbollah's founders were mostly young Shi'a, some with affiliations to Amal, others with educational experience in Shi'a religious schools. Hasan Nasrallah was but 22 in 1982, and his mentor, Abbas al-Musawi, was 30, as was Raghib Harb. Subhi Tufayli, Hezbollah's first secretary general, was 34 in 1982.[8] They held deep suspicion for both the United States and the Soviet Union, along with the Lebanese government (considered by Hezbollah to be deeply corrupt), and other militias, including Amal.[9]

Paradoxically, Hezbollah, which became one of Israel's more dangerous enemies, gained life and power because of the 1982 Israeli invasion of Lebanon. Earlier Israeli invasions had not radicalized the Lebanese Shi'a, but the 1982 invasion came on the heels of the 1979 Iranian Revolution, as Amal Saad-Ghorayeb observes, "Another factor explaining the Shi'a's non-resistance and the non-materialization of the Islamic Resistance during the 1978 invasion was the fact that the Islamic revolution in Iran had not yet taken place. That the Shi'is reacted militantly to the 1982 invasion, after the revolution's occurrence in 1979, is proof of this observation."[10]

The 1982 Israeli invasion of Lebanon drew in the United States and France, which dispatched peace-keepers, as noted in Chapter 1. Hezbollah, viewing the move as an effort to support both Israeli and Lebanese Christian power, struck back. First, a wing of Hezbollah bombed the U.S. embassy in Beirut in March 1983, and then a Hezbollah truck bomber destroyed the U.S. Marine Corps barracks, killing 241 American military personnel, while simultaneously hitting French peace-keepers and Israeli military positions. Sheik Fadlallah denied responsibility for planning or sanctioning the bombings, yet he praised the actions at the same time. In 1985 three Hezbollah operatives hijacked an American commercial airliner and flew it to Beirut after killing a U.S. Navy diver who was traveling as a passenger on the plane. Such actions drew international condemnation, but for many young Lebanese Shi'a in particular, they burnished the path that Hezbollah took to enter Lebanese political space.

HEZBOLLAH ENTERS LEBANESE POLITICAL SPACE

Hezbollah self-styled itself a "resistance group," operating outside the borders of Lebanese mainstream politics, consistent with the tradition of many other "resistance" groups in and out of Lebanon, including most of Lebanon's militias.

Fadlallah had openly called for the establishment of an Islamic state in Lebanon, yet he understood how unacceptable such a plan was not only to Lebanese Christians, but also for the Sunnis, who would be suspicions of any Islamic state built on the Iranian model that declared the Twelver School of Shi'a as the official religion of the state.[11] Whether such rejection also included the refutation of Shi'a guardianship, or *Vilayat al-faqih*, was uncertain. Bilal Y. Saab claims that Hezbollah does embrace *Vilayat al-Faqih* as a central tenant of Shi'a authenticity.[12] However, in an interview, Fadlallah specifically rejects the guardianship principle for Lebanon:

> I don't believe that Welayat al-Faqih has any role in Lebanon. Perhaps some Lebanese commit themselves to the policy of the Guardian Jurist, as some of them commit themselves to the policy of the Vatican (Lebanon's large Maronite community is Catholic). My opinion is that I don't see the Guardianship of the Jurist as the definitive Islamic regime.[13]

Lebanon's other Shi'a group, Amal, specifically rejects the formation of a Shi'a state for Lebanon, along with the doctrine of *Vilayat al-Faqih*.[14] Other Lebanese Shi'a also reject *Vilayat al-Faqih*, claiming that the doctrine is inconsistent with Arab identity. Noted Muhammad Ali al-Husayni, secretary general of the Islamic Arab Council in Lebanon, a critic of Hezbollah, "It is true that Hezbollah has a Lebanese identity but its decisions come from outside Lebanon. They come from the *vali-e faqih* in Iran and it works for the interests of Iran and not those of Lebanon."[15]

In 1992, Hezbollah decided to contest national elections. While Ghorayeb argued that the decision was about gaining political legitimacy, "The need to legitimize its resistance was one of the principal motivations that induced Hizbollah to enter the political mainstream in 1992"[16]; it was also the case that integration into the formal Lebanese political system allowed Hezbollah to spread its influence into the national web of Lebanese governance, giving it access to resources and a veto on national policy. The decision was not without its hiccups, as Syria reminded Hezbollah of its expectations. Hezbollah leader Nasrallah tried and failed to get Amal to join a Shi'a coalition of both parties and thus announced that Hezbollah would run candidates without Amal. But shortly before the summer 1995 elections, Syrian leaders summoned both Nasrallah and Nabhi Berri to Damascus and "corrected" them on their "separate path" stances. Shortly thereafter both parties announced a joint list of candidates in Beqaa and south Lebanon, though the results cost Hezbollah two parliamentary seats.[17] As time wore on, the two groups appeared to compromise more, particularly as Hezbollah eclipsed Amal after the 2006 summer war with Israel. However, Hezbollah leaders also recognized that it was important to cooperate with Amal where possible, partially to avoid the old conflicts between the two groups that led to bloodshed and mutual weakness. Thus in the run-up to the 2009 election, a Hezbollah candidate withdrew in favor of the Amal candidate. Hezbollah candidate MP Amin Sherri officially withdrew his candidacy for the Shi'ite seat in the Beirut II district, in favor of the Shi'ite Amal Movement candidate for the same seat, Hani Qobessi, stating,

> Since Hizbullah's leadership is committed to preserving the strength of the (Lebanese national) opposition and its coherence and harmony, especially with the approaching of the elections, I hereby withdraw my candidacy for the Shiite seat in Beirut II in favor of the Amal Movement candidate, Hani Qobeissi.[18]

In August 2008, the Lebanese parliament approved the so-called "unity cabinet," which allocated Hezbollah 11 of the 30 cabinet positions, giving it veto power. The parliament also debated the issue of disarming Hezbollah, but the body affirmed the cabinet lineup without conditions, which gave Hezbollah yet another political victory.[19] Hezbollah demonstrated the fruits of that victory shortly after, when Lebanese foreign minister Fawzi Sallukh remonstrated that Hezbollah must retain its weapons, citing an unready Lebanese military as the reason: "Weapons of the resistance cannot be removed before the Lebanese army is fully prepared with military equipments, such as armoured vehicles, tanks and missiles in order to be able to counter any aggression from outside, particularly from the usurping state of Israel, whose violations still continue in spite of Resolution 1701."[20]

Because Hezbollah also portrays itself as a social movement inside Lebanon, it must also divert resources to addressing the considerable poverty of the Shi'a residents. That message was reinforced by the position taken by Subhi Tufayli, a secretary general of Hezbollah who left the party and campaigned successfully in the 1998 local elections. Tufayli accused Hezbollah of ignoring the plight of Shi'a farmers whose livelihood was being lost to cheap Syrian food imports in the 1990s, leading the so-called "revolt of the hungry," and accusing Nasrallah of being an Iranian intelligence agent. His rhetoric and position resonated with other Shi'a poor and reminded Hezbollah that it could not take local Shi'a poverty for granted.[21] This was an important critique, because Lebanon's government is not noted for its efficient provision of public goods, as noted in Chapter 3. In the slums of Beirut and the impoverished villages in the Beqaa Valley, the Shi'a, though the largest of Lebanon's confessional groups, are often on the bottom of official government services, creating a ready climate for Hezbollah's social programs. Hezbollah operates hospitals in Shi'a areas, distributes food during hard times, provides free education where there are few government schools, and provides reconstruction efforts to rebuild from Lebanon's multiple destructive events. Hezbollah provides such mundane things as recreation, parks, health and fitness lessons, and a multitude of other services that are normally unavailable in poor sections of Lebanon. Additionally, Hezbollah is widely seen in Lebanon as an honest provider, unlike so many elements in the Lebanese state system, where a bribe or the influence of a *za'im* is needed to get a job, or a bed in a hospital, or a village road repaired. And even though Hezbollah's emphasis is on provisions to Lebanese Shi'a, Hezbollah also distributes goods to other confessional groups, with the stress on economic level rather than on religious status. The message is that Hezbollah benefits Lebanon's poor, and with a 20 percent unemployment rate, and an estimated 28 percent of Lebanon's population considered "poor" (with 8 percent in "extreme poverty"),[22] there is a clear demand for Hezbollah's civic works.

While some might argue that these are valued items that reflect Hezbollah's primary mission, improving the lives of Lebanon's Shi'a community, others might claim that these activities are but a front to improve Hezbollah's image publicly while allowing it to gain more recruits who are ultimately funneled into its resistance/terrorist activities. Others suggest that such programs ultimately delegitimize the state and nation of Lebanon. The very success of Hezbollah demonstrates the failure of the Lebanese state, and thus Hezbollah's successes in replacing state functions encourages a shift from Lebanese to Hezbollah identity and loyalty. At the same time, though, the state of Lebanon may be delegitimizing itself by its failures to provide adequate levels of the basic services expected of any modern state.

HEZBOLLAH AND AMAL

Hezbollah has had a mixed relationship with Amal, the older Lebanese Shi'a group, now headed politically by Nabhi Berri. Berri regards the south of Lebanon as his political province and has resented Hezbollah's presence there, preferring to see the Lebanese Army deployed there as a defense against Israeli incursions.[23] As Samir Khalaf has observed,

> Among Shi'ites, the infighting between Syrian-supported Amal and Iranian-supported Hizbullah was equally ferocious (as other militia conflicts). These conflicts were exacerbated by their shifting global and regional sponsors. For example, when Iran became suspicious of Syria's rapprochement with Washington, after 1988, it gave Hizbullah a freer hand in undermining Syria's proxy powers within the Shi'a community.[24]

The rivalry in south Lebanon became particularly critical when Hizbollah kidnapped American Marine officer William R. Higgins in early 1988 on a road near Tyre, in Amal-protected territory. Embarrassed by a rival's action on its turf, Amal initially fired its chief of security, but the conflict between the militias turned violent in April 1988 as the two groups contested for control of Nabatiye, the largest city in south Lebanon. Bloody clashes broke out in the city before Amal ousted the Hizbollah fighters. This was more than a footnote in Lebanon's factional rivalry; it also revealed the growing contest between Syria, which supported Amal, and Iran, which inspired Hezbollah, revealing the degree to which even the poor south of Lebanon was increasingly controlled by forces supported by foreigners.[25] Still, Amal and Hezbollah disagreed, as noted above, on the role that outside powers, particularly Iran, should take in Lebanese political discourse, with Amal preferring to underscore Lebanese national identity and secular governance, though Hezbollah has also tried to keep Iranian influence at arms' length, as when it limited the number of Iranian preachers coming to Lebanon during Ashura.[26]

HEZBOLLAH AND THE SALIFIST

Hezbollah's dealings with Sunni Salafist groups have veered between cooperation and conflict. During the 2006 conflict with Israel, al-Qaeda praised Hezbollah and called upon all Muslims to support the Hezbollah positions, even in the face of al-Qaeda's labeling of the Shi'a as heretics. In 2008, Hezbollah briefly entered in an unspecified "pact" with Sunni Salafist groups in Lebanon, but found the pact came under criticism from some Salafists within the umbrella group, which had to repudiate it. A delicately worded statement from Hezbollah captured the situation: "Hizbullah appreciates Sheikh Hassan al-Shahhal's courage and is aware of the special circumstances that forced him to decide to freeze the memorandum of understanding."[27] The purpose of the agreement was to suspend conflict between Muslim groups and to base incitement on religious reasons rather than secular reasons, something that would benefit Hezbollah, but its potential allies in the Sunni movement appeared unwilling to make the sacrifice, placing Hezbollah on the side of practicality over religious zeal. However, when a suicide bomber attacked the Saıda Zaynab mosque in Damascus, Hezbollah ordered its members to leave Syria, apparently fearing that the attack was the work of Sunni Salifist militants who were targeting Shi'a.[28]

HEZBOLLAH AND THE 2006 WAR WITH ISRAEL

During most of the 2000s, Israeli security focused on the threat of internal terrorist acts by militia Palestinians. Israel security decision makers appeared to be so focused on this menace that they appeared to downplay the growing Hezbollah presence on their northern border.[29] Hezbollah had moved into the border region next to Israel after the Israeli troop withdrawal, and reports held that Hezbollah was importing missiles and other weapons into south Lebanon. There were occasional skirmishes between Israeli military forces and Hezbollah militia forces, but those usually involved the abduction of Israeli soldiers, who would then be exchanged for Hezbollah prisoners held by Israel. Apparently Hezbollah leader Nasrallah believed that a July 12, 2006, raid on an Israeli force would not turn out any differently. Thus Hezbollah forces crossed the Israeli border, ambushed an Israeli patrol, and abducted two Israeli soldiers. This time, instead of engaging in backdoor diplomacy to secure the soldiers release, Israel launched a massive attack on Hezbollah areas of Lebanon, and against Lebanese infrastructure, again trying to pressure Lebanese political factions to withhold support for Hezbollah. The Israeli attack had apparently been planned for some time, because, according to Trita Parsi, a senior Israeli officer was giving PowerPoint briefings on Israel's planned campaign against Hezbollah in Lebanon in 2005.[30]

The campaign on both sides, as noted in Chapter 1, dragged on for days, with intense fighting on both the ground and in the air. While Israel apparently did have a war plan developed at least a year earlier, Hezbollah did not appear to have anything more than a generic plan that did not allow Hezbollah to adapt quickly to Israeli moves.[31] The way that Hezbollah fought during the conflict also raised questions about what its overall strategic aims were. As Stephen Biddle and Jeffrey A. Friedman observe,

> It is also possible that Hezbollah's strategy was the product of religio-cultural self-expression rather than an instrumentally rational plan to counter an Israeli threat via strategic coercion and operational brute force. A culture of struggle and resistance can be expressed in many ways; perhaps the observed pattern of tactics and operations is uniquely attributable to Hezbollah's particular belief system and world view. It is clear that the ultimate result was a strategic program that at least mimicked a rationally instrumental design with considerable fidelity.[32]

Israeli commentators complained that, two years after the passage of UN Resolution 1701, Hezbollah continued rearming and the United Nations Interim Force in Lebanon (UNIFIL) was not capable of stopping the return of Iranian-supplied missiles to Lebanon. Complained one columnist, UNIFIL, "whose forces were augmented to prevent Iran's preparations for a missile attack on Israel from Lebanon, has become the guardian of Hezbollah—the executor of the Iranian plan—against an attempt by Israel to foil it with a preemptive strike."[33]

In July 2008, Hezbollah delivered the remains of two Israeli soldiers in exchange for the Israeli release of Samir Kuntar, a Lebanese Druze convicted of murdering an Israeli citizen and members of his family in 1979, along with other Hezbollah prisoners and the bodies of Hezbollah members and Palestinians killed by Israeli forces. The result was a considerable triumph for Hezbollah, which abducted the two Israeli soldiers (their deaths remained unexplained as Nasrallah had said they were alive when captured), and ultimately got back Kuntar, and other Lebanese and Palestinian prisoners. Their return, along with the coffins of the dead, generated massive celebrations in areas where Hezbollah is popular, and almost all Lebanese political leaders showed up to the Hezbollah-sponsored welcome, including President Michel Suleiman, Prime Minister Fuad Siniora, and the speaker of parliament, Nabhi Berri.[34]

Hezbollah probably had mixed objectives: it wanted a release of its prisoners, and, after the first skirmish escalated greatly, Hezbollah ramped up its own efforts to pursue that original goal. Hezbollah also appeared to appreciate the difficulty that democracies face when they take civilian casualties, though it is never clear if a democracy will fold its cards when casualties become too high, or if it will lash out with even more ferocity because its citizens demand revenge.

HEZBOLLAH'S GOALS FOR LEBANON

Do Hezbollah's goals include a Lebanon governed by Shi'a clerics, or at least by Shi'a religious understanding? Or is Hezbollah more interested in gaining its fair share of Lebanese political and economic power? Hezbollah leaders deny wanting political control over Lebanon. Hassan Nasrallah stated in May 2008, "We don't want authority in Lebanon. We don't want to control Lebanon. We don't want to impose our ideas on the Lebanese people."[35] There has been little effort by Hezbollah to convert other Lebanese to the Shi'a faith or to impose Shi'a jurisdiction over them. However, Hezbollah does appear to be strengthening its influence over Lebanon's Shi'a population. Its organizations reach out to all segments of the Shi'a in Lebanon. The "Mahdi Scouts," with over 60,000 followers, is Hezbollah's youth movement that inculcates young Shi'a into Hezbollah, and some graduates go on to serve in Hezbollah's militia. Hezbollah runs a network of schools, from elementary to university education, so that Lebanese Shi'a youth never leave Hezbollah education. It has special programs for women, who are more likely to be included in Hezbollah than in other Islamist organizations (this attests to the predominate role of historical women figures in Shi'a tradition, such as Fatima, the mother of Ali, and Zaynab, the sister of Hussein ibn Ali).[36] Hezbollah uses such religious-based training and socialization to deepen its ties to Lebanon's Shi'a population in a way that other secular groups have not been able to match. It would appear that Hezbollah is preparing for a future where well-indoctrinated followers will be even more prepared to compete for power and influence within Lebanon's quilted political and social system. It is on track to do so. Farid el Khazen says of Hezbollah,

> In a way, Hizballah is the only party in Lebanon whose success is measured more by the large measure of autonomy is has from government authorities in political and security affairs rather than from the power it exercises in government . . . No other party in Lebanon or in any other country . . . enjoys the kind of status and privileges that Hizballah has had since the end of the (civil) war.[37]

HEZBOLLAH, IRAN, AND SYRIA

From the time of its founding onward, Hezbollah has been linked to both Iran and Syria. While the Israeli invasion of Lebanon in 1982 was the most important spark in the creation of Hezbollah, the Iranian Revolution of 1979 influenced its founders, including Sheik Muhammad Hussein Fadlallah. Fadlallah developed his own vision of a revolutionary Shi'a political discourse before 1979, but the Iranian Revolution took abstractions to the level of actuality.[38] While Fadlallah maintained theological differences with Iran's religious leadership (on the necessity for clerical rule, where Fadlallah disagreed, for example), Iran still had reasons to support Hezbollah. Iran was isolated from the rest of the Middle East due to its burgeoning conflict with Iraq (which exploded into a bloody war in 1981), and thus Hezbollah was an potential entry into an Arab country, where Iran could support its claim that its mission was to offer protection to Shi'a everywhere, particularly those living in the Arab world.[39] Lebanon's Shi'a became a particular cause for Iran largely due to the impoverishment of the rural Shi'a in south Lebanon and the Beqaa Valley, and their particularly disproportionate casualties after Israeli attacks into those places. Thus, as Gary Sick argues, Iran's ambassador to Syria, Ali Akbar Mohtashemi, provided the seed money for the founding of Hezbollah in the early 1980s. As Hezbollah's success against Israel grew after its founding, Sick notes that "Iran takes pride in its continued support for Hizballah as a national resistance organization but denies having operational control over decisionmaking."[40] That may be true, but Iran flows funds into Lebanon to support Hezbollah, prompting counteroffers from Iranian regional rivals such as Saudi Arabia. One advisor to the Saudi Arabian government stated bluntly, "We are putting a lot into this. We're supporting candidates running against Hezbollah, and we're going to make Iran feel the pressure."[41] At least some Lebanese politicians seemed fine with the foreign intervention, particularly when it gushed into their campaign coffers. One party leader stated that Saudi Arabian funds were a "significant source" of support for his election bid, and that "I need tools to fight back, and if the Saudis have an interest in building a state here, why shouldn't I take advantage of that?"[42]

SYRIA AND HEZBOLLAH

Syria saw its connections to the Arab world loosen, particularly after 1979, when Egypt's peace agreement with Israel began the long collapse of Syria's position that those states losing territory to Israel should never agree to a peace agreement with the Jewish state. Syrian hopes that Ba'athist socialism would allow Syria a leading role in the Arab world also weakened as personal differences between Hafiz al-Asad and Saddam Hussein prevented any collaboration. Other Arab countries increasingly found the Ba'ath ideals a recipe for failure as they gradually turned to market economies and limited democracy. Thus Syria was the only Arab country to back Iran in its war with Iraq, and, later, Syria would join the 1990–1991 coalition against Saddam Hussein after the Iraqi invasion of Kuwait.

Syria, which coveted a dominant role in Lebanon, found that Hezbollah might be a willing partner, even though Hezbollah's Shi'a focus contrasted with the secular nature of the Ba'ath. Syria had staked out a similar position with Amal after Nabih Berri had claimed that Syria had a special economic and political relationship with Lebanon that focused on Israel as the Lebanese enemy.[43] William Harris stated Syrian policy toward the Shi'a organizations succinctly:

> Hafiz al-Asad cultivated Syria's ties with Shiite parties, both Hezbollah and Amal, while making sure that the Sunnis and Maronites maintained advantages that guaranteed Shiite dependence on Syria. Israel's occupation of a "security zone" in southern Lebanon anchored Syrian hegemony over the Lebanese. It invited Shiite resistance and enabled Syria and its friends to smear Lebanese criticism of Syrian hegemony as treason. Confrontation with Israel justified Hezbollah's private army and reinforced the Party of God's efforts to expand its popular base and exact money from Lebanese Shiites at home and abroad.[44]

For Syria, Hezbollah provided a tie to the Shi'a community that, if empowered, could potentially weaken the power of Syria's foes in Lebanon (primarily the Maronite factions) and allow Syria more authority in its neighboring country. However, Syrian-Hezbollah relations had their limits. Syria, fearful of an Israeli reaction to Hezbollah provocations, reigned in Hezbollah actions. Hezbollah also provoked Syria when its agents kidnapped and later murdered a U.S. military officer in 1988, as noted in Chapter 1, and Syrian clashes with Hezbollah happened on several occasions in the 1980s.[45] Syria also had to broker clashes between Hezbollah and Amal, as it did in the 1996 elections when Amal tried to limit Hezbollah participation.[46]

Still, Syria appreciated that it needed Hezbollah not only to strengthen its foothold in Lebanon, but also as a bargaining chip against Israel. Syria's primary foreign policy objective since 1967 has been the return of the Golan region, taken by Israel in the 1967 War. One of the negotiating points that President Hafiz al-Asad wanted to keep on the table was an offer to disband Hezbollah's militia wing and to integrate it into the Lebanese Army, but the seriousness of the offer, which might have been valuable to Israel if it was credible, is uncertain. Noted one analyst, "Hizballah's future was never explicitly put on the table, and there is no clear indication that Syria was asked to offer written guarantees to that end. Hizballah's own statements were contradictory enough to wonder whether its leadership even knew the endgame."[47] Hezbollah did not have much incentive to submerge its own identity and the political power of its militia force for the benefit of Syria. However, Syria did want Israel to believe that it did have control over Hezbollah's actions and that it had the power to reign in the organization and its attacks on Israeli targets if Israel would reciprocate in negotiations over Golan. That position, however weak it might have been, has been negated even further by Syria's withdrawal from Lebanon in 2005. Syria clearly has less leverage over Hezbollah, and Hezbollah, having been strengthened by its 2006 performance over Israel, needs Syria less. Moreover, Syria, like most non-Shi'a countries in the Middle East, has become concerned about the rising power of Iran.[48]

Syria's role in Lebanon was eclipsed with the death of Hafiz al-Asad in 2000, to Iran's comparative benefit. Still, Syria was able to influence the number of seats Hezbollah could win in the 2000 elections, as Augustus Richard Norton observed that Hezbollah might have won 4 seats at Amal's expense, but the "Syrian ceiling" limited Hezbollah participation and forced Hezbollah and Amal into an alliance (that nevertheless won all 23 seats available to it in south Lebanon).[49] The assassination of Rafiq Hariri in February 2005 further reduced Syrian influence as Syrian troops (if not intelligence personnel) left Lebanon after massive protests against alleged Syrian complicity in the Hariri killing. Iranian support for Hezbollah increased as advanced weapons flowed into Hezbollah arsenals, and Hezbollah's performance in the 2006 conflict with Israel allowed Iran to take some of the credit.

Abbas William Samii argues, however, that despite Syrian and Iranian ties to Hezbollah, Hezbollah is increasingly pursuing its own agenda in Lebanon at the expense of both its patrons. The political stalemate engineered by Hezbollah that left Lebanon without a president between 2006 and 2008 ultimately required Iranian-Saudi Arabian cooperation to end it. Said Samii, "It can be argued reasonably that the walkout reflected Hizbullah's political ambitions, and it did not serve the short or medium-term interests of either the Iranian or Syrian regimes."[50] That appears to support Hezbollah's own contention that Hezbollah is, first and foremost, a Lebanese entity. Saab appears to disagree, arguing that Hezbollah serves at the pleasure of Iran, and that "Hezbollah's future role as an armed force will be determined by Iran."[51] Hezbollah did benefit from Iranian largesse following the 2006 war, allowing Hezbollah to take credit for some of the rebuilding that it sponsored. Of course, Hezbollah leader Fadlallah did take responsibility for what he seemed to indicate was a miscalculation that started the war, so it was unclear how many Lebanese actually gave Hezbollah or Iran much credit for reconstructing what they may have been partially responsible for destroying.

There is evidence that Iranian funds and weapons flow to Hezbollah, with the funding conduit running through Iranian banks. For example, officials from both the U.S. Treasury and State departments argued that American sanctions against Bank Sepah under Executive Order 13382 imposed in January 2007 disrupted funding to Hezbollah, as did earlier sanctions against Iranian Bank Saderat, Iran's second largest bank. The sanctions prevented both banks from engaging in dollar transfers, thus cutting them off from much international finance.[52] However, these officials do not cite amounts of money allegedly lost to Hezbollah because of sanctions against these banks, nor do they explore the possibility that Iran simply found other sources of funding to send to Hezbollah.

Unsurprisingly, Iran also denies supporting Hezbollah. According to Israeli sources, Iran acknowledges providing "spiritual" support while denying that it gives military or financial aid to the regime. Indeed, the Iranian Supreme Leader Ali Khamenei took pains to support the entire Lebanese "resistance" effort against "Zionism": "Iran believes that the strength of all Lebanese groups lies in national unity for effectively confronting the Zionist regime."[53]

Others disagree, though, about the position that Hezbollah is dependent on Iranian and Syria for its support and its ideology. Graham Fuller argues that while Hezbollah would not have risen to prominence without Iranian help, "Hizballah today does not operate at the command of the Iranian government," noting that it gets much more of its funding from wealthy Shi'a benefactors in places such as West Africa, South America, and the United States.[54]

Hezbollah is much more a creation and reflection of Lebanon's factious society, where most groups seem to require militias (if only to protect themselves from the militias of other groups), and a civil society element to replace the often-missing services of the official Lebanese state. Iran and Syria will take advantage of Hezbollah's presence and success in Lebanon, using it for Iranian national purposes, as the French take advantage of their support for Maronite groups, and the United States the factions that it supports. Lebanon appears to be too important to have its various groupings left alone, and too weak to collectively limit the range of outside interference in Lebanon's affairs.

HEZBOLLAH: A GLOBAL REACH?

As noted earlier, Hezbollah is believed by some analysts to be responsible for two terrorist bombings in Argentina in the early 1990s, acts that first alerted the world to the potential global presence of Hezbollah. Hezbollah was also allegedly involved in raising money through illegal drug smuggling in the "tri-border" area of Argentina, Paraguay, and Brazil. More recently, reports surfaced that Hezbollah has also been forming a base of operations in Venezuela. As Venezuelan-Iranian ties increased under Venezuelan President Hugo Chávez, evidence mounted that Iran was bringing Hezbollah into the mix. U.S. Treasury officials accused Lebanese-born Venezuelan diplomat Ghazi Nasr al-Din of using his position to support Hezbollah activities, including transporting Hezbollah members from Venezuela to Iran for training and for raising funds for Hezbollah.[55]

Hezbollah's global reach is also facilitated by global public communication, particularly through its television station, al-Manar. Hezbollah opened al-Manar in 1991 as a local broadcasting station, but by 2000 al-Manar became a satellite-based operation. It now broadcasts worldwide and has become one of the top stations in the Arab world as both a "station of resistance" and as a source of news, which tends to be unbiased.[56] There are emphases: Syria tends to get favorable treatment while Saudi Arabia gets criticism for corruption and miserliness, but subjects involving Christians are treated respectfully and town-hall meetings get broadcast coverage even though some of the topics may be controversial. Around half of the announcers are women, and not all women appearing on al-Manar are wearing the *hijab*, or headscarf.[57] While al-Manar is quite popular within the larger Arab world, enhancing the reach of Hezbollah, the U.S. station Alhurra, established during the George W. Bush administration, has failed to attract a significant Arab audience, for a variety of reasons, including poor programming choices and a widespread belief that it is simply a mouthpiece for the United States and for Israel.[58]

Hizbollah's reach beyond Lebanon also extends to its popularization of the tactic of suicide bombing. Says Gilles Kepel, "This terrorist organization (Hezbollah) introduced the concept of suicide bombings, which were very popular in Iranian revolutionary Shiism, into the vernacular of Arab political culture, where previously they had been little more than an oddity."[59] The tactic was passed on to Palestinian militants initially after Israel had deported some of them to Lebanon, but it was emulated widely after Palestinian suicide bombers began to attack targets in Israel, spreading to Iraq, Pakistan, and beyond.

Hezbollah's effort to expand its horizons ran into obstacles beyond those erected by Israel. After Egyptian authorities arrested members of a Hezbollah cell in Cairo in April 2009, the general secretary of the ruling National Democratic Party, Safwat Sherif, issued a blunt statement about that organization's welcome in Egypt: "We say to the Hezbollah group who exports terrorism to our territories: Egypt cannot be a field where you experiment your ideas and plans. The blow that security authorities dealt to the terrorist Hezbollah group is a warning message to anyone who might think of messing with Egypt's security."[60] That arrest, apparently triggered by a Mossad investigation shared with Egyptian policy, led authorities in Egypt to conclude that the Hezbollah cell was planning to attack targets on the Suez Canal and in Tel Aviv, where it planned large-scale suicide attacks.[61]

Hezbollah's success in Lebanon reflects not only its unique ability to transform, to mobilize support, and to capitalize on its opponent's mistakes, but also the reality that most Lebanese political organs sustain themselves on foreign support. Many countries both close to and distant from Lebanon have tentacles that reach deep into Lebanese political and social space. The following chapter highlights those actors and their Lebanese interests and influences.

NOTES

1. Roschanack Shaery-Eisenlohr, *Shi'ite Lebanon: Transnational Religion and the Making of National Identities* (New York: Columbia University Press, 2008), 24.

2. Rodger Shanahan, *The Shi'a of Lebanon: Clans, Parties, and Clerics* (London: Tauris Academic Studies, 2005), Chap. 1.

3. Majed Halawi, *A Lebanon Defied: Musa al-Sadr and the Shi'a Community* (Boulder, CO: Westview Press, 1992), 130–134; Shaery-Eisenlohr, *Shi'ite Lebanon*, 26–27.

4. Shaery-Eisenlohr, *Shi'ite Lebanon*, 37.

5. There are other "Hezbollah's" in the Muslim world, including Turkish "Hezbollah," which has no connections to the more well-known Lebanese Shi'a party.

6. Martin Kramer, "The Oracle of Hizbullah: Sayyid Muhammad Husayn Fadlallah," in *Spokesmen for the Despised: Fundamentalist Leaders of the Middle East*, ed. R. Scott Appleby (Chicago: University of Chicago Press, 1997), 83–181.

7. David Hirst, "South Lebanon: The War That Never Ends?" *Journal of Palestine Studies* 28 (Spring 1999): 11.

8. Augustus Richard Norton, *Hezbollah: A Short History* (Princeton, NJ: Princeton University Press, 2007), 34.

9. Ibid., 36–38.

10. Amal Saad-Ghorayeb, "Factors Conducive to the Politicization of the Lebanese Shi'a and the Emergence of Hizbu'llah," *Journal of Islamic Studies* 14, no. 3 (2003): 313.

11. Kramer, "The Oracle of Hizbullah," 127–128.

12. Bilal Y. Saab, "Rethinking Hezbollah's Disarmament," *Middle East Policy* 15 (Fall 2008): 95.

13. "The Weekend Interview with Muhammad Hussein Fadhlullah: A Dialogue with Lebanon's Ayatollah," *Wall Street Journal*, March 14, 2009.

14. Augustus Richard Norton, *Amal and the Shi'a: Struggle for the Soul of Lebanon* (Austin: University of Texas Press, 1987), 72–73; Shaery-Eisenlohr, *Shi'ite Lebanon*, 108.

15. "Lebanese Shi'i Figure Blames Iran's Velayet-E Faqih Regime for Crisis," BBC Monitoring Middle East, February 28, 2008. "*Vali*" is the Arabic form of the Persian *Wilayat*. The Islamic Arab Council was founded in 2007, which appears to emphasize the connection between Arab identity and Islam. It is headquartered in Beirut.

16. Amal Saad-Ghorayeb, "The Paradox of Hezbollah's Arms," Arab Reform Bulletin, September 2005, http://www.carnegieendowment.org/arb/index.cfm?fa=show&article=21139.

17. Graham Usher, "Hizballah, Syria, and the Lebanese Elections," *Journal of Palestinian Studies* 26 (Winter 1997): 59–60.

18. "More Parties Announce Electoral Lists as Elections Race Intensifies," *Daily Star* (Beirut), April 23, 2009.

19. "Lebanese Parliament Approves Unity Cabinet," *New York Times*, August 12, 2008.

20. "Resistance Weapons Lebanon's "Internal Affair," Says Foreign Minister. OpenSource, GMP20080911950040 Cairo *Voice of the Arabs*, in Arabic, September 11, 2008.

21. Norton, *Hezbollah*, 105–106.

22. Heba Laithy, Khalid Abu-Ismail, and Kamal Hamdan, "Poverty, Growth, and Income Distribution in Lebanon," International Poverty Centre, Country Study 13, January 2008, 4–5.

23. Judith Harik, "Syrian Foreign Policy and State/Resistance Dynamics in Lebanon," *Studies in Conflict & Terrorism* 20 (July 1997): 254.

24. Samir Khalaf, *Civil and Uncivil Violence in Lebanon: A History of the Internationalization of Communal Conflict* (New York: Columbia University Press, 2002), 46.

25. "Shiite Militia Routs its Pro-Iran Rival in Lebanon," *New York Times*, April 8, 1988.

26. Shaery-Eisenlohr, *Shi'ite Lebanon*, 196–197.

27. "Hizbullah 'Understands' Salafists' Froze Pact under Pressure," *Daily Star* (Beirut), August 22, 2008. Sheik al-Shahhal was the leader of the particular Salafist group.

28. "Hizbollah Orders Members out of Syria," *Jerusalem Post*, October 1, 2008. Saida Zaynab was the sister of Hussein Ali and a significant figure in the lore of Shi'a Islam.

29. In March 2005, the author noted Hezbollah flags on the hills over the Israeli-Lebanon border, but, when queried about them, Israeli military officials downplayed any concerns, noting that Israel had suffered much more loss of life from Palestinian suicide attacks than from Hezbollah.

30. Trita Parsi, *Treacherous Alliance: The Secret Dealings of Israel, Iran, and the U.S.* (New Haven, CT: Yale University Press, 2007), 274.

31. Stephen Biddle and Jeffrey A. Friedman, *The 2006 Lebanon Campaign and the Future of Warfare: Implications for Army and Defense Policy* (Carlisle, PA: Strategic Studies Institute, 2008), 54–55.

32. Ibid., 53–54.

33. Israel Harel," The Sole Achievement Has Been Erased," *Ha'aretz*, July 10, 2008.

34. "Prisoner's Homecoming a Triumph for Hezbollah," *New York Times*, July 17, 2008. In a postscript, Ghassan bin Jiddo, Beirut bureau chief for *Al Jazeera*, referred to Kuntar as a "pan-Arab hero," and after Israel protested and threatened to boycott *Al Jazeera* unless the station apologized, *Al Jazeera's* program director issued a statement, claiming that "elements of the program violated [the station's] Code of Ethics," and he "regards these violations as very serious." "*Al-Jazirah* Admits Unethical Coverage of Kuntar," *Haaretz*, August 7, 2008. In May 2009, Kuntar's name appeared on a British list of 16 persons (8 of them Muslims) barred from entering the country.

35. "Hezbollah Leader Plays Down Group's Political Aims in Lebanon," *New York Times*, May 8, 2008.

36. "Hezbollah Seeks to Marshal the Piety of the Young," *New York Times*, November 21, 2008.

37. Farid el Khazen, "Political Parties in Postwar Lebanon: Parties in Search of Partisans," *Middle East Journal* 57 (Autumn 2003): 617–618.

38. Kramer, "The Oracle of Hezbullah: Sayyid Muhammad Husayn Fadlallah," 83–182.

39. Arshin Adib-Moghaddam argues that the traditional view of Arab-Persian enmity was exaggerated by the tragic and costly Iran-Iraq War between 1981 and 1988. Arshin Adib-Moghaddam, *Iran in World Politics: The Question of the Islamic Republic* (New York: Columbia University Press, 2008), Chap. 3.

40. Gary Sick, "Iran: Confronting Terrorism, *The Washington Quarterly* 26 (Autumn 2003): 85.

41. "Foreign Money Seeks to Buy Lebanese Votes," *New York Times*, April 23, 2009.

42. Ibid.

43. Norton, *Amal and the Shi'a*, 68.

44. William Harris, "Crisis in the Levant: Lebanon at Risk," *Mediterranean Quarterly* 28 (Spring 2007): 48.

45. Abbas William Samii, "A Stable Structure on Shifting Sands: Assessing the Hizbullah-Iran-Syria Relationship," *The Middle East Journal* 62 (Winter 2008): 39.

46. Ibid., 42–43.

47. Emile El-Hokayam, "Hizballah and Syria: Outgrowing the Proxy Relationship," *The Washington Quarterly* 30 (Spring 2007): 38.

48. Ibid., 47–48.

49. Norton, *Hezbollah*, 102.

50. Samii, "A Stable Structure on Shifting Sands," 52.

51. Saab, "Rethinking Hezbollah's Disarmament," 104.

52. *Iran Sanctions: Impact in Furthering U.S. Objectives Is Unclear and Should Be Reviewed.* Report to the Ranking Member, Subcommittee on National Security and Foreign Affairs, House Committee on Oversight and Government Reform. Washington, DC: United States Government Accountability Office, December 2007, 20.

53. "Iran's Khamenei: Lebanon Needs Unity to 'Confront the Zionist Regime,'" *Ha'aretz*, November 25, 2008.

54. Graham Fuller, "The Hizballah-Iran Connection: Model for Sunni Resistance," *The Washington Quarterly* 30 (Winter 2006–2007): 143.

55. "Hezbollah Presence in Venezuela Feared," *Los Angeles Times*, August 27, 2008.

56. Anne Marie Baylouny, "Al-Manar and Alhurra: Competing Satellite Stations and Ideologies," Occasional Paper Series No. 2, George C. Marshall European Center for Security Studies, Garmisch-Partenkirchen, Germany, October 2006, 9.

57. Ibid., 13.

58. Ibid., 15–17.

59. Gilles Kepel, *The War for Muslim Minds* (Cambridge, MA: Harvard University Press, 2004), 100. Bloom cites evidence that Hezbollah may have actually learned the tactic from Lebanese Christians, who used primarily women operatives in attacks against Israeli occupation. Mia Bloom, *Dying to Kill: The Allure of Suicide Terror* (New York: Columbia University Press, 2005), 122.

60. "Cairo Calls Hezbollah Terrorist Organization," *Los Angeles Times*, April 13, 2009.

61. "Mossad Tip Led to Capture of Hezbollah Cell in Sinai," *Ha'aretz*, April 16, 2009; "Hezbollah Planned Huge Terror Attacks in Tel Aviv," *Ha'aretz*, April 16, 2009.

FURTHER READING

Harel, Amos, and Avi Isacharoff. *34 Days: Israel, Hezbollah, and the War in Lebanon.* New York: Macmillan Palgrave, 2009.

Harik, Judith Palmer. *Hezbollah: The Changing Face of Terrorism.* New York: I. B. Tauris, 2004.

Jaber, Hala. *Hezbollah: Born with a Vengeance.* New York: Columbia University Press, 1997.

Norton, Augustus Richard. *Hezbollah: A Short History.* Princeton, NJ: Princeton University Press, 2007.

CHAPTER 5

The Lebanese Regional Neighborhood

There are few places in the world that have as much instability as does the eastern Mediterranean, and Lebanon is located right in the middle of it. Thus a part of Lebanon's chronic instability is a function of its neighbors' quarrels and the influx of population of peoples into Lebanon who carry those quarrels into the country as they arrive.

To Lebanon's south is Israel, and to its east and north is Syria, two countries that have fought numerous wars and skirmishes. It is likely that more Lebanese than Syrians and Israelis have died in struggles between Israel and Syria, fought on Lebanese soil. Jordan does not border Lebanon, but after the September 1970 uprising of the Palestine Liberation Organization (PLO) in Jordan, the Hashemite government of Jordan crushed the PLO and many of its leaders and followers migrated to Lebanon. All these countries have, in their own ways, contributed to Lebanon's chronic instability, as they view Lebanon as tied to their own national interests. This chapter describes Lebanon's difficult relations with its neighbors and the influence that those neighbors have had on Lebanese politics.

Lebanon is in a rather unique situation relative to its foreign policy. While Lebanon considers itself a sovereign country, it has traditionally been under partial or full control of Syria. The situation was epitomized by the fact that Syria and Lebanon did not recognize each other diplomatically until the summer of 2008, and normally, the Lebanese foreign minister had to depart on international travel from Damascus instead of Beirut, symbolically reinforcing Syria's powerful influence in Lebanon. Moreover, while many Arab countries proudly emphasize their sovereignty by cutting ties to powers that try too hard to dominate them (Egypt removed Soviet advisors in 1972 when they became too influential, for example), Talal Nizameddin observes, "In Lebanese politics, paying lip service to the dominant foreign powers was, historically speaking, part and parcel of the way of doing business."[1] Thus Lebanon has found itself pulled between dominant powers, often having to make significant compromises. Moreover, these powers reach into Lebanon's diverse population to find favorite clients and thus serve as divisive agents for a country that already has large fissures. Iran courts Hezbollah, and Israel courted various Maronite factions, as did France before it. When U.S. Secretary of State Condoleezza Rice visited Lebanon in July 2006, she visited Sunni Muslim Prime Minister Fuad Siniora but not Maronite Christian President Emile Lahoud. Thus Lebanon must be very careful in its foreign relations, as it is not only a small and vulnerable country, but its very sovereignty and unity is threatened by powerful countries near and far.

SYRIAN INTERESTS IN LEBANON

Both Syria and Lebanon are modern countries, results of the breakup of the Ottoman Empire after World War I. The British and French redrew the borders of the old Ottoman areas into sphere of influence, with France getting greater Syria, and, in August 1920, decreeing the new country of Lebanon, as noted in Chapter 1. The Syrian elite in Damascus never acceded to the partition, and to this day, Syrian maps show Lebanon as a part of Syria. Syrian Ba'athist ideology rejected the concept of Lebanon as a capitalist state with ties to the West, pressing instead for pan-Arab nationalism and the self-sufficiency that Ba'ath socialism promised (but never delivered).

As Judith Harik indicates, Syria views Lebanon as both a problem and an asset. Syria's goal is to keep Israel out of Lebanon, which is an avenue into Syria, and thus Syria uses its ability to manipulate a relatively weak country by exploiting the sectarian divisions inside the country.[2] Syria, like Israel, used both direct and indirect methods to accomplish its aims in Lebanon, inserting troops and intelligence operatives to manipulate Lebanese politics, and supporting a variety of Lebanese political actors, including Hezbollah. Syria facilitated the supply of weapons and civilian supplies from Iran, which usually landed at the Damascus International Airport[3] or arrived at Syrian seaports.

While Syria has always claimed Lebanon, the Ta'if Accord empowered and legitimized Syria's growing role in enforcing Ta'if. That role included Syrian peace-keepers (who were unsurprisingly effective given their willingness to use overwhelming force), and Syrian control over Lebanese politics and the Lebanese economy. Syria called the tune, with most political deals in the post-Ta'if era sealed only with an approving phone call from Damascus. Syria bolstered its flagging economy by sending Syrian workers to Lebanon, where they took jobs in the post–civil war construction boom. Syria sold its own products in Lebanon, thus often squeezing local producers out of their own market. Lebanese anger grew proportionately to the growth of Syrian influence and exploded after the assassination of Rafiq Hariri, and the visible part of Syrian power left shortly after a second massive anti-Syrian demonstration in Beirut following the Hariri funeral.

As Syrian influence in Lebanon continued even after the pullout of Syrian forces in 2004, some Arab governments reacted with anger. Saudi Arabia, in particular, threatened to boycott an Arab summit meeting scheduled to be held in Damascus. Said a Saudi Arabian government official,

> There's a new initiative to completely isolate Syria and weaken its destructive influence in Lebanon. We're not going to pull them away from Iran by talking to them. We're going to take them away from Iran by making them feel the pressure and making them understand that this time it's as real as it can get.[4]

Some of the differences were personal: Saudi Arabian King Abdullah and Syrian President Bashar Asad did not like each other, partly fueled by Asad's comment about the Saudi Arabians and other Gulf Arab leaders being "half-men" during the 2006 Hezbollah conflict. However, Saudi Arabian fears of Syria as a proxy for Iran, its Gulf rival, allowing Iran to extend its influence into Lebanon, and Saudis' anger over the assassination of Harari, which they blamed personally on Bashar Asad (whose father allegedly protected Harari), fueled the dispute.[5] Other Saudi allies, including Jordan and Yemen, followed Saudi Arabia's lead, further isolating Syria and reducing to almost nothing the long-standing Syrian identity with pan-Arabism.

One of Syria's potential proxy forces in Lebanon was Hezbollah. Under Sheik Muhammed Hussein Fadlallah, Hezbollah had departed from the Khomeini understanding of Shi'a as requiring clerical rulers, but still received support from Iran (see Chapter 4). Syria and Hezbollah shared common goals in limiting Israeli power in Lebanon, though they diverged. While Hezbollah wanted a Shi'a Lebanese state (albeit not ruled by clerics), Syria's vision for a Lebanese state converged with its own Ba'athist socialism. Syria's ruling Ba'ath Party viewed political Islam as a threat, having crushed a Sunni Muslim Brotherhood revolt in Hama in February 1982 with particular brutality. However, Syria and Fadlallah both understood that open conflict between Syria and Hezbollah would only benefit Israel, and Hezbollah and Syrian opponents in Lebanon. Fadlallah engineered what he called a "special relationship" with Syria, taking Syrian cooperation and assistance, while denying that Syria had Lebanese annexation objectives in mind.[6] Syria was also wary of the possible danger that Hezbollah actions against Israel might pose for Syria, As Volker Perthes notes, Syria was unwilling to let Hezbollah drag it into a conflict with Israel and feared the possibility that Israel would use Hezbollah actions to attack Syria.[7] While this did not happen in 2006, Syrian fears are not unjustified, with memories of the past when Israel attacked targets in Syria in the 1982 invasion that largely targeted the PLO.

In June 2008, newly elected president Michel Suleiman argued that Syria was ready to establish diplomatic relations with Lebanon, though he offered little evidence to support his claim.[8] Shortly thereafter, French President Nicolas Sarkozy, seeking to enhance France's role in the Middle East, convened a meeting in Paris, attended by all Middle East countries except Libya, and, during the meeting, Syria and Lebanon announced that they would open embassies in each other's capital. But mysterious events continued to confuse the relationship. In September 2008, Bashar Asad claimed that unspecified forces in Lebanon were trying to destabilize Syria and massed troops on Lebanon's northern border with Syria. Syrian spokespersons connected a bomb blast directed at Lebanese troops in Tripoli in early September 2008 to a bombing several days later in Damascus. The Syrians then linked both bombings to Sunni extremists who, they believed, were targeting Alawites.[9] The day after that blast, another bomb killed five Lebanese soldiers, again in Tripoli, causing Damascus to repeat its warning that Sunni militants were mobilizing in northern Lebanon and possibly were receiving Saudi Arabian support. Some Syrians speculated that this rise in Sunni extremism in Lebanon was related to Hezbollah's rise after the 2006 war.[10]

Although Syria had symbolically withdrawn from Lebanon in 2004–2005, Damascus continued its war of words with elements in Lebanese politics and with Saad Hariri's Future Movement in particular. Accusing it of supporting terrorism (presumably Sunni extremists that Syria claims are funded by Saudi Arabia), newspaper *Al Baath* (Damascus) opined, "Everyone near and far knows that he [Al-Hariri] and his lackeys were the first to find it easy to sacrifice a city they all colluded to prepare as a safe haven for local and foreign armed men and fighters, only because they have their own calculations about the resistance [Hizballah]."[11] According to Syrian dissident sources, Syrian officials may have had reason to suspect Saad Hariri if revenge was the motive, and the bombing in Damascus was indeed the Palestine branch of the Syrian intelligence service whose deputy chief, Brigadier General Abd-al-Karim Abbas, was a suspect in the Rafiq Hariri assassination.[12] None of these accusations are provable, of course, without documentation, but they illustrate the tensions that continue between Syria and its Lebanese opponents. They also indicate some Syrian fears that violent extremism may spill from Lebanon into Syria. One Web site reported, for example, that Syrian officials arrested Shakir al-Absi, leader of the Fatah al-Islam Movement, in the al-Malihah area, south of Damascus, after he reportedly escaped the Lebanese siege of his camps outside of Tripoli a few months before. The same source also reported that four suicide bombers were planning a revenge attack by bombing the Al-Abbasiyin Stadium during a soccer match, but Syrian officials caught them before they could commit the act.[13]

The American reaction to Syrian concerns was swift, with U.S. Department of State spokesperson Robert Wood stating that "the recent terrorist attacks that took place in Tripoli and Damascus should not serve as a pretext for, you know, further Syrian military engagement or as—should not be used to interfere in Lebanese internal affairs."[14] Questions remained about how much authority Syria actually had over the jihadists. As Iraqi and coalition forces began to succeed against foreign jihadists in Iraq, many who had originally come through Syria (many from Palestinian refugee camps in Lebanon) returned back through Syria into Lebanon. Syria increased its border patrols along its frontier with Iraq, generating suspicions that the suicide bombing in Damascus in September 2008, noted earlier, was a consequence of jihadist elements targeting Syrian intelligence for trying to stem the crossings of jihadist groups back and forth from Iraq. As jihadists moved back to Lebanon, they found an unlikely part-ally in Saad Hariri, who appeared to court the Sunni jihadists as a hedge against the rising power of the Shi'a Hezbollah.[15] That prompted one commentator to note, "Hariri has been paying *jihadis* not to be *jihadis*, but they've been rebelling against him. You don't play Ghandi with a *jihadi*."[16]

Syria's offer of diplomatic relations might have encouraged speculation that Syria was at last prepared to consider Lebanon as a sovereign country and to treat it as an equal rather than as a dependent. But there were few signals from Syria to that effect. In a rambling interview with the Syrian show *Circle of Events* in 2008, Syrian Deputy Foreign Minister Faysal al-Miqdad stated, "This is a central process, for it to have relations with Syria and Lebanon, with Syria as a main player in the region."[17] Moreover, some analysts suggest that Syria is first and foremost seeking a peace deal with Israel over Golan, taken in the 1967 War, before it seriously revisits its policy with Lebanon.[18]

ISRAELI INTERESTS IN LEBANON

As Israel proclaimed its independence in the spring of 1948, the area it claimed had no commonly recognized borders. Thus some of the leaders of the Zionist movement envisioned southern Lebanon as a possible part of Israel. Chaim Weitzman reportedly wanted access to the Litani River, but the British and French, in the 1916 Sykes-Picot Agreement, agreed that the Balfour Declaration of 1917 did not include what were then French lands in Lebanon. Some early Zionists then hoped for the next best thing for them, a Christian state in Lebanon that would not pose a threat to Israel. When the Lebanese Civil War of 1958 empowered radical Arab groups, Israel directly supplied Maronite forces with assistance and allowed Jordanian troops, intervening as a part of the Baghdad Pact, to get to Lebanon through Israel to curb Syrian influence on the Arab population.[19] Israel's more significant problem in Lebanon, though, was the Palestinian refugee population. Palestinians carried their grievances against Israel into their new country and retained their insurgency organizations, which resumed the pattern of attacking Israel from bordering countries, as they had earlier from Jordan and Egypt. Palestinians also mobilized to attack Israeli targets outside of Israel, focusing on civil airline hijackings in particular. Thus the Israelis responded in similar ways to the attack patterns, by punishing the "host" countries for attacks against Israeli targets by Palestinian groups from Lebanon, as they had previously retaliated against Jordan and Egypt. Thus in 1968, Israeli forces attacked the Beirut International Airport in retaliation for an attack on an Israeli passenger plane in Athens, which the Popular Front for the Liberation of Palestine, based in Lebanon, took credit for.[20]

The situation worsened for Israel when the Cairo Agreement of November 1969 formalized the Palestinian presence in Lebanon. The Maronite elite opposed the Cairo Agreement provisos, the election of Suleiman Frangieh, a powerful *za'im* and family friend of Hafiz Asad, lessened Christian opposition because Frangieh needed to work with Muslim elements and thus found it inconvenient to oppose Cairo. However, Lebanon's Palestinian problem, and thus Israel's, became more serious in September 1970 when the Jordanian government cracked down on the Palestinian Liberation Army (PLA) in Jordan, and thousands of PLA members and their headquarters moved to Lebanon. Israel continued to focus on Lebanon, raiding periodically when Palestinians infiltrated from Lebanon to attack in Israel; thus in March 1978, Israel launched "Operation Litani" in response to a Palestinian attack on a bus on an Israeli coastal highway.[21]

Syria was wary of fighting Israel directly in Lebanon and thus avoided support to the Palestinians when it threatened to draw in Israeli forces. In 1982, when a combination of factors indicated another Israeli invasion of Lebanon, Hafiz al-Asad attempted to avoid a clash with the incoming Israeli forces, but Israel attacked Syrian antiaircraft positions in Lebanon and then decimated the Syrian Air Force, downing scores of Syrian fighters without any Israeli losses.[22] Syrian ground forces entered the fray and performed well, unlike the air components, until the cease-fire of June. Israel broke the cease-fire of early June in order to drive out Palestinians from Lebanon and secure the presidency for Bashar Gemayel. In the end, Asad could do little as the Israeli forces besieged Yasser Arafat and the PLO in Lebanon, and the result deepened the fissure between Asad and Arafat.[23] The siege of Beirut lasted for weeks, and ultimately U.S. President Ronald Reagan openly called for Prime Minister Menachem Begin to end it and to allow the PLA to evacuate. French President François Mitterrand joined the call for a cease-fire, and both the United States and France sent in peace-keepers, but withdrew them after the Israelis announced a withdrawal from Beirut. However, in September 1982, President Bashar Gemayel died in a bomb blast, and his militia, blaming the Palestinians, attacked two refugee camps under Israeli control. The resulting massacre at the camps horrified both the United States and France, who sent peace-keepers back to Lebanon while publically blaming Israel for the tragedy.[24]

For Israel, the cost of the invasion was offset partially by the dramatic reduction of the Palestinian base in Lebanon. But the Israel Defense Forces (IDF) continued to aspire to higher goals, including the creation of a pro-Israeli Lebanese government (an ambition not thwarted initially by the assassination of Bashar Gemayel), and a semipermanent security zone in south Lebanon. However, the Israeli forces faced determined resistance by a Syrian-Druze coalition that weakened the authority of Amin Gemayel, pressuring him to abrogate the original Israeli agreement in March 1984. Israel faced a growing insurgency in its remaining occupation areas in south Lebanon, and the cost in casualties and resources was mounting; as a consequence Israel decided to limit its occupation to a strictly antiterrorist campaign in a smaller security zone of 25 to 40 kilometers in extreme south Lebanon.[25] They had hoped to rely largely on the renegade "South Lebanon Army" (SLA) under Major Saad Haddad, who had defected (or been removed, depending on the source) from the Lebanese military. Haddad died of cancer, though, in 1984, and his successor in the SLA, Antoine Lahad, was appointed by President Camille Chamoun. Lahad adopted the Lebanese *za'im* tradition in south Lebanon, becoming a local politician in addition to his military role. During the 1990s, Lahad imported expensive Israeli gasoline, earning an estimated $7,000 a day on it, levied a 2 percent tax on all goods going in and out of his area, and even banned Lebanese ice cream, claiming it was a "security risk."[26]

The SLA was in many ways an Israeli creation, sustained by Israeli funds. Its methods were sometimes brutal, and it, along with the remaining Israeli troops in south Lebanon, grew as targets for Shi'a militias, particularly Hezbollah. The Israeli casualties grew, stimulating protest in Israel both by ministers of parliament and by civil society members, including those representing families of those killed or wounded in Lebanon. Public support in Israel grew to withdraw the forces, and in the May 1999 election, Labor Party candidate Ehud Barak, a retired IDF chief of staff, promised to remove the troops, a promise he kept when the withdrawal was completed in May 2000.[27]

Israel contributed to Lebanon's problems in another way when it began to expel Palestinians suspected of militancy. The deportations, which apparently began in January 1988, reached 125 by the time that the United Nations, joined by the United States, condemned the action in April of that year. While the Palestinians had no previous connection or citizenship with Lebanon, it appeared to be an expedient way for Israel to dispense with militant Palestinians. Some Israeli officials justified the measures as deterrence: said then-foreign minister Shimon Peres, "It has been proven in the past that deportation is one of the most effective means of deterrence there is, and we try not to use it too much."[28] However, many of the deported Palestinians wound up in the Beqaa Valley (as these particular individuals did), where they came into contact with Hezbollah. Hezbollah operatives reportedly taught the refugee Palestinians suicide tactics, something that Palestinian militants had not used before the 1990s. When the Palestinians eventually returned to the Occupied Territories, they brought those tactics with them. By the mid-1990s, the wave of suicide bombings in Israel reached a crescendo, with one particularly violent period of four bombings right before the March 1996 Israeli elections, swinging those election results in favor of Benyamin Netanyahu of the Likud Party. His Labor Party rival was the same Shimon Peres who had defended the expulsion of Palestinians to Lebanon as a deterrent measure.

Hezbollah attacks from south Lebanon also continued in the 1990s. Israeli Prime Minister Peres, facing an election, and four terrorist bombings in Israel in March 1996, decided to take strong measures, launching "Operation Grapes of Wrath" in April of that year. Along with other weapons, Israel brought 155 mm howitzers that mistakenly shelled a UN refugee camp, killing hundreds of refugees. Though Israel attempted to blame Hezbollah for the tragedy, Lebanese anger targeted Israel instead, with all major Lebanese factions united in at least temporary support for Hezbollah. Yet another cease-fire came shortly, and Israeli voters, unimpressed by Peres's purported toughness, voted in Benyamin Netanyahu as prime minister.

Netanyahu's Likud Party won with a razor-thin majority, but Netanyahu put together a coalition based largely on religious parties (Shas, Ahdut Ha'Torah, and the National Religious Party), while excluding Labor. Thus the governing coalition took a rightward tilt, freed from the normal limits of a coalition of Labor and Likud. The focus, though, was on the Palestinian situation, which remained fluid because of different Israeli positions over the implementation of the 1993 Oslo Accords. Netanyahu's relations with the Palestinians were inflamed initially in September 1996 when an Israeli move to open an ancient tunnel under the Muslim part of the old city of Jerusalem led to rioting and loss of lives on both sides. Netanyahu finally agreed to glacially implement parts of Oslo, evacuating as agreed the Israeli areas of Hebron, though losing some of his cabinet support in doing so. He also alienated many Arab countries that had previously tried to breach their own gaps with Israel, including Jordan and Egypt. Part of his problem was his own personality and leadership style; one assessment of his governance held that

> [f]or all his tough talking, Netanyahu has made a hesitant and uncertain start as prime minister. In an effort to please his various constituencies, he has succeeded in alienating them. Netanyahu gives the impression of being a prime minister distrustful of all but a few close advisers. He has failed to cultivate allies within his own government and has been unwilling to co-opt members of the coalition into the heart of the decisionmaking process and negotiations with the Palestinians.[29]

Possibly to offset small compromises on the Palestinian front, Netanyahu did not show much flexibility in Lebanon, where Israeli troops remained. Their status remained in limbo without an exit strategy. Israel had not viewed the stationing of its troops in Lebanon as permanent, but conditions for withdrawal were very difficult politically and strategically. Israel's stated requirement for security from Lebanon was an agreement with Lebanon that its territory would not be used for raids into Israel, but neither Lebanon nor Israel was willing to sign such an agreement for two reasons: first, Syria, then in virtual control of Lebanese foreign policy, would not allow such an agreement, and, second, Israel would have to fully accept UN Resolution 425, which called for Israel to withdraw from Lebanese territory.[30] Consequently, Israeli troops remained in south Lebanon, and, as Hezbollah strengthened and became more aggressive, Israeli casualties mounted. As they did, pressure mounted in Israel for their withdrawal, and as Netanyahu dragged his feet on the issue, even some hard-line Likud members began to question the mission. Ariel Sharon, who had not initially received a cabinet post in the Netanyahu government, formulated a plan for a phased Israeli military withdrawal from Lebanon, which although rebuffed by the Defense Ministry,[31] began the process of deliberation, fueled by Israel's most notable hawk. The process accelerated as Netanyahu wore out his support in Israel, and in May 1999 a new government headed by Labor Party head and former general Ehud Barak took the reins. Barak had campaigned on a promise to seek new solutions with Israel's neighbors, and in May 2000, Israeli forces left Lebanon, at least temporarily.

Hezbollah did not respond to the withdrawal with its own concessions, nor did Syria, and efforts later in the year by Barak to seek peace with Syria and with the Palestinian administration failed. Hezbollah moved in to the former areas occupied by Israel and strengthened its position both politically and militarily to the point where Hezbollah flags were clearly visible in Lebanese mountains across the Israeli border.[32]

For Israel, the focus for 2006 was on the Palestinians, resulting in a policy that was to surround Israel with a "security obstacle" to keep out Palestinian militants, but attention also turned increasingly to Iran, whose mercurial president, Mahmoud Ahmadinejad, increased his fiery rhetoric against Israel, sponsored a Holocaust denial conference (attended by members of the American Ku Klux Klan, among others), and refused to halt an Iranian nuclear development program, or open it for international inspection. Iran thus complicated Israel's security problems by threatening nuclear weapons that could strike Israel from Iran with long-range missiles that Iran was also developing and also by Iran's support for Hezbollah. Thus when Hezbollah operatives captured two Israeli soldiers along the Lebanese-Israel border in the summer of 2006, Israel launched an all-out assault on Lebanon, as discussed in detail in Chapter 2.

If Israel's strategic objectives in 2006 were to send a message of determination to Iran through Hezbollah, it most likely failed and, indeed, may have backfired. Noted one editorial,

> If Israel's primary objective back in the summer of 2006 was the Iranian nuclear program, it was a grave blunder to channel national and security resources for a wide-scale military operation against Hizballah. It was a gross waste, which makes the military option against Iran in the summer of 2008 far more difficult and expensive.[33]

After the Doha solution of spring 2008, which strengthened Hezbollah's position in Lebanese politics, Israel announced that it had opened peace talks with Syria. Israel and Syria had not attempted peace negotiations since the fateful 2000 efforts led by then U.S. President Bill Clinton in West Virginia, which came to a halt after several days of fruitless efforts. The United States initially opposed the talks, hoping to continue a policy aimed at isolating Syria, but the Israelis made it clear that they wanted to press ahead with the discussions, so the United States relented. What spurred the decision to open discussions, which were aided by Turkish mediation, was not clear, but the continuing rise of Hezbollah power in Lebanon and the hope that Syria might be moved away from Hezbollah's major backer, Iran, seemed to be prime factors.[34]

Israel had hoped that its openings with Damascus might allow talks with Lebanon, which technically could be more fruitful since Israel did not occupy a significant part of Lebanon, as it did Syria's Golan. But in early June 2008, the caretaker Lebanese government rejected the prospects raised by Prime Minister Ehud Olmert in a cabinet meeting. Lebanon insisted that Israel return the Shabaa Farms area before any talks could even begin. Shabaa Farms was a tiny enclave between Syria and Lebanon that Israel continued to occupy after it left Lebanon, stating that it regarded Shabaa as a part of Golan. Earlier, French President Nicolas Sarkozy, visiting in Lebanon, proposed that Shabaa Farms come under the control of the United Nations, but Hezbollah member of parliament Mohammad Raad rejected that bid as well.[35] That position changed in a matter of weeks, though, in mid-June 2008 when Israel and Lebanon opened talks on Shabaa Farms, ending the Lebanese position that no talks with Israel were possible until Shabaa Farms was returned to Lebanese control.

In early 2009, Israeli elections resulted in the usual indeterminate outcome. The "center" Kadima Party won one more seat in the Knesset than did the rightist Likud, but because more right-wing parties emerged as the top vote-getters, Likud leader Benyamin Netanyahu was asked to form a government. He succeeded with a coalition of mostly right-wing parties, with the exception of Labor, which sank to 14 seats in the 120-seat Knesset. The election left Israel's future policy toward Lebanon unclear. While Likud has a hawkish reputation, it was also the case that Likud Prime Minister Menachim Begin signed a peace treaty with Egypt and Ariel Sharon unilaterally withdrew Israeli forces from the Gaza Strip. Whether Netanyahu would match his swearing-in rhetoric with actions conducive to relaxed tensions between Israel and Lebanon remained a mystery.

IRANIAN INTERESTS IN LEBANON

Prior to the 1979 Islamic Revolution in Iran, the Persian state had little interaction with Lebanon. The founding of the Islamic Republic of Iran would change that relationship as the Iranian narrative changed from secular Persian nationalism to a Shi'a political foundation. Embracing the Shi'a story, Iran's Ayatollah Ruhollah Khomeini exhorted the vision of a global mission to protect Shi'a communities in parts of the Middle East. The importance of the religious mission is easy to neglect if state interests are considered paramount, but Shi'a identity was Iran's revolutionary fuel: "What gave Iran's revolutionary narrative its force was its religious passion . . . Glorifying the symbols of Iranian and Shia romanticism—the aesthetics of *shahadat* (martyrdom), the suffering of Imam Hussein, the just age of the Imam Mahdi—they extracted, channeled, and dispersed the emotional energy onto the receptive revolutionary masses."[36] Iranian policy began emphasizing the spread of Islamic revolution to all Muslim lands, but given the traditional Shi'a-Sunni cleavage, Iran had success only in countries with significant Shi'a populations. Even there, Iran failed to launch a successful revolution in Iraq and Bahrain, two Arab countries with Shi'a majorities. However, Israel's invasion of Lebanon in 1982 suddenly handed Iran's revolutionary leaders the Arab world plum they were seeking. While Lebanese Shi'a largely gave the Israeli invasion quiet welcome, Israeli attacks against Shi'a communities quickly gave birth to Hezbollah, whose founders and ideologues had close Iranian connections. Iran was thus able to establish a toehold in southern and eastern Lebanon that remains to this day.

Kenneth M. Pollack argues that Iran, perceiving weakness from the United States relative to its inability to resolve its dual hostages crises in Lebanon and Iran, decided to challenge American influence in Lebanon: "It seems fairly certain that this impression of weakness contributed to Iran's decision to challenge the United States in Lebanon in the 1980s."[37] Iranian agents built ties with a group of Lebanese Shi'a who had studied in Iranian religious schools under Sheikh Muhammad Hussein Fadlallah and Ayatollah Khomeini and had left for Lebanon after Saddam Hussein expelled them from Iraq in 1977.[38] They were ready in 1982 when the Israeli invasion of Lebanon spawned Hezbollah, allowing Iran to attach itself to that movement. The scope of Iranian influence or control over Hezbollah is disputed, making it difficult to apportion accountability for actions attributed to Hezbollah, but, for Pollack, the September 1982 suicide bombings against American, French, and Israeli targets, "what everyone seems to agree on, including senior Hezbollah leaders, is that a man named Imad Mughniyah and the Iranians were ultimately behind it."[39] There is some evidence from Argentina that Iranian agents had some responsibility through Hezbollah for two bombings, noted earlier, against Jewish and Israeli targets in that country in 1992 and again in 1994.[40] Argentine officials actually indicted Imad Mughniyah for the crime, though he was never arrested, dying instead in a massive car bomb explosion in Damascus in February 2008, with accusations directed at the usual suspects, including Israel's Mossad, Syrian political figures, and rival Shi'a factions.

Lebanon and Iranian Regional Interests

For analysts in the West, Israel, and many Arab countries, Iran's interest in Lebanon is but a small part of a larger Iranian regional ambition. Jordan's King Abdullah II openly discussed the danger of a "Shi'a Crescent," originating in Tehran and linking Iraq, Syria, and Lebanon, constructed out of the cloth of Shi'a loyalty to the perceived dominance of Iran over that faith. Egyptian officials worry about the growing influence of Iran over Syria, Hezbollah, and, perhaps curiously, Qatar, which they view as too friendly to Iranian interests.[41] That concern over Qatar was echoed in Jordan,[42] though the concern about Qatar as a friend of Iran may mask the effort taken by the Qatari ruling family to remain above regional political frays, with Qatar one of the few Gulf Arab countries to maintain economic ties to Israel, for example.

Whether or not Iran saw Lebanon as a hinge in a Shi'a crescent, as predicted by Abdullah II, or whether Iran was acting defensively in Lebanon to facilitate protection of the Lebanese Shi'a remained a matter of debate. For Vali Nasr, Iran became a magnet that Shi'a in the region became attracted to for both protection and inspiration: "Shias from Lebanon to Iraq, the Gulf, and Pakistan looked to Shi regional power to protect and further their particular communal interests."[43] Moreover, Iran has taken advantage of U.S. efforts to topple rogue Sunni regimes that persecuted Shi'a. The fall of Saddam Hussein and the Taliban regime in Afghanistan, again according to Nasr, "Iranians have welcomed the collapse of the Sunni wall around them since 2001 and see the Shia revival as a means of preventing its return."[44]

There were reasons for such concern. Iran was also reaching out to the predominately Sunni Palestinian diaspora populations, including those in Lebanon. In the spring of 2009, Iranian aid programs began a reach to the Palestinian refugee camps in Lebanon, with 33 truckloads of relief supplies going to the al-Barid and al-Baddawi camps, which arrived along with Iranian expressions of support from the Iranian charge d'affaires, who stated, "We support the Palestinian people and their right to freedom, independence, and sovereignty over the whole Palestinian soil. We extend our congratulations for their divine victory in Gaza."[45]

As this chapter indicates, Lebanon is located in a highly unstable part of the world. Normally countries that exist in dangerous places rely at least partly on a viable professional military to enhance their security. Lebanon, though, never developed strong state institutions, and thus its military, the focal point of the next chapter, has been chronically weak, though it also has the potential to serve as one of the country's few points of unity.

NOTES

1. Talal Nizameddin, "The Political Economy of Lebanon under Rafiq Hariri: An Interpretation," *The Middle East Journal* 60 (Winter 2006): 98.

2. Judith Harik, "Syrian Foreign Policy and State/Resistance Dynamics in Lebanon," *Studies in Conflict & Terrorism* 20 (July 1997): 250.

3. Author's observations, March 1996 and March 1997.

4. "Arab Leaders, Angry at Syrian President, Threaten Boycott of Arab Meeting," *New York Times*, March 8, 2008.

5. Ibid.

6. Martin Kramer, "The Oracle of Hizbullah: Sayyid Muhammad Husayn Fadlallah," in *Spokesmen for the Despised: Fundamentalist Leaders of the Middle East*, ed. R. Scott Appleby (Chicago: University of Chicago Press, 1996), 141–144.

7. Volker Perthes, *Syria under Bashar al-Asad: Modernization and the Limits of Change.* Adelphi Paper 366, the International Institute for Strategic Studies, 2004, 57.

8. "Suleiman Touts Prospects for Diplomatic Ties with Damascus," *Daily Star* (Beirut), June 2, 2008.

9. "Syrian Blast 'Was Suicide Attack,' " *Al Jazeera*, September 29, 2008.

10. "4 Soldiers Killed in Lebanon Bombing," *New York Times*, September 29, 2008.

11. "Traitors, Even in Their Statements," OpenSource GMP20081002627001 Damascus *Al-Ba'ath (Internet Version-WWW)* (in Arabic), October 2, 2008.

12. Faris Khashshan, "The Damascus Bombing: Al-Asad Regime Tampers with Scene of Crime and Accuses Lebanon: What Happened to Palestine Branch Headquarters? Who Is the Brigadier General Who Was Killed? Why Are the Wounded Less Than the Dead?" OpenSource, GMP20080929663002 *Free Syria* (in Arabic) September 28, 2008.

13. "Shakir al-Absi Is Detained in Damascus; and a Major Terrorist Operation Has Been Foiled," OpenSource, GMP20081002637003 Damascus *All4Syria* (in Arabic), September 28, 2008.

14. Originally at "Daily Briefing, Deputy Spokesman Robert Wood, U.S. Department of State, October 6, 2008, http://www.state.gov/r/pa/prs/dpb/2008/oct/110643.htm," which is no longer available. See http://www.licus.org/blog/usarchive/2008_10_01_usblog_archive.html.

15. "Jihadist Blowback," *The Economist*, October 4, 2008, 50–51.

16. Ibid.

17. Syrian Space Channel Talk Show Discusses Lebanese, Syrian Diplomatic Exchange, OpenSource, GMP20081110689008 Damascus *Syrian Space Channel Television* (in Arabic) October 20, 2008.

18. Author's interview, Cairo, Egypt, March 2009.

19. Kirsten E. Schultze, *Israel's Covert Diplomacy in Lebanon* (New York: St. Martin's Press, 1998), 61–62.

20. Ibid., 71.

21. Schulze, *Israel's Cover Diplomacy in Lebanon*, 102.

22. The Syrian Air Force adopted Soviet air combat tactics of utilizing ground control over its fighters, with ground officers guiding the fighters through radar impressions. Thus when the Israeli aircraft struck down the Syrian ground radars, the Syrian pilots in the sky were left with no control and had not been trained to fight independently. They were thus decimated by Israeli pilots who had been taught American tactics of pilot independence.

23. Patrick Seale, *Asad: The Struggle for the Middle East* (Berkeley: University of California Press, 1988), Chap. 22.

24. Pia Christina Wood and David S. Sorenson, "Alliance Theory, Risk Assessment, and Peacekeeping Operations: The French and U.S. MNF to Lebanon, 1982–1985," International Studies Association Annual Conference, San Diego, CA, April 1996.

25. Avraham Sela, "Civil Society, the Military, and National Security: The Case of Israel's Security Zone in South Lebanon," *Israel Studies* 12 (Spring 2007): 61.

26. David Hirst, "South Lebanon: The War That Never Ends?" *Journal of Palestine Studies* 28 (Spring 1999): 28.

27. Sela, "Civil Society, the Military, and National Security," 67–72.

28. "8 Arabs Deported to South Lebanon by Israeli Order," April 11, 1988.

29. Joel Peters, "Under Netanyahu: The Current Situation in Israeli Politics," *Middle East Review of International Affairs* 1 (January 1997), http://meria.idc.ac.il/journal/1997/issue1/jv1n1a2.html.

30. Simon Murden, "Understanding Israel's Long Conflict in Lebanon: The Search for an Alternative Approach to Security during the Peace Process," *British Journal of Middle Eastern Studies* 27 (May 2000), 35.

31. Murden, "Understanding Israel's Long Conflict in Lebanon," 41–42.

32. Author's observations, March 2005. When asked by the author if Israeli concern about an apparent buildup was growing, the answer came back that Israel was far more concerned with the Palestinian threat than it was with Hezbollah, a response that partly suggested why Israel appeared so unprepared for the conflict with Hezbollah that came a year later.

33. "The Answer to Hizballah—in the Diplomatic Realm," *Maqor Rishon* (Tel Aviv) (in Hebrew), Open Source Center, July 11, 2008.

34. "Israel Holds Peace Talks with Syria," *New York Times*, May 22, 2008.

35. "Lebanon: Israel Must Quit Shaba Farms If It Wants Peace," *Haaretz* (Tel Aviv), June 11, 2008.

36. Arshin Adib-Moghaddam, *Iran in World Politics* (New York: Columbia University Press, 2008), 55.

37. Kenneth M. Pollack, *The Persian Puzzle: The Conflict between Iran and America* (New York: Random House, 2004), 176.

38. Ibid., 200–201.

39. Ibid., 203.

40. Nikki R. Keddie, *Modern Iran* (New Haven, CT: Yale University Press, 2003), 268.

41. Author's interview, government agency, Cairo, Egypt, March 2009.

42. Author's interview, Amman, Jordan, March 2009.

43. Vali Nasr, *The Shia Revival* (New York: W. W. Norton, 2006), 173.

44. Ibid., 222.

45. Al-Manar Television, OpenSource, GMP20090317637003, March 17, 2009.

FURTHER READING

Adib-Moghaddam, Arshin. *Iran in World Politics: The Question of the Islamic Republic.* New York: Columbia University Press, 2008.

Parsi, Trita. *Treacherous Alliance: The Secret Dealings of Israel, Iran, and the United States.* New Haven, CT: Yale University Press, 2007.

Pollock, Kenneth M. *The Persian Puzzle: The Conflict between Iran and America.* New York: Random House, 2005.

CHAPTER 6

Lebanon's Military Forces

Unlike most of the militaries in the eastern Mediterranean, Lebanon's military did not participate in the numerous wars that have marked the history of the area since World War II. Thus Lebanon's small army has neither the honor that comes from victory nor the shame that accompanies defeat. There are few statues of military heroes in Lebanon as there are in places such as Syria, Jordan, and Egypt, where most public squares have a bronze image of a great general astride a horse. There are no large military cemeteries in Lebanon, though the civilian graveyards are swollen with casualties from Lebanon's numerous civil conflicts. Indeed, most of the wars involving Lebanon have been fought by private militias, with the professional Lebanese military standing on the sidelines.

Lebanon's military does have a political tradition, though. In May 2008, General Michel Suleiman became Lebanon's president after a long delay, and General Michel Aoun remained a powerful figure in Lebanese politics. Both had previously served as the commander of the Lebanese Army. Other presidents also have served in the Lebanese military, including Fouad Chehab, and Émile LaHood, who both also served as chief of staff of the army.

THE ORIGINS OF THE LEBANESE MILITARY

Like many other postcolonial countries, Lebanon's armed forces are a legacy of its colonial past. Thus in 1916 the French created the units that ultimately became the Lebanese armed forces, romantically calling the unit "The Legion of the Orient." After France received the League of Nations mandate to govern Lebanon, it created the *Troupes Spéciales du Levant*, a military commanded by

French officers that fought for both the Vichy French forces and later the Free French in the Levant. Some Lebanese army units came under control of the Lebanese government in 1943 to maintain domestic order, but most of the army remained under French control until France's final departure in August 1945. However, that force never became significant politically after independence. There was concern among the Christian political elite that the army might seek political power and become a rival to the militias that the most powerful families controlled. Thus the military remained underfunded, capable only of maintaining domestic order, though most Lebanese leaders were reluctant to engage the armed forces in domestic politics.

Christian officers traditionally led the Lebanese military at the senior officer corps level. The reason for these favored positions was societal: Christians held a substantial economic advantage in Lebanon compared to other religious groups, and many of them were able to afford good education for their offspring, which qualified them to become officers in the army, while the Muslim communities often lacked access to such levels of education. Members of the Muslim communities were also hesitant to see their sons join a force that had its origins in the French Mandate period.[1] Thus in a sense the Lebanese military became a support force for the Maronite political establishment, and one of its most important functions was supplying intelligence on other Lebanese political actors to Maronite leaders through the military intelligence branch, the *Deuxième Bureau*. Lebanon's armed forces also became a social platform for the Maronite elite to advance through the ranks to political prominence, with several high-ranking Maronite officers rising to high political office, including the presidency.

The Narrative of Military Tradition

Lebanon remained officially neutral during the 1948 war, but elements of the Lebanese military who wanted to join the Arab cause were allowed to join the "Liberation Army," a volunteer militia. The Liberation Army participated in the Battle of Malikiyya in June 1948, and when Israeli units cut off the Liberation Army's supply lines, elements of the regular Lebanese military intervened to reopen the lines. It was one of a limited number of successful operations by an Arab army against Israeli military forces, and thus it became a powerful source of mythology for the larger Lebanese community. Its narrative has reemerged throughout modern Lebanese history as a signal of resistance, as when Amal leader Nabih Berri called upon the army to return to its Malikiyya roots when it was ordered to demolish homes in the largely Shi'a areas in south Beirut. Its unification effect on the army itself came after the Ta'if Accord, when the army became a coalescing force to reconstruct a national Lebanon, because Makikiyya was fought by a multireligious army.[2] And because the unifying theme of "Palestine" was a key element in the Malikiyya narrative, it remained useful to bridge confessional lines,

The Lebanese Army used its one semi-successful battle in the 1948 war against Israel's formation, the battle of Malikiyya, as the foundation myth serving to unite the many confessions. The power of this battle turned the armed forces into a national institution, from its origins as a colonial army, and created a collective identity to prevent fragmentation during most of the civil war.[3]

During the 1958 civil war, which ultimately evoked intervention by U.S. military forces, the army remained on the sidelines, disobeying an order by President Camille Chamoun's orders to fight Muslim forces that had rebelled against the government's resistance to joining the Egyptian-Syrian–led United Arab Republic. Some elements of the army briefly fought in the civil war, but after the Christian-dominated air force bombed Muslim areas, Muslim elements of the Lebanese military split from it to form their own militias, taking revenge on Christians for the bombing. Christian army units did stave off a Muslim militia attack on the port area of Beirut, but the instigation for the action came from Christian military commanders rather than from the divided government. In an important way, Lebanon's armed forces were building a foundation for a future role as a force for national unity, though subsequent conflict would weaken the professional military as an institution before it could emerge after Ta'if as a force for national accord.

One consequence of the 1958 civil war was an effort by Fouad Chehab to distribute administrative posts (except at the top level) equally between Muslims and Christians, and the military followed the distribution, which would help it later in claiming a position as national unifier.[4] Moreover, during the Chehab presidency, more Muslims, particularly Shi'a, joined the military, giving it more national legitimacy in the eyes of Lebanese Muslims.[5]

Lebanon's civil war almost emasculated the Lebanese military, however, removing it from any unity role. A poor decision to involve the army in the early stages of the civil war cost it national legitimacy and ultimately paved the road for the militias that took its place. Some soldiers simply deserted, while a larger number joined the militia of their choice. Ultimately a 1976 Arab League Summit to restore peace to Lebanon actually allowed Syrian forces, under the guise of peace-keeping, to occupy the country, thus almost replacing the Lebanese military as Lebanon's "protector." As Syrian forces chased remnants of Palestinian militias into south Lebanon, Israel became concerned that the Syrians might cross the Lebanese border into Israel and thus created yet another Lebanese militia, the South Lebanon Army. Lebanon's military largely stayed out of the conflict, though it did get a minor role after Israeli forces invaded south Lebanon in 1987, and the United Nations authorized outside peacekeeping forces under UN Resolution 425. While most of the 4,000 troops came from outside Lebanon, the Lebanese Army sent 700 of its own to assist in the restoration of security in the south.

Both before and after the Ta'if Accord, Syrian military and intelligence penetrated the Lebanese military, gradually trying to take control of its functions.

The *Deuxième Bureau*, which once supplied Maronite parties with internal intelligence, came under Syrian pressure to infiltrate those Lebanese who opposed
Syrian power in Lebanon. Syrian motives appeared to focus on either weakening
the Lebanese armed forces or eliminating them altogether so that they would not
complicate Syrian political objectives for the control of Lebanon. However, the
Lebanese armed forces tried to remain loyal to their Lebanese roots, and during
the 2005 mass demonstrations against Syria following the Rafiq Hariri assassination the armed forces refused to obey an order from Prime Minister Omar
Karami to disperse the anti-Syrian demonstrations.[6] They also refused Syrian
efforts to command Lebanese forces with Syrian officers and to equip the army
with Syrian-supplied equipment.

Following several failed efforts, the Lebanese armed forces began a gradual
rebuilding after the civil war and the withdrawal of most foreign forces.
In 1983 the United States began to supply the army with a $150 million arms
package and advanced training. While the air arm remained weak and
ill-equipped, the army grew steadily in size and capability.[7]

The 2006 Hezbollah-Israel War returned the Lebanese armed forces to the
bystander role they played during the civil war. But though the army did little
actual fighting (except for a few antiaircraft shots), it did play a significant role
in assisting displaced populations and coordinating relief efforts. The military
also got a policing mission to monitor and enforce the cease-fire between the
two sides. The military, in this case, had to act as a neutral broker, a role it had
been assigned at independence. Two years later, it got a similar responsibility
when the government called upon the military to restore order after Hezbollah
defied the government's effort to cut its communications network, sending
Hezbollah supporters into the streets to clash with government supporters. While
it took the army almost a week to decide to intervene, it did, for almost the first
time, act to stop fighting between two internal Lebanese groups.[8]

The Army and Lebanon's Factions

Lebanon is a nation of factions, a fact that poses particular problems for its
military. As in many other countries, the armed forces can be a unifying force
to help bridge internal divisions and, to a degree, the Lebanese armed forces have
attempted to become such a binding influence, even though their origins were
very much tied to leading Maronite families. Yet the military is also a source of
power and influence, and the different factions have all tried to pull the armed
forces into their political orbits. The Lebanese Army also had close ties to the
Lebanese Front, a Maronite militia group whose power grew during the civil
war.[9] Those ties were cemented partially because Camille Chamoun, who had
served as chief of staff of the Lebanese armed forces, was a key member of the
Lebanese Front with his National Liberal Party.

Lebanon's army traditionally received support from Amal, the Shi'a political group. As Augustus Richard Norton indicates, the support was a part of Amal's overall support for the establishment and maintenance of the central government's authority that would bring not only security but also an expectation of political rewards.[10] For its opponents, Amal's support of the Lebanese armed forces brought suspicions that it had secret ties to the military intelligence branch, *Deuxième Bureau*.[11] Such suspicions played into the hands of Hezbollah, which could argue that Amal was just another part of the Lebanese political establishment and not interested in supporting the Shi'a community in Lebanon or the greater Shi'a cause beyond Lebanon.

The Lebanese army's relationship with Hezbollah is somewhat more complicated. The 2006 conflict, in particular, highlighted the dilemma that the military faced in its relationship with Hezbollah:

> The 2006 war between Israel and Hizbullah was a sour wake-up call for the LAF (Lebanese Armed Forces). While it was a unifying force at a time of increasing socio-political and sectarian tension, the LAF was acutely aware that Hizbullah did not factor in what could be the reaction of Lebanon's legitimate military forces if the Shi'a group carried out its attack on Israel. Hizbullah, like many other players in the Lebanese political environment, took for granted that what the LAF would or would not do was irrelevant, and that the LAF—fearful for its integrity and force cohesion—did not need to be consulted. The LAF and supporters of a more robust national military apparatus learned the hard way that in order to discourage, contain and block future Hizbullah cross-border operations that do not enjoy the full support of Lebanon's various political actors, the LAF would have to become a force that cannot be side-stepped by Hizbullah or any other Lebanese faction in the context of Lebanon's sovereignty and national security.[12]

The military did step in to police the cease-fire after the 2006 conflict; however, the Lebanese political leadership reached a consensus that Hezbollah would not have to disarm because it was a national defense element that both frustrated and limited the role of the Lebanese armed forces. The Lebanese military risked breaching civil-military relations if they tried to disarm Hezbollah, and, at the same time, Hezbollah's claimed position as Lebanon's defender was a direct challenge to the authority of the national military. They faced a similar challenge two years later when the Sunni prime minister decided to dismantle Hezbollah's communication network, and a battle between Lebanese Sunni forces loyal to the prime minister and Hezbollah resulted. The army largely stayed out of the fray until the government reversed its positions, though some reports held that a number of Sunni military officers resigned from the armed forces after the incident.[13]

THE STRUCTURE OF THE LEBANESE MILITARY

Like most modern militaries, Lebanon's armed forces are broken into three services, though the army is the largest. There is also a paramilitary force,

Table 6.1 **Components of the Lebanese Armed Forces**

Force	Personnel
Army	53,900
Navy	1,100
Paramilitary	20,000
Air Force	1,000

following the French gendarmerie tradition. The military structure is shown in Table 6.1.[14]

The army operates around 310 main battle tanks, which are all obsolete former Soviet Union or American-made, along with around 1,200 armored personnel carriers (more appropriate for civil and countermilitia operations), along with some artillery pieces. The Lebanese Navy is equipped with a handful of small patrol and landing craft, while the air force has a small number of helicopters and training aircraft. Taken as a whole, Lebanon has one of the smallest militaries in the entire Middle East, useful only for domestic operations. Even this role is limited by Lebanon's obsolete military equipment, which is decades old and limited in capability. The handicap posed by its poor gear became apparent during the conflict with Israel in the summer of 2006, and thus at the time of the Paris III Lebanon donor's conference in January 2007, the United States pledged over $770 million in grants, with $220 million specifically for the Lebanese armed forces.[15] However, the next year found Lebanese forces struggling against Palestinian militants at the Nahr al-Bared refugee camp near Tripoli. The fight lasted for three months and caused heavy casualties on both sides. As a consequence, the United States increased its military assistance package to $410 million, but the hope of the Lebanese military that the program would include better weapons was only partially fulfilled. Apparently concern about the Israeli reaction to sophisticated weapons that might go to Hezbollah was causing divisions in the U.S. Department of State and Dpartment of Defense. "There are differing points of view," said one Department of State official, in the face of conflicting Israeli concerns that Lebanon's military needed to contain Hezbollah, but that some weapons transferred to the military might wind up in Hezbollah arsenals.[16] Lebanese senior military officials expressed dismay at the delay, noting that they lacked modern combat helicopters, unmanned aerial vehicles, and night-vision equipment that would have helped them in combating the militants at Nahr al-Bared. One Lebanese officer noted, "Nahr al-Bared lasted 105 days. If we had attack helicopters, it would have been over in 15 days."[17]

There were limits, though, on the types of technologies that the United Stares was willing to supply Lebanon. While Israel wanted the Lebanese Army to be strong enough to cope with internal militia groups that might threaten Israel, there were also concerns in Tel Aviv that if Lebanon's army got too strong, it might pose a future threat to Israel. The concerns seemed far-fetched, though, given Israeli military superiority. However, American limits were clearly in place. Said Chris Straub, the U.S. deputy assistant secretary of defense for Near East and South Asian affairs, "We don't have a conversation on these matters without considering the concerns of Israel and Israel's qualitative edge. That's a commitment we take very seriously."[18] So the United States, with a $400 million arms sales package since 2006, sent primarily trucks, humvees, 155 millimeter howitzers, M-60 tanks (no match for Israel's Merkava 4 tanks, said a U.S. military spokesperson), night vision equipment, and aerial drones.[19] The M-60 tanks were originally in the Jordanian military, but, with funds supplied by the United Arab Emirates, the tanks were transferred from Jordan to Lebanon.[20]

Lebanon's air force, noted earlier, consists of a small number of obsolete fixed-wing aircraft and helicopters. American plans for its modernization consisted of selling several single engine propeller-driven Cessna "Caravan" observation aircraft. Russia, on the other hand, was thinking big. In December 2008 Russia announced that it was offering Lebanon's air force the advanced MiG-29 fighter, a plane often compared to the U.S.-operated F-16. American officials were surprised at the offer by Russia for 10 MiG-29s, arranged after a trip to Moscow by Defense Minister Elias Murr.[21] Russia sweetened the deal by offering the planes for free, yet it was unclear what Lebanon would do with them (they are not well equipped for urban warfare, for example). Moreover, there was alarm both in the United States because Lebanon had traditionally bought American weapons and in Israel since the MiG-29 would give Lebanon's 1950s-era air force a new punch.[22] The deal also offered new access for Russia into Middle East affairs, a region where the former Soviet Union once had considerable influence, but lost it decades ago.

The Lebanese Military as an Integrative Force

As the previous chapters indicate, Lebanon is one of the most divided countries in the Middle East. It lacks, among other things, an integrative national force to bring its populations closer together. Thus it is somewhat remarkable that the Lebanese military has become more representative of Lebanon's population mix than other institutions. At the time of its founding in 1945, a majority of the officers in Lebanon's army were Maronite Christians, reflecting their dominant political influence. However, according to Oren Barak, the percentage of Christian officers was around 71 percent before 1945, dropping to 55 percent in the 1958–1971 period, and to 47 percent during the 1991–2004 period. This was partly due to concerted efforts to make the Lebanese Army more ethnically balanced after the civil war, which stand in contrast to the reality that Lebanon's political institutions only became more representative in the late 1980s.[23] It was also a consequence of the overall decline of Lebanon's Maronite population relative to the other religious groupings over time.

Lebanon's military would take a much more visible and definitive stand in January 2000 when it engaged a small group of violent militants belonging to *Takfir wal-Hijra* in the mountains of Dinnieh. When members of *Takfir wal-Hijra* overran a small Christian village in the area, thousands of army troops and weapons mobilized to free hostages taken during the fight. This was one of the first fights against jihadist Sunni groups, but it would not be the last.[24]

The army's role in domestic politics did increase considerably after the 2006 Hezbollah war with Israel, when, in response to the cease-fire, it entered Hezbollah-controlled areas to police the terms of the agreement. The Lebanese military also deployed against drug dealers in the Beqaa Valley, which sometimes put it at odds with local families who benefited from the drug trade. In April 2009 four soldiers died at the hands of drug dealers, an event that generated celebratory gunfire in the village of the Jaafar family, suspected of supporting the transport of drugs in the Valley.[25] Minister of the Interior Ziad Baroud reacted harshly to the incident, "The military is a red line that should not be crossed by anyone. It is unacceptable that the military be dealt with in the manner it was today. We shall strike with an iron fist to prevent this from happening again."[26] He backed up his words with a military raid into Baalbek, sweeping up 69 suspected drug gang members, and killing several. They also confiscated drug-producing equipment and the car that they believed was used by the gang members who killed the soldiers.[27] The operation demonstrated, among other things, that the armed forces of Lebanon had emerged as a significant player in Lebanon's internal security, perhaps unwilling to again cede the national stage to the militias. Such a position could only enhance the power of the armed forces as an institution that could enhance national unity, indeed perhaps the only such institution in Lebanon's political mosaic. The chief of staff of the Lebanese armed forces, Brigadier General Shawqi al-Masri, seemed to appreciate the national unification role that his forces could play when he told his troops on Army Day, "Lebanon's unity and power emerges from your own unity and power."[28] The general continued by arguing that the military protection of national unity ultimately led to the end of the months-long stalemate that ended in the summer of 2008 with a presidential selection.[29] Still, the army's inability to control the Hezbollah-instigated violence in Beirut and beyond in May 2008 also indicates that limits to a unity role for the military still remain.

Lebanon's armed forces also have allowed the United States to build a relationship with the country at large because of American interests in supplying Lebanon's military with arms and training. That relationship builds on what has been a zigzag relationship between Lebanon and the United States, which is the focus of the next chapter.

NOTES

1. Oren Barak, "Commemorating Malikiyya: Political Myth, Multiethnic Identity, and the Making of the Lebanese Army," *History & Memory* 13 (Spring/Summer 2001): 65.

2. Ibid., 71–74.

3. Anne Marie Baylouni, "Al-Manar and Alhurra: Competing Satellite Stations and Ideologies," Occasional Paper Series, George Marshall European Center for Security Studies, 2 (October 2006): 7.

4. Oren Barak, *The Lebanese Army: A National Institution in a Divided Society* (Albany: State University of New York Press, 2009), 27–28.

5. Ibid., 65.

6. Aram Nerguizian, *The Lebanese Armed Forces: Challenges and Opportunities in Post-Syria Lebanon* (Washington, DC: Center for Strategic and International Studies, 2009), 9.

7. Barak, *The Lebanese Army*, 125.

8. "Lebanese Army Says It Will Use Force to Quell Fighting," *New York Times*, May 13, 2008.

9. Lewis W. Snider, "The Lebanese Forces: Their Origins and Role in Lebanon's Politics," *Middle East Journal* 38 (Winter 1984): 30.

10. Augustus Richard Norton, *Amal and the Shi'a: Struggle for the Soul of Lebanon* (Austin: University of Texas Press, 1987), 67.

11. Ibid.

12. Nerguizian, *The Lebanese Armed Forces*, 13.

13. Ibid., 20.

14. *The Military Balance, 2009*, International Institute for Strategic Studies (London: Routledge, 2009), 254–256.

15. "Donors Gather to Help Lebanon's Government," *New York Times*, January 25, 2007.

16. "U.S. Resupplies Lebanon Military to Stabilize Ally," *New York Times*, October 26, 2008.

17. Ibid.

18. "US Mindful of Israel when Aiding Lebanese Army," *Daily Star* (Beirut), December 3, 2008.

19. Ibid.

20. Author's interview, Amman, Jordan, March 2009.

21. "Russia, Testing U.S. Sway, Offers Lebanon 10 Warplanes," *New York Times*, December 18, 2008.

22. Ibid.; "Russia to Supply Lebanon with 10 MiG-29 Fighter Jets," *Haaretz* (Tel Aviv), December 17, 2008.

23. Oren Barak, "Towards a Representative Military? The Transformation of the Lebanese Officer Corps Since 1945. *Middle East Journal* 60 (Winter 2006): 75–94.

24. Nicholas Blanford, *Killing Mr Lebanon* (London: I. B. Tauris, 2006), 195.

25. "Four Lebanese Killed in Ambush," *New York Times*, April 13, 2009.

26. "Lebanon's Drug Mafia Blamed in Death of 4 Soldiers," *Los Angeles Times*, April 13, 2009.

27. "Lebanese Army Rounds Up 69 Suspects in Bekaa Raids," *Daily Star* (Beirut), April 16, 2009.

28. "A United Army Assures Lebanese Unity, Says Acting LAF Commander," *Daily Star* (Beirut), August 1, 2008.

29. Ibid.

FURTHER READING

Barak, Oren. *The Lebanese Army: A National Institution in a Divided Society.* Albany: State University of New York Press, 2009.

Nerguizian, Aram. *The Lebanese Armed Forces: Challenges and Opportunities in Post-Syria Lebanon.* Washington, DC: Center for Strategic and International Studies, 2009.

CHAPTER 7

The United States and Lebanon

The United States is a relative latecomer to the Middle East because it was distant and nonessential for American interests and because it was largely the province of European powers. The end of World War II and America's entry into global politics would make the Middle East rise in importance, though it would take a while before the Middle East would consume more attention than did Europe or Asia in the American pantheon of attention. Generally American Middle East priorities have focused on the following:

- Reducing the influence of global competitors in the Middle East
- Preserving Israeli security
- Anchoring states that might serve as local pillars for American interests
- Preventing the rise of states or nonstate groups that could challenge American regional interests
- Preventing the spread of weapons of mass destruction into the region (selectively)
- Preserving access to petroleum

To achieve these objectives, the United States sought "anchor" states to provide both political and military support for them. Clearly larger states could be better anchors, so the United States built preferential relations with Egypt (after 1973), Iran (before 1979), and Saudi Arabia (after 1973). Some smaller states also got the American embrace, such as Jordan and the smaller Arab Gulf countries, and Israel received large quantities of both financial and military aid after 1967. In this expansion of interests, other small states such as Lebanon got left behind because they were either too resource-poor or too fragile, and Lebanon met both tests.

The United States and Lebanon have a long history, dating back almost to the founding of the American republic. American missionaries and explorers found their way to the eastern Mediterranean in efforts to establish both religious and commercial influence, though such efforts often ended in disappointment.[1] The United States also became home to thousands of Lebanese, mostly Christian, who began immigrating to America beginning in the late nineteenth century, and now they make up more than half of the Arab-American population. These Lebanese-Americans have distinguished themselves in all walks of American life, as noted in the Introduction. Their connections to the land of their ancestors is tenuous, though, because like many other so-called "hyphenated Americans," their forbearers often cast off ties to the old country when they arrived in the United States. Thus the voices of Lebanese-Americans are relative mute regarding American policy toward Lebanon, in comparison to Jewish-Americans or Armenian-Americans, for example.

For the United States, policy toward Lebanon has been inconsistent and inchoate, partly because American strategy toward the eastern Mediterranean has been shaped by the logic of the Cold War and, later, by the so-called "Global War on Terror" during the George W. Bush administration. And while Lebanese-American public opinion has been relatively quiescent about the region, the views of the Israel Lobby have been more influential, no matter what the debate on the nature and validity of those pressure groups.[2]

THE U.S. FOCUS ON LEBANON: THE EARLY YEARS

Following World War II, U.S. policy focused more on Europe and Asia than on the Middle East. As William R. Polk noted, the United States had little commercial or political interest in the Middle East and resisted British efforts to engage it more fully in the area.[3] The perceived Soviet threat to U.S. interests loomed larger in postwar Europe and Asia, ravaged by war and vulnerable to radical political movements. A 1947 document argued, for example, that the Middle East was of "secondary strategic importance," and only Turkey ranked in the top 16 strategically important countries.[4] But as Soviet interests grew in the Mediterranean and Caspian regions, the United States began to take note, responding with stronger efforts to bolster regional countries considered to be strategic.[5] But Lebanon got relatively little attention even as the firestorm of the 1948 Arab-Israeli War was opening a strident debate on what position to take on Israeli independence. Truman barely mentioned Lebanon during his administration, nor did Eisenhower until the 1958 crisis.

Following the violent overthrow of the Iraqi monarchy in the summer of 1958, President Camille Chamoun requested troops from the United States, believing that his regime would be the next to fall to an Arab nationalist movement. Said Eisenhower, "President Chamoun made clear that he considered an immediate United States response imperative if Lebanon's independence, already menaced from without, was to be preserved in the face of the grave developments which occurred yesterday in Baghdad whereby the lawful government was violently overthrown and many of its members martyred."[6] Eisenhower added that the troops were also being sent to protect American lives in Lebanon (stating that there were around 2,500 Americans in the country), but added Cold War narrative to the reasoning by noting the revolt in northern Lebanon which, Eisenhower argued, was "encouraged and strongly backed by the official Cairo, Damascus, and Soviet radios which broadcast to Lebanon in the Arabic language."[7] Eisenhower cited previous efforts by communists to take over Greece, China, Czechoslovakia, Korea, and Indochina, thus using the logic of the "domino theory" to justify the first commitment of American troops to the Middle East after World War II.[8] Eisenhower was also alarmed by the appeal of Egyptian President Gamal Abdul Nasser, particularly after Nasser spoke in Damascus in the spring of 1958, attended by thousands of Lebanese Muslims. Eisenhower's top advisors warned that Nasser was trying to take over the entire region and was particularly interested in denying Middle East oil to the West.[9] For Eisenhower, other alternatives, including an anticommunist propaganda campaign, were not feasible partly due to a congressional refusal to fund such policies, even though the president realized that the cost of a military commitment was higher than preventative measures would have been.[10]

Eisenhower's successors in the White House did not follow his Middle East activism. John F. Kennedy found himself preoccupied with U.S.-Soviet relations after the 1962 Cuban Missile Crisis and the 1961 Bay of Pigs fiasco, and he later focused on Southeast Asia prior to his assassination. Lyndon B. Johnson saw his presidency swallowed by the Vietnam War, and his focus was hardly interrupted even by significant events such as the 1967 War. Richard M. Nixon succeeded Johnson, and, in an effort to extricate the United States from its Southeast Asian commitments in particular, articulated the so-called "Nixon Doctrine" in 1969, which called for the United States to rely more on regional powers to provide for their own defense, instead of relying on American might and influence for their safety. Nixon articulated the doctrine in February 1970: "America cannot—and will not—... undertake all the defense of the free nations of the world."[11] Nixon reluctantly did become more involved in the Middle East during and after the 1973 Arab-Israeli War, but that involvement did not include Lebanon, which had not been a party to the war. Nixon would soon become entangled in the Watergate political crisis and would leave the White House to Vice President Gerald Ford in 1974. The next year began Lebanon's civil war, but most of the American policy for that war would fall on the shoulders of President Jimmy Carter, who took office in 1977. Carter, one of the first presidents to have a genuine interest in the Middle East, learned firsthand of the conflict from his new ambassador to Lebanon.

Richard B. Parker, who presented his ambassadorial credentials in February 1977, saw some of the worst of the conflict. He understood that a role for the United States in the conflict would have been extremely difficult:

> The Americans were willing to help, but they were stymied by the inability of the Lebanese themselves to work together in support of national conciliation. It was all very well to urge the United States to do something, but it could not impose domestic peace on Lebanon unless it was willing to commit a substantial US military force to do the job (my estimate was that 50,000 men would have been required), and that was out of the question. If there was to be a political, as opposed to a military solution to the civil war, the first requirement was that the Lebanese themselves be ready to bury the hatchet.[12]

Parker was correct about the impossibility of committing 50,000 troops (or fewer, for that matter) in the wake of the unpopular Vietnam war, which the United States had finally terminated only two years previous. Parker also understood the other lesson from Vietnam for the United States: if a country is torn by internal conflict fueled by centuries of domestic division, external forces are incapable of even making a small dent on that conflict. Moreover, as Parker further observes, the United States was unwilling to put pressure on either Syria or Israel to withdraw or lessen their respective presence in Lebanon.[13] Ultimately the United States decided not to commit peace-keepers to help terminate the civil war, and thus while American audiences watched televised images of the pulverization of Beirut, the United States remained aloof from the internal conflict. It was clear to President Carter that there was little that the United States could do to curb the violence and return stability to Lebanon, and, preoccupied with Egyptian-Israeli peace and the Iranian hostage crisis in his last year of office, Carter had little time to devote to Lebanon.

His successor, Ronald Reagan, brought a conservative mindset to the White House, but lacked experience in foreign affairs. Taking office in 1981, Reagan was initially preoccupied with the former Soviet Union, using a combination of tough language and defense dollars to repair what Reagan and his advisors judged to be a weak and conciliatory approach to American-Soviet relations by Carter. The Middle East did not enter Reagan's political calculations until 1982 when Israel invaded Lebanon and drove to the outskirts of Beirut (Chapter 1). Reagan was increasingly concerned about the costs to the United States of the Israeli moves and increasingly pressured Prime Minister Menachem Begin to exercise restraint. Under pressure from the United States, Israeli forces began to withdraw and the United States, fearful that Syria might follow them back to the border, sent in U.S. peace-keepers. The mission was poorly defined and the justification changed frequently, but as the Israeli troops withdrew, the U.S. Department of Defense ordered the troops back to their ships off the Lebanese coast. Then came the Sabra-Shatilla massacre, and Reagan immediately sent them back. The mission, now adjusted to protect Lebanese civilians, remained vague, with troops placed in vulnerable positions and with unsure operational instructions. The bombing by Hezbollah of the U.S. embassy and the Marine barracks in October 1983 shattered Reagan's hopes of influencing events in Lebanon, and American forces withdrew some months later. The message for Reagan's successors was that Lebanon was a dangerous place for American interests, and thus presidents George G. W. Bush and Bill Clinton downplayed a role in Lebanon, preferring to concentrate on containing Iran in the Gulf, challenging Saddam Hussein in Kuwait, and, in Clinton's case, attempting unsuccessfully to construct peace between Israel and Syria, and Israel and the Palestinians. President George H. W. Bush did make a concerted effort to construct a regional peace in the eastern Mediterranean after the 1990–1991 Gulf War, endorsing peace efforts initiated in Oslo, Norway, and Madrid, Spain. Bush had hoped to include Syria in such peace efforts, and in an effort to lure Syria into possible discussions with Israel over Golan, Bush tacitly endorsed Syria's violation of the Ta'if Accord, permitting Syria to retain its forces and influence in Lebanon.

George W. Bush entered the White House with very little foreign policy experience, and thus it was likely that he hoped that Lebanon would not appear too large on his presidential radar screen, but the events of September 11 and the rise of Hezbollah in Lebanon would alter those plans.

After September 11, the so-called "Global War on Terror" brought a new focus on Islamist groups such as Hezbollah. While Hezbollah had no ties to al-Qaeda, which regarded the Shi'a as apostates, the distinction did not appear to matter to Bush administration planners, who did not specialize in knowledge about the general Middle East and its complexity. Thus Bush urged Congress to push for a harsh policy against states that he believed were supporting Islamist terror groups, including Hezbollah. Thus in 2003 Congress passed the Syria Accountability and Lebanese Sovereignty Restoration Act of 2003, and in May 2004 President George W. Bush added through an executive order adding more sanctions against Syria for a variety of allegations, including its support for Hezbollah. The sanctions had few real teeth because U.S.-Syrian commercial trade was almost nonexistent; for example, the acts precluded Syrian banks from holding assets in American banks, which they did not have anyway, and a prohibition on Syrian Arab Airlines from commercial routes to the United States, which it did not fly. Still, the reason for the sanctions, as is so often the case, was to create at least the appearance of action against Syria.

U.S. POLICY AND THE 2006 WAR

President Bush had already sharpened both rhetoric and policy toward Iran, Syria, and Hezbollah when the summer 2006 war between Israel and Hezbollah (and, ultimately much of Lebanon itself) broke out, as described in Chapter 1. For the United States and the Bush II administration, the 2006 war helped to reify Iran's efforts to expand its influence in the Middle East, and thus efforts to link Hezbollah to Iranian motives and direction grew during the 2006 conflict. President George W. Bush said in a joint press conference with then-Prime Minister Tony Blair of the United Kingdom, "Prime Minister Blair and I discussed the crisis in the Middle East. In Lebanon, Hezbollah and its Iranian and Syrian sponsors are willing to kill, and to use violence to stop the spread of peace and democracy—and they're not going to succeed."[14] Six month later, Bush repeated the accusation:

> While Lebanon's friends seek to help the Lebanese government build a free, sovereign, and prosperous country, Syria, Iran, and Hizballah are working to destabilize Lebanese society. Their goals are clear. They foment violence in order to prevent the establishment of a Special Tribunal in response to former Prime Minister Hariri's assassination, to prevent full implementation of U.N. Security Council resolutions calling for Hizballah's disarmament, and to bring down Lebanon's democratically elected government, in violation of its constitution.[15]

Thus the administration wasted no time in choosing sides, giving Israel strong verbal support early in the conflict. Diplomatic support also came quickly as U.S. ambassador to the United Nations (UN) John R. Bolton vetoed a Security Council resolution criticizing Israel and worked to block efforts to impose a UN-sponsored cease-fire. Congress joined the administration by passing non-binding resolutions condemning Hezbollah while supporting Israel. While some of this support may have reflected traditional U.S. support for Israel and a strong dislike of Hezbollah (remembered for the 1983 Marine Corps barracks bombing), the so-called "Israel Lobby" also stimulated support. The American Israel Public Affairs Committee (AIPAC) fought efforts by members of Congress to work for a cease-fire and criticized what AIPAC considered as "unfair" reporting about Israeli tactics and motives during the war.[16] Whether or not the Israel Lobby was key to sustaining American support for Israel during the 2006 war is difficult to demonstrate, though it should be noted that there was almost no parallel effort by the Lebanese-American community or other American-Arab organizations to challenge U.S. support for Israel during the conflict.

The 2006 Lebanon War did provide lessons for the United States military, though there was considerable debate over what those lessons might be. The American military sent numerous teams to Israel to interview Israeli participants, wrote long narratives on prospective lessons, and included the Lebanon scenario in select wargames: "I've organized five major games in the last two years, and all of them have focused on Hezbollah," said a staff member of the Marine Corps Warfighting Laboratory in Quantico, Virginia.[17] The "lessons" also highlighted the friction within the U.S. military between those who saw it as a textbook example of the low-intensity war that the military should be preparing for and those who prefer to hold out and arm for a conventional enemy down the road.[18] Analyst Stephen Biddle put it well when he noted, "The Lebanon war has become a bellwether. If you are opposed to transforming the military to fight low-intensity wars, it is your bloody sheet. It's discussed in almost coded communication to indicate which side of the argument you are on."[19]

Regardless of the lessons learned from the 2006 war, the United States found itself dealing with new realities in Lebanon. It could be argued that American neglect for Lebanon and Hezbollah might have helped fuel the crisis, so the Bush administration tried to refocus its Lebanese policies. First, the administration approved new reconstruction aid money to partially offset the criticism that the United States had refused to limit Israeli strikes on the country. However, American aid to Lebanon following the 2006 war was quite limited in scope and value, particularly in comparison to the more than $1 billion promised by Iran. According to Director of U.S. Foreign Assistance Ambassador Randall Tobias, U.S. aid to Lebanon concentrated on a few reconstruction projects:

- Reconstructing the Fidar Bridge in Jbeil, a key link in Lebanon's coastal highway between Beirut and the northern city of Tripoli;
- Removing debris from the southern road between Marjeyoun and Nabatyeh;
- Procuring materials and hiring local workers to repair damaged homes;
- Cleaning and repairing schools in preparation for the coming school year;
- Providing new nets, hooks, and other trade material to fishermen whose equipment was damaged; and
- Supporting local fishermen working to clean up the oil slick that now pollutes 90 miles of the Lebanese coastline.[20]

While these projects were certainly worthwhile in their own right, they represented only a small fraction of Lebanon's needs in the post-2006 period. There were calls for more spending and more activity from the United States, partly because Hezbollah was clearly spending more, much more, than was the United States. Noted Senator John Kerry (D-MA),

> The other day, I was told the story of our National Security Adviser, former Marine Commandant Jim Jones, who was commenting how we have powerful, enormous ships off the shores of Lebanon, but Hezbollah is building schools and building homes and winning the hearts and minds of people in that divided and volatile country by doing so. In effect, he described a situation where, as powerful as our military is, we are not able to win the contest for ideas at the center of security issues today . . . . We also might mention again the importance of standing up with respect to Iran. When you look back at what happened in the war with Israel and Lebanon, the southern part of the country of Lebanon was significantly damaged. Iran, using its surrogate Hezbollah, immediately painted flags on the houses—their flags, Hezbollah flags—and essentially asserted: Don't worry, we are here, and we are going to rebuild this.[21]

Kerry's comments came almost three years after the 2006 war (and his thrust was increasing aid to Pakistan), though his point was that the United States was allowing itself to be outspent and outimaged by Hezbollah and its financial patron, Iran.

The United States also tried to expand political development activities under the Middle East Partnership Initiative (MEPI), which the Bush administration had founded to help implement the administration's push for democratization in the Middle East. Small grants went to nongovernmental organizations such as the Lebanese Center for Policy Studies for studies of transitional democracy, the Lebanese Transparency Association, and Statistics Lebanon to train students and professionals about the nuances of democracy, civil law, and media reporting.[22] While MEPI does not provide details of the funding for such grants, the total funding for the five MEPI countries (Algeria, Egypt, Lebanon, Morocco, and Tunisia) for 2005–2006 totaled $617,936.[23] Whether or not such projects might assist in stabilizing Lebanon remain to be seen, but the small size of the grants did not offer much optimism.

THE POST-2006 RELATIONSHIP WITH LEBANON

Besides some limited reconstruction and military assistance, the Bush administration tended to put 2006 behind it, focusing instead on Iraq and Afghanistan. Lebanon did not emerge at all during the 2008 presidential campaign that saw Barack Obama win the election, and thus there was little indication of how Obama might craft Lebanon policy once in office, or, in the larger arena, would shape U.S. policy toward Hezbollah's patron, Iran.

OBAMA TAKES OVER

There were growing concerns in Congress after January 2009 about whether the Obama administration would be as harsh on the Iranian government as had the Bush II regime. Complained Republican Representative Pete Olson (R-TX), "The President did not call on the Iranian Government to give up uranium enrichment. He did not insist that the Iranian Government stop arming Hezbollah in Lebanon and Hamas in Gaza. He did not insist that the Iranian Government stop threatening Israel."[24] However, the United States did take steps less than six months into the Obama administration to curtail funds to Hezbollah, freezing the assets under U.S. jurisdiction of Kassim Tajideen and Abd Al Menhem Qubaysi, two Africa-based supporters of Hezbollah, and prohibiting American citizens from engaging in any transactions with them.[25] Obama UN ambassador Susan Rice also had harsh words for Hezbollah:

> Hizballah has now admitted supporting militants in Egypt and exhorting the Egyptian military to defy its political leaders. These actions are further reminders that Hizballah

is a threat not only to Lebanon but to the region at large. And so we join the Secretary-General in condemning Hizballah's "unwarranted interference in the domestic affairs of a sovereign state."[26]

In late May 2009, Vice President Joseph Biden arrived in Beirut right before the June elections. Biden's visit reflected American concern that Hezbollah would add to the 14 seats it already held in the 128-seat parliament. While Biden professed to represent U.S. neutrality in the Lebanese election ("I do not come here to back any particular party or any particular person. I come here to back certain principles"), he also indicated that the United States had genuine concerns about the possible outcome and would adjust its policy accordingly: "We will evaluate the shape of our assistance programs based on the shape of the new government."[27]

The symbolism of Vice President Biden's visit to Lebanon went beyond his comments on the elections. Biden was the highest ranking American official to visit Lebanon since the early 1980s, when the spate of kidnappings and murders of Americans and other officials made travel there difficult at best. It is clear that America's strategic focus on the Middle East in the past two decades has concentrated on Israeli-Palestinian relations, Iran, Iraq, the so-called "Global War on Terrorism," and concerns over the proliferation of weapons of mass destruction. Lebanon has played a peripheral role in this focus, even when it has been wracked by violence from both internal and external sources. Such lack of attention by the world's leading superpower is sometimes difficult to understand, given Lebanon's strategic location and its role as a microcosm of many of the larger political and social challenges of the larger Middle East region.

U.S. POLICY TOWARD LEBANON: THE FUTURE

In 2007, a report by the Congressional Research Service (CRS) tried to capture U.S. interests in Lebanon:

> The United States and Lebanon have traditionally enjoyed good relations, rooted in long-standing contacts and interaction beginning well before Lebanon's emergence as a modern state. Factors contributing to this relationship include a large Lebanese-American community (a majority of Arab-Americans are of Lebanese origin); the pro-Western orientation of many Lebanese, particularly during the Cold War; cultural ties exemplified by the presence of U.S. universities in Lebanon; Lebanon's position as a partial buffer between Israel and its principal Arab adversary, namely Syria; Lebanon's democratic and partially Christian antecedents; and Lebanon's historic role as an interlocutor for the United States within the Arab world. Two U.S. presidents have described Lebanon as of vital interest to the United States, President Eisenhower in 1958 and President Reagan in 1983.[28]

The latter sentence is probably more telling about U.S. interests in Lebanon than the former paragraph. The reality is that most Lebanese-Americans have been in the United States for generations and have weakened their ties to the old country.

They cannot match the power and influence of the Israel lobbies, and since a majority of Lebanese-Americans are Maronite or other Christian denomination, they do not necessarily oppose the actions of AIPAC or other pro-Israeli activities in the United States. It is also significant that the CRS report mentions presidents Eisenhower and Reagan, who were the only presidents to commit force in an effort to stabilize Lebanon or to protect it from enemies, real or imagined. Perhaps the other occupants of the Oval Office knew better than to make a determined stand for the United States in a country as difficult to manage or even define as Lebanon.

NOTES

1. Michael B. Oren, *Power, Faith, and Fantasy: America in the Middle East, 1776 to the Present* (New York: W. W. Norton, 2007); Ussama Makdisi, *Artillery of Heaven: American Missionaries and the Failed Conversion of the Middle East* (Ithaca, NY: Cornell University Press, 2008); Zachary Lockman, *Contending Visions of the Middle East: The History and Politics of Orientalism* (Cambridge: Cambridge University Press, 2004); Douglas Little, *American Orientalism: The United States and the Middle East since 1945* (Chapel Hill: University of North Carolina Press, 2002).

2. See John J. Mearsheimer and Stephen M. Walt, *The Israel Lobby and U.S. Foreign Policy* (New York: Farrar, Straus, and Giroux, 2007). This book was severely criticized after its publication, with some of the criticism devolving to simple name-calling by well-known scholars and pundits. While this author disagrees with some of the *Israel Lobby* conclusions (U.S. support for Israel has not prevented a number of Arab countries from giving strong support to the U.S. military, such as Qatar and Jordan), the author agrees with the proposition that much of the work of the Israel Lobby has been harmful to both American and Israel interests.

3. William R. Polk, *The United States and the Arab World*, 3rd ed. (Cambridge, MA: Harvard University Press, 1975), 363–365.

4. "United States Assistance to Other Countries from the Standpoint of National Security, JCS 1769/1, April 29, 1947, in *Containment: Documents on American Policy and Strategy, 1945–1950*, ed. Thomas H. Etzold and John Lewis Gaddis (New York: Columbia University Press, 1978), 171–179.

5. Bruce Robellet Kuniholm, *The Origins of the Cold War in the Near East* (Princeton, NJ: Princeton University Press, 1980); John P. Miglietta, *American Alliance Policy in the Middle East, 1945–1992* (Lanham, MD: Lexington Books, 2002).

6. "Statement by the President on the Lebanese Government's Appeal for United States Forces," Document 171, *Public Papers of the Presidents of the United States: Dwight D. Eisenhower, 1957*, 549.

7. "Special Message to the Congress on the Sending of United States Forces to Lebanon," Document 172, *Public Papers of the Presidents of the United States: Dwight D. Eisenhower, 1957*, 551.

8. "Statement by the President Following the Landing of United States Marines at Beirut," Document 173, *Public Papers of the Presidents of the United States: Dwight D. Eisenhower, 1957*, 555.

9. H. W. Brands, Jr., "Decisions on American Armed Intervention: Lebanon, Dominican Republic, and Grenada," *Political Science Quarterly* 102 (Winter 1987–1988): 610–611.

10. John Lewis Gaddis, *Strategies of Containment* (New York: Oxford University Press, 1982), 177–178.

11. Quoted in Barry Rubin, "US Policy, January–October 1973," *Journal of Palestine Studies* 3 (Winter 1974): 99.

12. Richard B. Parker, "Kawkaba and the South Lebanon Imbroglio: A Personal Recollection, 1977–1978," *Middle East Journal* 50 (Autumn 1996): 548.

13. Ibid.

14. "President Bush and Prime Minister Blair of the United Kingdom Participate in Press Availability," The White House, Washington, D.C., July 28, 2006, http://www.whitehouse .gov/news/releases/2006/07/20060728-1.html.

15. "President's Bush's Statement on the Situation in Lebanon," America.gov., http:// www.america.gov/st/texttrans-english/2007/January/20070129180353MBzemoG0.9362299 .html.

16. Mearsheimer and Walt, *The Israel Lobby and U.S. Foreign Policy*, 326–330.

17. "Short '06 Lebanon War Stokes Pentagon Debate," *Washington Post*, April 6, 2009.

18. Ibid.

19. Ibid.

20. Jeremy M. Sharp, *Lebanon: The Israel-Hamas-Hezbollah Conflict* (Washington, DC: Congressional Research Service, 2006), 14.

21. Congressional Budget for the United States Government for Fiscal Year 2010. *Congressional Record*, Congressional Record: April 1, 2009 (Senate), http://frwebgate3.access .gpo.gov/cgi-bin/TEXTgate.cgi?WAISdocID=53734525762+0+1+0&WAISaction=retrieve.

22. "MEPI in Lebanon," MEPI Regional Office Tunis, http://www.medregion.mepi.state .gov/about_lebanon.html.

23. "Lebanese Associations Receive MEPI Funding," Embassy of the United States, Beirut, Lebanon, October 24, 2006, http://lebanon.usembassy.gov/pr20061024.html.

24. "Threat from Iran Is Real," Congressional Record: March 25, 2009 (House), H3840.

25. "Treasury Targets Hizballah Network in Africa," TG-149, United States Department of the Treasury, http://www.ustreas.gov/press/releases/tg149.htm.

26. Susan E. Rice, "Remarks on Lebanon and Resolution 1559," United States Department of State, May 7, 2009, http://www.state.gov/p/io/rls/rm/2009/123084.htm.

27. "Biden Arrives in Beirut Ahead of Vote," *New York Times*, May 22, 2009.

28. Alfred Prados, *Lebanon* (Washington, DC: Congressional Research Service, 2007), 2.

Epilogue

If there is a single theme for this book, it is that Lebanon's political system is fraught with division that produces stalemates at the center and thus empowers both civil society and regional power brokers. The national parliamentary election in June 2009 was symptomatic. Like most previous Lebanese elections, the 2009 election produced mixed results, and, again like past elections, confounded expectations.

Prior to the elections, Hezbollah and its ally, General Michel Aoun's Free Patriotic Movement, were expected to gain seats in the assembly. Instead the "March 14 Coalition" retained a majority of the seats, 71 in the 128 seat majority. The rival "March 8 Coalition" won 57 seats. There were both immediate and long-term implications of the outcome: the immediate was that Lebanon would likely continue to cooperate with the international investigation of the Hariri assassination, which the opposition indicated it would not support.[1] The longer-term product of the election was that the strengthened March 14 alliance might gain enough support to begin the process to pare back Lebanon's still massive debt. The biggest loser was General Aoun's Free Patriotic Movement, which foundered. As one analysis held, "Mr. Aoun, on the other hand, walks away with less than when he entered the race. The Sunni and Shiite communities are largely united behind their respective parties. Mr. Aoun gambled that he would be able to bring the majority of Christian voters with him into the alliance with Hezbollah, and appears to have been rejected by his intended constituents."[2] Some found slight reason for optimism in the Lebanese outcome, suggesting that the electoral defeat of Hezbollah was a triumph for U.S. President Barack Obama, particularly since it came right after the president's powerful speech in Cairo calling for, among other things, a rejection of political extremism in the Middle East and beyond. Said one editorial,

[W]eekend elections in Lebanon delivered a blow to the Hezbollah Islamic movement. Hezbollah forces stood at the very doorway to political control of Lebanon until the country's voters Sunday turned them back and instead gave continued control of Parliament to a Western-leaning coalition. That outcome does many good things all at once. It provides the perfect and immediate response to President Barack Obama's speech to the Islamic world last week urging the Islamic street to reject extremism; it vindicates the American decision to try to tip the balance toward the Western-leaning parties; and it makes it easier for the U.S. to deal with Israel, which now will be slightly less nervous, and with Syria, which now is a chastened sponsor of Hezbollah.[3]

The election also signaled Lebanon's continuous rise in the world of personal communications. Facebook and Twitter became essential tools for candidates and parties, along with personal texting and other forms of communication unknown to previous generations of Lebanese politicians. As one report noted,

Politicians have recognized the importance of an online presence and have attempted to participate in social media during this round of elections. The majority of candidates have registered domains in their names, created a website that hosts their election term programme, activities and TV/radio appearances leading up to the election . . . The candidates have referenced their websites on print advertisements such as street ads.[4]

The rhetoric from the June election was initially positive. Both Hassan Nasrallah and Saad Hariri pledged to accept the results, and Hariri hoped that conciliation would prevail:

We extended our hands to everyone (in his speech on Sunday-Monday night) because we believe we must come together somewhere. All of us, whether it is the 14 March forces or the 8 March forces, must listen to each other's voice. Did not these voices go to the ballot boxes and which we must respect? From this premise, we believe there is a need for us to come together so that we can all work for Lebanon's interest. This victory for the 18 March forces is not directed against anyone. It is in the interest of the country and stability.[5]

In June 2009, Saad Hariri got the post of prime minister, showing the influence of the Future bloc, though the outcome was not without its clashes in the streets. Supporters of Amal and the Future bloc clashed in late June, and the army, dispatched to curb the violence, warned darkly that perpetuators of bloodshed would be shot: "Orders have been given to [the army] to open fire on any armed person appearing on the streets and it will not tolerate any breach of security."[6]

More evidence for the "more of the same" attitude in Lebanese politics came in early August 2009, when Walid Jumblatt took his Progressive Socialist Party out of the anti-Syrian March 14 Coalition. The *Daily Star* (Beirut), no friend of Jumblatt, put it bluntly,

The political chameleon Walid Jumblatt has once again changed colors, dumping the March 14 coalition to ingratiate himself with Syria and Hizbullah, whom he sees as the political heavyweights of the moment . . . Jumblatt said to an extraordinary congress of his Progressive Socialist Party (PSP) Sunday that he had joined the anti-Syrian March 14 camp out of necessity and the current form of their partnership must end.[7]

According to Jumblatt, he had changed his position because the British had decided to open negotiations with Syria, though Jumblatt was able to point out that Saad Hariri was also planning to meet Syrian leadership in Damascus. The very next day Jumblatt announced that he would continue to support President Suleiman in the cabinet while "I will examine the conditions when I have to vote in Parliament."[8]

The point here is that Lebanon's inchoate political gamesmanship continued after the 2009 elections even as it had since Lebanon's founding. Prominent politicians move conveniently from political flower to flower, seeking the best deal. The bargaining may be more intense and the loyalties lower in Lebanon than in other polities, but the most important part of it is that it happens peacefully. Jumblatt and his political peers may jockey for the spoils by trying to outmaneuver rivals and constantly testing the political winds (particularly those that blow from Damascus), but they are doing it without killing each other. That is Lebanon's best hope. Given the country's bloody history, it is very likely that Lebanon's citizenry will gladly put up with political shenanigans as long as the conflict is limited to words in the *Daily Star*.

NOTES

1. U.S. Backed Alliance Wins in Lebanon," *New York Times*, June 8, 2009.

2. Ibid.

3. Gerald F. Seib, "Some Victories Emerge in Fight against Islamic Extremism," *Wall Street Journal*, June 9, 2009.

4. "Social Networking Media's Role in Lebanon's Election," BBC Monitoring, June 10, 2009.

5. "Al-Hariri to 'Al-Hayah': Nasrallah's Speech Is Positive, Head of Government Is My Decision, and My Bloc Is for Sulayman," Al-Hayah Online in Arabic. OpenSource, GMP20090610825006, June 10, 2009.

6. "Army Warnings Follow Beirut Unrest," *Al-Jazeera*, June 29, 2009.

7. "Analysts Attribute Jumblatt's Change of Heart to International Shift toward Syria," *Daily Star* (Beirut), August 3, 2009.

8. "Jumblatt Says He'll Join Sleiman's Bloc in Upcoming Cabinet," *Daily Star* (Beirut), August 4, 2009.

Biographies

AOUN, MICHEL

Position: Military commander, prime minister, September 1988–October 1990, leader of "Free Patriotic Movement"
Date and Place of Birth: February 19, 1935, Haret Hreik, Lebanon
Education: Military Academy, College Des Frères, École Supérieure de Guerre, France
Religion: Maronite Christian
Background: Michel Aoun commanded forces briefly during the Lebanese Civil War and became Lebanese army commander in 1984. In 1988 Aoun became prime minister of a divided government after President Amine Gemayel dismissed the government of Prime Minister Salim Hoss, though Aoun's appointment violated the tacit understanding of the 1943 national pact that the prime minister should be a Sunni Muslim. Aoun's military forces fought with Syrian forces in Beirut, with Aoun accepting arms from Syria's rival, Saddam Hussein. Aoun denounced the Ta'if Accord of 1989 and Syrian forces defeated his army, sending him into exile in France in 1990. He returned to Lebanon in May 2005, and his Free Patriotic Movement won 21 of 58 seats in the Lebanese parliament. In February 2006, he joined forces with Hezbollah.

BERRI, NABIH

Position: Speaker of parliament
Date and Place of Birth: January 28, 1938, Freetown, Sierra Leone

Education: BA, Ecole de la Sagesse, Beirut, law degree, Lebanese University, 1963
Religion: Shi'a Muslim
Background: Nabih Berri was born in Sierra Leone to Lebanese parents, though the family moved back to Lebanon in the 1940s. He received a degree in law in 1968, and in 1975, Berri and Shi'a religious leader Musa al-Sadr jointly formed the Amal militia. He became the secretary general of Amal in 1978, which gave him a significant role in the Lebanese Civil War. He took several ministerial positions, including Minister of Justice and of Electrical and Hydraulic Resources, and was elected to the National Assembly in 1991 and selected as its speaker in December 1992. Stories about Berri's association with corruption are common in Lebanon. He is also politically powerful, having enough influence to force the resignation of Prime Minister Rafiq Hariri in 1997. Berri was an ally of Syria, but a strong rival to Hassan Nasrallah, the spiritual founder of Hezbollah.

CHAMOUN, CAMILLE

Position: President of Lebanon, 1952–1958
Date and Place of Birth: April 3, 1900, Dayr al-Qamar, Lebanon
Date of Death: August 8, 1987
Education: Legal education, France
Religion: Maronite Christian
Background: Camille Chamoun began his political career as a member of the Constitutional Bloc, which was predominately Christian. Denied an opportunity to become president in 1948, Chamoun formed an alliance with Druze leader Kamal Jumblatt, leader of the Progressive Socialist Party, in 1952, the same year that the resignation of President Bashara al-Khouri allowed Chamoun the job. Chamoun allowed considerable political freedoms in Lebanon, but also allowed the old patronage networks to flourish. In 1956, Chamoun refused demands to break ties to Britain and France, which had invaded the Egyptian Sinai. Two years later, Chamoun called upon the United States to intervene in Lebanese politics to quell rioting by mostly Muslim elements in Beirut and beyond. Chamoun survived demands that he resign, but he did leave office after his presidential term expired in 1960, and, after a brief retirement, returned to serve in several ministerial positions. He survived numerous assassination attempts, dying of heart failure in 1987.

CHEHAB, FOUAD

Position: President of Lebanon, 1958–1964
Date and Place of Birth: 1903 in Ghazir in Kisrwan district
Date of Death: April 1973

Education: Military academy in Damascus, later studied in France at L'Ecole d'Application de L'Infanterie à Saint Maixent and at L'Ecole Supérieure d'Etat-Major de Versailles and L'Ecole Supérieure de Guerre
Religion: Maronite Christian
Background: Fouad Chehab was born into a powerful Maronite family and chose a career in the military; he became a primary founder of the Lebanese Army. He studied at the French War College and led Lebanese forces attached to the French in several European campaigns. Later he built the Lebanese military into a non-sectarian force, becoming its commander. He became prime minister temporarily in 1952, and as the compromise candidate for president in 1958, he ended the crisis of that year by replacing Camille Chamoun. He built bridges to Egypt's Nasser, thus reducing the threat of Arab nationalism in Lebanon, while at the same time reforming Lebanon's civil service. He ended his term in September 1964 and declined to run again in 1970, dying in 1973.

FRANGIEH, SULEIMAN

Position: President of Lebanon, 1970–1976
Date and Place of Birth: June 10, 1915, Zgharta, Lebanon
Date of Death: July 1992
Education: Private schools, Beirut
Religion: Maronite Christian
Background: Suleiman Frangieh was born to a prominent Maronite family who lived near Tripoli, and he followed his father into politics. The National Assembly elected him president in August 1970. Suleiman Frangieh also maintained the Marada militia under the command of his son, Tony, which was originally a part of the Lebanese Front. Frangieh broke with the National Front in 1978, spawning a feud with the rival Gemayel family, resulting in the assassination of Tony Frangieh, his family, and 25 of his followers in June 1978. The Frangieh family revenged the killings with the murder of Bashar Gemayel in 1982. Suleiman Frangieh's presidency ended in 1976, and, after an unsuccessful comeback effort, he died in 1992.

GEAGEA, SAMIR

Position: Leader of Lebanese Forces, key element of March 14 Coalition
Date and Place of Birth: October 25, 1952, Beirut
Education: St. Joseph's University
Religion: Maronite Christian
Background: Samir Geagea was the son of an army officer, and he attended both the American University in Beirut and St. Joseph's University pursuing a medical degree. Instead, he joined the Phalangist Party, rising quickly through the ranks

under the tutelage of Bashar Gemayel. Geagea became a leader in the Phalangist militia, Kata'ib, which later evolved into the Lebanese Forces. When the leader of the rival Frangieh family aligned with Syria in the mid-1970s, Geagea participated in a raid on the Frangieh home that resulted both in the death of Tony Frangieh, patriarch Suleiman Frangieh's son, and the wounding of Geagea, which elevated his status within the Lebanese Forces. Geagea then took command of the Lebanese Forces, remaining allied with Bashar Gemayel until his assassination in 1982. Following attempts by the Phalange to take over the Lebanese Forces under Bashar's brother Amin, Geagea took control of it. He dramatically increased his power, and with the ouster of General Michel Aoun by Syria in October 1990, Geagea became one of the most powerful Maronite leaders in Lebanon. An explosion in the Church of Sayyidet Al Najet in February 1994 clipped Geagea's power as the authorities accused the Lebanese Force of the attack. While acquitted of the church bombing case, the courts convicted Geagea of several assassination attempts and sentenced him to 11 years in prison. Geagea's supporters claimed that his rivals trumped up the charges, and he was ultimately freed after the general amnesty of 2005. The Lebanese Forces joined the March 14 Coalition, and Geagea thus became one of the more powerful political leaders in the country to the point of traveling to France and the United States, where Geagea met with U.S. Secretary of State Condoleezza Rice at the White House in March 2008.

HARIRI, RAFIQ

Position: Prime Minister of Lebanon, 1992–1998; 2000–2004
Date and Place of Birth: November 1, 1944, Sidon, Lebanon
Date of Death: February 2005
Education: Beirut Arab University
Religion: Sunni Muslim
Background: Rafiq Hariri established a construction firm in the 1960s, and after almost failing in Lebanon, he partnered with a French firm to contract for construction in Saudi Arabia. His company soon became the favored firm for Saudi Arabian building, and he became a multibillionaire. Hariri's firm also began a massive rebuilding of Lebanon after the end of the civil war in 1989, and Hariri also established a number of charitable foundations to support education and other social needs. Hariri reportedly cultivated ties to the Asad regime in Syria to enhance Hariri's standing in Lebanon, but also reportedly helped to broker the Ta'if Accord through his long-standing ties to Saudi Arabia. His ties to Damascus allegedly helped him to become prime minister in 1992, but Syrian dissatisfaction with him (over charges of corruption and excessive public spending) is supposed to have led to his replacement by Salim al-Hoss in 1998. He returned to the prime ministership in 2000, resigning in October 2004. A massive car

bomb took Hariri's life (and 21 others) in February 2005 as his motorcade drove through Beirut, though the assassins were never identified. Upon his death, Hariri's fortune was estimated to be over $16 billion.

HARIRI, SAAD ED DEEN RAFIQ

Position: Leader, Future Movement
Date and Place of Birth: April 18, 1970, Riyadh, Saudi Arabia
Education: Georgetown University, Washington, D.C.
Religion: Sunni Muslim
Background: Saad Hariri is the son of former Prime Minister Rafiq Hariri who took control of his father's political movement after the latter died in a car bombing in February 2005. Hariri also took over his father's numerous businesses and is ranked on the Forbes 400 billionaires list. He is a possible candidate for prime minister himself.

JUMBLATT, WALID

Position: Leader of Progressive Socialist Party
Date and Place of Birth: August 7, 1949, Beirut, Lebanon, or Moukhtara, Shuf, depending on source
Education: Bachelor's degree, American University of Beirut, 1973
Religion: Druze
Background: Walid Jumblatt is the son of Kemal Jumblatt, and he the latest prominent person of the powerful Druze Jumblatt family, which traces its roots to Kurdish Syria. The Jumblatt family became powerful and famous in the Mount Lebanon region for its resistance during the Ottoman Empire, and even today, the language of Druze leader Walid Jumblatt rings with nationalist verbiage, which is partly derived from the long tradition of repression.

Assassins felled Kemal Jumblatt in 1977, and Walid Jumblatt took over the Progressive Socialist Party after Kemal's death. He was appointed a member of parliament in June 1991 and elected to the same post in 1992, 1996, 2000, and 2005. He held numerous cabinet positions, including Minister of Tourism, Minister of Transport and Public Works, Minister of State, and Minister of Displaced. He also has served as the leader of the Parliamentary Democratic Meeting Bloc and chairman of the Board of Ciment de Cibline.

LAHOUD, ÉMILE

Position: President of Lebanon, November 1998–November 2007
Date and Place of Birth: January 12, 1936, Baabdate, Lebanon
Education: Lebanese Military Academy

Religion: Maronite Christian
Background: Emile Lahoud was born to the family of General Jamil Lahoud, a leader in the Lebanese independence movement and, like his father, chose a career in the armed forces. He rose through the ranks, studying at the U.S. Naval War College after studying naval engineering in the United Kingdom, and became commander of the Lebanese armed forces in 1989, an unusual assignment for a Lebanese naval officer (the army is the most powerful force). Lahoud later served as president and was at odds with both Prime Minister Rafiq Hariri and the United States for his support for Syria.

NASRALLAH, HASSAN

Position. Secretary General of Hezbollah
Date and Place of Birth: 1960, East Beirut
Education: Seminary, Najaf, Iraq
Religion: Shi'a Islam
Background: Born in 1960 in the Bourji Hammoud neighborhood of East Beirut, Hassan Nasrallah first met Sayyad Abbas Musawi as a student in a Shi'a seminary in Hajaf, Iraq. When both returned to Lebanon in 1978, Musawi started a religion school where he invited Nasrallah to teach. Nasrallah initially joined Amal, but when that organization proposed joining the National Salvation Front, which had relations with Israel, Nasrallah left Amal and joined Hezbollah. Nasrallah rose in Hezbollah's ranks and fought against the Israelis after their invasion of Lebanon in 1982. Nasrallah initially opposed Syrian support to Hezbollah, but later apparently changed his mind. He became secretary general of Hezbollah after the Israeli assassination of Musawi, though he lacked his former teacher's religious credentials. He compensated for this lack by embarking on populist social programs for Lebanon's impoverished Shi'a, gaining Hezbollah popular support. Nasrallah was reportedly behind the Hezbollah attacks on Israeli soldiers in 2006 that kindled a bloody conflict between Hezbollah and Israel, though he acknowledged that had he known that the conflict would have escalated as it did, he would have not carried out the provocation. Israel has attempted to assassinate Nasrallah, bombing his house in July 2006. Nasrallah once called for Lebanon to become a Shi'a state run by Hezbollah, but suspended that platform after the 2006 war; after the conflict, he has served to broker agreements between Lebanon's factious parties.

SALAM, SAEB

Position: Prime Minister, May–August 1953; 1960–1961
Date and Place of Birth: January 17, 1905, Beirut, Lebanon
Date of Death: January 2000

Education: American University of Beirut, London School of Economics
Religion: Sunni Muslim
Background: Saeb Salam was born to a prominent Sunni Muslim family. In the 1950s he was active in the Arab Nationalist Movement in Lebanon and served six times as prime minister. Salam played a conciliatory role in the Lebanese Civil War, which led to his significant part in the Ta'if Accord with Saudi Arabia in 1989. He was also a primary negotiator in the evacuation of Yasser Arafat and the PLO leadership from Lebanon after the Israeli invasion of 1982. Salam also founded Lebanon's national airline, Middle East Airlines, in 1943. He died in 2000 at age 95.

SINIORA, FOUAD

Position: Prime Minister, July 19, 2005–present
Date and Place of Birth: April 14, 1943, Sidon, Lebanon
Education: Business degree, American University of Beirut
Religion: Sunni Muslim
Background: Fouad Siniora was born to a Muslim family and, following his university education, entered the banking business before joining Hariri's firm. His business background served him well when he served as finance minister from 1992 to 1998 and again from 2000 to 2004, negotiating the Paris II financial package in November 2002.

Siniora became prime minister in July 2005, giving a tone of stability to an office that had been occupied briefly by Omar Karami and Najim Mikati.

SULEIMAN, MICHEL

Position: President of Lebanon, June 2008–present
Date and Place of Birth: November 21, 1948, Amchit-Caza, Lebanon
Education: Lebanese University
Religion: Maronite Christian
Background: Michel Suleiman was born in Amchit-Caza, a town on the coast around 40 miles north of Beirut, in a predominately Maronite area. He joined the Lebanese military in 1967 and rose quickly through the ranks. He became chief of military intelligence in the Mount Lebanon area, commanded an infantry brigade, and in 1998 was appointed commander of the Lebanese armed forces.

Suleiman believed that Lebanon's military should remain free from the national political fights and, against Syrian wishes, refused to use the military to quash the massive demonstrations that followed the 2005 assassination of Rafiq Hariri. Suleiman's most notable conflict came in 2007, when he led Lebanese forces against Fatah al-Islam, a Palestinian radical group based in the Nahr al-Bared refugee camp. The conflict, lasting from May to December, resulted in a defeat for Fatah al-Islam and increased the stature of both the Lebanese military and General Suleiman. Suleiman was careful to not affiliate himself with either the March 14 or the March 8 factions, and thus he was one of the few senior figures who could bring an end to the factional fighting that had paralyzed Lebanese politics. Thus on May 25, 2008, the parliament elected Suleiman president.

Suleiman's tenure as chief of the Lebanese armed forces has not been without controversy. He commanded the Lebanese military during Syria's control over the country, and his brother-in-law was spokesman for Hafiz al-Asad. He also praised Hezbollah during its 2006 war with Israel. Shortly after he assumed the presidency, he called for diplomatic ties to Syria, confirming what some of his critics feared, a continuation of Syrian influence over Lebanon through diplomatic means, though it could also be argued that Syrian recognition of Lebanon as a sovereign state would reduce such influence.

Chronology

5000 BCE	First human settlements
3500–1200 BCE	Canaanite period
2750 BCE (?)	Founding of the city of Tyre
1200–900 BCE	Phoenician Period
555–333 BCE	Persian Period
332 BCE	Alexander the Great conquers Tyre
332–64 BCE	Hellenistic Period
64 BCE–399 CE	Roman Period
399–636	Byzantine Period
636–661	Arab Conquest Period
661–750	Umayyad Period
750–969	Abbasid Period
969–1169	Fatimid Period
1099–1291	Crusades Period
1169–1250	Ayyubid Period
1287	Lebanon becomes part of the Mameluke Sultanate of Egypt
1250–1516	Mamluke Period
1516	Lebanon becomes part of the Ottoman Empire
1585–1590	Direct Ottoman rule
1832	Is annexed by Egypt
1840	Ottoman rule is restored

1842	Mount Lebanon emirate ends; Ottomans divide Lebanon administratively, creating a Christian district in the north and an area under Druze control in the south
1860–1861	France occupies Lebanon
1861	Special status is created for the Mount Lebanon area within the Ottoman Empire
1918	Syria annexes Lebanon
October 1918	France and Britain occupy Lebanon
1920	State of Lebanon is proclaimed
1926	Lebanese Representative Council approves a constitution and declares the Lebanese Republic
1932	Last Lebanese census is taken
1940	Vichy France takes over Lebanon
1941	Free French occupy Lebanon
1941	Lebanon declares independence from France
1941–1946	France and Britain occupy Lebanon
1943	France recognizes Lebanese independence
October 1948–March 1949	Israeli troops occupy 13 villages in Lebanon
1958	U.S. troops land in Beirut
1975–2005	Syrian troops occupy Lebanon
1975–1991	Lebanese Civil War
March 1978–June 1978	Israeli troops occupy southern Lebanon
1982–2000	Israeli troops occupy southern Lebanon
July 2006–October 2006	Conflict between Hezbollah and Israel

Documents

DOCUMENT 1

Preamble of the 1926 Lebanese Constitution

a. Lebanon is a sovereign, free, and independent country. It is a final homeland for all its citizens. It is unified in its territory, people, and institutions within the boundaries defined in this constitution and recognized internationally.
b. Lebanon is Arab in its identity and in its association. It is a founding and active member of the League of Arab States and abides by its pacts and covenants. Lebanon is also a founding and active member of the United Nations Organization and abides by its covenants and by the Universal Declaration of Human Rights. The Government shall embody these principles in all fields and areas without exception.
c. Lebanon is a parliamentary democratic republic based on respect for public liberties, especially the freedom of opinion and belief, and respect for social justice and equality of rights and duties among all citizens without discrimination.
d. The people are the source of authority and sovereignty; they shall exercise these powers through the constitutional institutions.
e. The political system is established on the principle of separation, balance, and cooperation amongst the various branches of Government.
f. The economic system is free and ensures private initiative and the right to private property.
g. The even development among regions on the educational, social, and economic levels shall be a basic pillar of the unity of the state and the stability of the system.

h. The abolition of political confessionalism is a basic national goal and shall be achieved according to a gradual plan.

i. Lebanese territory is one for all Lebanese. Every Lebanese has the right to live in any part of it and to enjoy the sovereignty of law wherever he resides. There is no segregation of the people on the basis of any type of belonging, and no fragmentation, partition, or colonization.

j. There is no constitutional legitimacy for any authority which contradicts the 'pact of communal coexistence'. This Constitutional Law shall be published in the Official Gazette.

DOCUMENT 2

Key Provisions of the Ta'if Accord

I. General Principles

A. Lebanon is a sovereign, free, and independent country and a final homeland for all its citizens.

B. Lebanon is Arab in belonging and identity. It is an active and founding member of the Arab League and is committed to the league's charter. It is an active and founding member of the United Nations Organization and is committed to its charters. Lebanon is a member of the nonaligned movement. The state of Lebanon shall embody these principles in all areas and spheres, without exception.

C. Lebanon is a democratic parliamentary republic founded on respect for public liberties, especially the freedom of expression and belief, on social justice, and on equality in rights and duties among all citizens, without discrimination or preference.

D. The people are the source of authority. They are sovereign and they shall exercise their sovereignty through the constitutional institutions.

E. The economic system is a free system that guarantees individual initiative and private ownership.

F. Culturally, socially, and economically-balanced development is a mainstay of the state's unity and of the system's stability.

G. Efforts (will be made) to achieve comprehensive social justice through fiscal, economic, and social reform.

H. Lebanon's soil is united and it belongs to all the Lebanese. Every Lebanese is entitled to live in and enjoy any part of the country under the supremacy of the law. The people may not be categorized on the basis of any affiliation whatsoever and there shall be no fragmentation, no partition, and no repatriation [of Palestinians in Lebanon].

I. No authority violating the common co-existence charter shall be legitimate

II. Political Reforms

A. Chamber of Deputies: The Chamber of Deputies is the legislative authority which exercises full control over government policy and activities.

1. The Chamber spokesman and his deputy shall be elected for the duration of the chamber's term.

2. In the first session, two years after it elects its speaker and deputy speaker, the chamber my vote only once to withdraw confidence from its speaker or deputy speaker with a 2/3 majority of its members and in accordance with a petition submitted by at least 10 deputies. In case confidence is withdrawn, the chamber shall convene immediately to fill the vacant post.

3. No urgent bill presented to the Chamber of Deputies may be issued unless it is included in the agenda of a public session and read in such a session, and unless the grace period stipulated by the constitution passes without a resolution on such a bill with the approval of the cabinet.

4. The electoral district shall be the governorate.

5. Until the Chamber of Deputies passes an election law free of sectarian restriction, the parliamentary seats shall be divided according to the following bases:

   a. Equally between Christians and Muslims.

   b. Proportionately between the denominations of each sect.

   c. Proportionately between the districts.

6. The number of members of the Chamber of Deputies shall be increased to 108, shared equally between Christians and Muslims. As for the districts created on the basis of this document and the districts whose seats became vacant prior to the proclamation of this document, their seats shall be filled only once on an emergency basis through appointment by the national accord government that is planned to be formed.

7. With the election of the first Chamber of Deputies on a national, not sectarian, basis, a senate shall be formed and all the spiritual families shall be represented in it. The senate powers shall be confined to crucial issues.

B. President of Republic: The president of republic is the head of the state and a symbol of the country's unity. He shall contribute to enhancing the constitution and to preserving Lebanon's independence, unity, and territorial integrity in accordance with the provisions of the constitution. He is the supreme commander of the armed forces which are subject to the power of the cabinet. The president shall exercise the following powers:

1. Head the cabinet [meeting] whenever he wishes, but without voting.

2. Head the Supreme Defense Council.

3. Issues decrees and demand their publication. He shall also be entitled to ask the cabinet to reconsider any resolution it makes within 15 days of the date of deposition of the resolution with the presidential office. Should the cabinet insist on the adopted resolution, or should the grace

period pass without issuing and returning the decree, the decree of the resolution shall be valid and must be published.

4. Promulgate laws in accordance with the grace period stipulated by the constitution and demand their publication upon ratification by the Chamber of Deputies. After notifying the cabinet, the president may also request reexamination of the laws within the grace periods provided by the constitution, and in accordance with the articles of the constitution. In case the laws are not issued or returned before the end of the grace periods, they shall be valid by law and they must be published.

5. Refer the bills presented to him by the Chamber of Deputies.

6. Name the prime minister-designate in consultation with the Chamber of Deputies speaker on the basis of binding parliamentary consultation, the outcome of which the president shall officially familiarize the speaker on.

7. Issue the decree appointing the prime minister independently.

8. On agreement with the prime minister, issue the decree forming the cabinet.

9. Issue decrees accepting the resignation of the cabinet or of cabinet ministers and decrees relieving them from their duties.

10. Appoint ambassadors, accept the accreditation of ambassadors, and award state medals by decree.

11. On agreement with the prime minister, negotiate on the conclusion and signing of international treaties which shall become valid only upon approval by the cabinet. The cabinet shall familiarize the Chamber of Deputies with such treaties when the country's interest and state safety make such familiarization possible. As for treaties involving conditions concerning state finances, trade treaties, and other treaties which may not be abrogated annually, they may not be concluded without Chamber of Deputies' approval.

12. When the need arises, address messages to the Chamber of Deputies.

13. On agreement with the prime minister, summon the Chamber of Deputies to hold special sessions by decree.

14. The president of the republic is entitled to present to the cabinet any urgent issue beyond the agenda.

15. On agreement with the prime minister, call the cabinet to hold a special session whenever he deems it necessary.

16. Grant special pardon by decree.

17. In the performance of his duty, the president shall not be liable unless he violates the constitution or commits high treason.

C. Prime Minister: The prime minister is the head of the government. He represents it and speaks in its name. He is responsible for implementing the general policy drafted by the cabinet. The prime minister shall exercise the following powers:

1. Head the cabinet.
2. Hold parliamentary consultations to form the cabinet and co-sign with the president the decree forming it. The cabinet shall submit its cabinet statement to the Chamber of Deputies for a vote of confidence within 30 days [of its formation]. The cabinet may not exercise its powers before gaining the confidence, after its resignation, or when it is considered retired, except within the narrow sense of disposing of affairs.
3. Present the government's general policy to the Chamber of Deputies.
4. Sign all decrees, except for decrees naming the prime minister and decrees accepting cabinet resignation or considering it retired.
5. Sign the decree calling for a special session and decrees issuing laws and requesting the reexamination of laws.
6. Summon the cabinet to meet, draft its agenda, familiarize the president of the republic in advance with the issues included in the agenda and with the urgent issues to be discussed, and sign the usual session minutes.
7. Observe the activities of the public departments and institutions, coordinate between the ministers, and issue general instructions to ensure the smooth progress of work.
8. Hold working sessions with the state agencies concerned in the presence of the minister concerned.
9. By law, act as the Supreme Defense Council's deputy chairman.

D. Cabinet:

The executive power shall be vested in the Cabinet.

The following are among the powers exercised by it:

1. Set the general policy of the State in all domains, draws up draft bills and decrees, and takes the necessary decisions for its implementation.
2. Watch over the implementation of laws and regulations and supervise the activities of all the state agencies without exception, including the civilian, military, and security departments and institutions.
3. The cabinet is the authority which controls the armed forces.
4. Appoint, dismiss, and accept the resignation of state employees in accordance with the law.
5. It has the right to dissolve the Chamber of Deputies at the request of the president of the republic if the chamber refuses to meet throughout an ordinary or a special session lasting no less than one month, even though it is summoned twice consecutively, or if the chamber sends back the budget in its entirety with the purpose of paralyzing the government. This right may not be exercised again for the same reasons which called for dissolving the chamber in the first instance.
6. When the president of the republic is present, he heads cabinet sessions. The cabinet shall meet periodically at special headquarters. The legal quorum for a cabinet meeting is 2/3 the cabinet members. The cabinet

shall adopt its resolutions by consent. If impossible, then by vote. The resolutions shall be adopted by a majority of the members present. As for major issues, they require the approval of 2/3 the cabinet members. The following shall be considered major issues: The state of emergency and it abolition, war and peace, general mobilization, international agreements and treaties, the state's general budget, comprehensive and long-term development plans, the appointment of top-level civil servants or their equivalent, reexamination of the administrative division, dissolving the Chamber of Deputies, the election law, the citizenship law, the personal status laws, and the dismissal of cabinet ministers.

E. Minister: The minister's powers shall be reinforced in a manner compatible with the government's general policy and with the principle of collective responsibility. A minister shall not be relieved from his position unless by cabinet decree or unless the Chamber of Deputies withdraws its confidence from him individually.

F. Cabinet Resignation, Considering Cabinet Retired, and Dismissal of Ministers:

1. The cabinet shall be considered retired in the following cases:
    a. If its chairman resigns.
    b. If it loses more than 1/3 of its members as determined by the decree forming it.
    c. If its chairman dies.
    d. At the beginning of a president's term.
    e. At the beginning of the Chamber of Deputies' term.
    f. When the Chamber of Deputies withdraws its confidence from it on an initiative by the chamber itself and on the basis of a vote of confidence.

2. A minister shall be relieved by a decree signed by the president of the republic and the prime minister, with cabinet approval.

3. When the cabinet resigns or is considered retired, the Chamber of Deputies shall, by law, be considered to be convened in a special session until a new cabinet is formed. A vote-of-confidence session shall follow.

G. Abolition of Political Sectarianism: Abolishing political sectarianism is a fundamental national objective. To achieve it, it is required that efforts be made in accordance with a phased plan. The Chamber of Deputies elected on the basis of equal sharing by Christians and Muslims shall adopt the proper measures to achieve this objective and to form a national council which is headed by the president of the republic and which includes, in addition to the prime minister and the Chamber of Deputies speaker, political, intellectual, and social notables. The council's task will be to examine and propose the means capable of abolishing sectarianism, to present them to the Chamber of Deputies and the cabinet, and to observe implementation of the phased plan. The following shall be done in the interim period:

a. Abolish the sectarian representation base and rely on capability and specialization in public jobs, the judiciary, the military, security, public, and joint institutions, and in the independent agencies in accordance with the dictates of national accord, excluding the top-level jobs and equivalent jobs which shall be shared equally by Christians and Muslims without allocating any particular job to any sect.

b. Abolish the mention of sect and denomination on the identity card.

III. Other Reforms

A. Administrative Decentralism:

1. The State of Lebanon shall be a single and united state with a strong central authority.

2. The powers of the governors and district administrative officers shall be expanded and all state administrations shall be represented in the administrative provinces at the highest level possible so as to facilitate serving the citizens and meeting their needs locally.

3. The administrative division shall be recognized in a manner that emphasizes national fusion within the framework of preserving common coexistence and unity of the soil, people, and institutions.

4. Expanded administrative decentralization shall be adopted at the level of the smaller administrative units [district and smaller units] through the election of a council, headed by the district officer, in every district, to ensure local participation.

5. A comprehensive and unified development plan capable of developing the provinces economically and socially shall be adopted and the resources of the municipalities, unified municipalities, and municipal unions shall be reinforced with the necessary financial resources.

B. Courts:

[1] To guarantee that all officials and citizens are subject to the supremacy of the law and to insure harmony between the action of the legislative and executive authorities on the one hand, and the givens of common coexistence and the basic rights of the Lebanese as stipulated in the constitution on the other hand:

1. The higher council which is stipulated by the constitution and whose task it is to try presidents and ministers shall be formed. A special law on the rules of trial before this council shall be promulgated.

2. A constitutional council shall be created to interpret the constitution, to observe the constitutionality of the laws, and to settle disputes and contests emanating from presidential and parliamentary elections.

3. The following authorities shall be entitled to revise the constitutional
   council in matters pertaining to interpreting the constitution and
   observing the constitutionality of the laws:

a. The president of the republic.

b. The Chamber of Deputies speaker.

c. The prime minister.

d. A certain percentage of members of the Chamber of Deputies.

[2] To ensure the principle of harmony between religion and state, the heads
of the Lebanese sects may revise the constitutional council in matters pertaining to:

1. Personal status affairs.

2. Freedom of religion and the practice of religious rites.

3. Freedom of religious education.

[3] To ensure the judiciary's independence, a certain number of the Higher
Judiciary Council shall be elected by the judiciary body.

D. Parliamentary Election Law: Parliamentary elections shall be held in
   accordance with a new law on the basis of provinces and in the light of rules
   that guarantee common coexistence between the Lebanese, and that ensure
   the sound and efficient political representation of all the people's factions
   and generations. This shall be done after reviewing the administrative
   division within the context of unity of the people, the land, and the
   institutions.

E. Creation of a socioeconomic council for development: A socioeconomic
   council shall be created to insure that representatives of the various sectors
   participate in drafting the state's socioeconomic policy and providing advice
   and proposals.

Second, spreading the sovereignty of the State of Lebanon over all Lebanese territories

Considering that all Lebanese factions have agreed to the establishment of a
strong state founded on the basis of national accord, the national accord
government shall draft a detailed one-year plan whose objective is to spread the
sovereignty of the State of Lebanon over all Lebanese territories gradually with
the state's own forces. The broad lines of the plan shall be as follows:

A. Disbanding of all Lebanese and non-Lebanese militias shall be announced. The
   militias' weapons shall be delivered to the State of Lebanon within a period of 6
   months, beginning with the approval of the national accord charter. The
   president of the republic shall be elected. A national accord cabinet shall be
   formed, and the political reforms shall be approved constitutionally.

B. The internal security forces shall be strengthened through:

1. Opening the door of voluntarism to all the Lebanese without exception,
   beginning the training of volunteers centrally, distributing the volunteers

to the units in the governorates, and subjecting them to organized periodic training courses.

2. Strengthening the security agency to insure control over the entry and departure of individuals into and out of the country by land, air, and sea.

C. Strengthening the armed forces:

1. The fundamental task of the armed forces is to defend the homeland, and if necessary, protect public order when the danger exceeds the capability of the internal security forces to deal with such a danger on their own.

2. The armed forces shall be used to support the internal security forces in preserving security under conditions determined by the cabinet.

3. The armed forces shall be unified, prepared, and trained in order that they may be able to shoulder their national responsibilities in confronting Israeli aggression.

4. When the internal security forces become ready to assume their security tasks, the armed forces shall return to their barracks.

5. The armed forces intelligence shall be reorganized to serve military objectives exclusively.

D. The problem of the Lebanese evacuees shall be solved fundamentally, and the right of every Lebanese evicted since 1975 to return to the place from which he was evicted shall be established. Legislation to guarantee this right and to insure the means of reconstruction shall be issued. Considering that the objective of the State of Lebanon is to spread its authority over all the Lebanese territories through its own forces, represented primarily by the internal security forces, and in view of the fraternal relations binding Syria to Lebanon, the Syrian forces shall thankfully assist the forces of the legitimate Lebanese government to spread the authority of the State of Lebanon within a set period of no more than 2 years, beginning with ratification of the national accord charter, election of the president of the republic, formation of the national accord cabinet, and approval of the political reforms constitutionally. At the end of this period, the two governments—the Syrian Government and the Lebanese National Accord Government—shall decide to redeploy the Syrian forces in Al-Biq'a area from Dahr al-Baydar to the Hammana-al-Mudayrij-'Ayn Darah line, and if necessary, at other points to be determined by a joint Lebanese-Syrian military committee. An agreement shall also be concluded by the two governments to determine the strength and duration of the presence of Syrian forces in the above-mentioned area and to define these forces' relationship with the Lebanese state authorities where the forces exist. The Arab Tripartite Committee is prepared to assist the two states, if they so wish, to develop this agreement.

Third, liberating Lebanon from the Israeli occupation

Regaining state authority over the territories extending to the internationally-recognized Lebanese borders requires the following:

A. Efforts to implement resolution 425 and the other UN Security Council resolutions calling for fully eliminating the Israeli occupation.
B. Adherence to the truce agreement concluded on 23 March 1949.
C. Taking all the steps necessary to liberate all Lebanese territories from the Israeli occupation, to spread state sovereignty over all the territories, and to deploy the Lebanese army in the border area adjacent to Israel; and making efforts to reinforce the presence of the UN forces in South Lebanon to insure the Israeli withdrawal and to provide the opportunity for the return of security and stability to the border area.

Fourth, Lebanese-Syrian Relations

Lebanon, with its Arab identity, is tied to all the Arab countries by true fraternal relations. Between Lebanon and Syria there is a special relationship that derives its strength from the roots of blood relationships, history, and joint fraternal interests. This is the concept on which the two countries' coordination and cooperation is founded, and which will be embodied by the agreements between the two countries in all areas, in a manner that accomplishes the two fraternal countries' interests within the framework of the sovereignty and independence of each of them. Therefore, and because strengthening the bases of security creates the climate needed to develop these bonds, Lebanon should not be allowed to constitute a source of threat to Syria's security, and Syria should not be allowed to constitute a source of threat to Lebanon's security under any circumstances. Consequently, Lebanon should not allow itself to become a pathway or a base for any force, state, or organization seeking to undermine its security or Syria's security. Syria, which is eager for Lebanon's security, independence, and unity and for harmony among its citizens, should not permit any act that poses a threat to Lebanon's security, independence, and sovereignty.

DOCUMENT 3

**Peter FitzGerald's report of the assassination of
former Prime Minister Rafiq Hariri
Report of the Fact-Finding Mission to Lebanon inquiring into the causes,
circumstances and consequences of the assassination of former Prime Minister
Rafiq Hariri
25 February–24 March 2005**

Executive Summary

On 14 February 2005, an explosion in downtown Beirut killed twenty persons, among them the former Prime Minister, Rafik Hariri. The United Nations'

Secretary-General dispatched a Fact-Finding Mission to Beirut to inquire into the causes, the circumstances and the consequences of this assassination. Since it arrived in Beirut on 25 February, the Mission met with a large number of Lebanese officials and representatives of different political groups, performed a thorough review of the Lebanese investigation and legal proceedings, examined the crime scene and the evidence collected by the local police, collected and analyzed samples from the crime scene, and interviewed some witnesses in relation to the crime.

The specific 'causes' for the assassination of Mr. Hariri cannot be reliably asserted until after the perpetrators of this crime are brought to justice. However, it is clear that the assassination took place in a political and security context marked by an acute polarization around the Syrian influence in Lebanon and a failure of the Lebanese State to provide adequate protection for its citizens.

Regarding the circumstances, the Mission is of the view that the explosion was caused by a TNT charge of about 1000 KG placed most likely above the ground. The review of the investigation indicates that there was a distinct lack of commitment on the part of the Lebanese authorities to investigate the crime effectively, and that this investigation was not carried out in accordance with acceptable international standards. The Mission is also of the view that the Lebanese investigation lacks the confidence of the population necessary for its results to be accepted. The consequences of the assassination could be far-reaching. It seems to have unlocked the gates of political upheavals that were simmering throughout the last year. Accusations and counter-accusations are rife and aggravate the ongoing political polarization. Some accuse the Syrian security services and leadership of assassinating Mr. Hariri because he became an insurmountable obstacle to their influence in Lebanon. Syrian supporters maintain that he was assassinated by "the enemies of Syria"; those who wanted to create international pressure on the Syrian leadership in order to accelerate the demise of its influence in Lebanon and/or start a chain of reactions that would eventually force a 'regime change' inside Syria itself. Lebanese politicians from different backgrounds expressed to the Mission their fear that Lebanon could be caught in a possible showdown between Syria and the international community, with devastating consequences for Lebanese peace and security. After gathering the available facts, the Mission concluded that the Lebanese security services and the Syrian Military Intelligence bear the primary responsibility for the lack of security, protection, law and order in Lebanon. The Lebanese security services have demonstrated serious and systematic negligence in carrying out the duties usually performed by a professional national security apparatus. In doing so, they have severely failed to provide the citizens of Lebanon with an acceptable level of security and, therefore, have contributed to the propagation of a culture of intimidation and impunity. The Syrian Military Intelligence shares this responsibility to the extent of its involvement in running the security services in Lebanon.

It is also the Mission's conclusion that the Government of Syria bears primary responsibility for the political tension that preceded the assassination of former Prime Minister Mr. Hariri. The Government of Syria clearly exerted influence that goes beyond the reasonable exercise of cooperative or neighborly relations. It interfered with the details of governance in Lebanon in a heavy-handed and inflexible manner that was the primary reason for the political polarization that ensued. Without prejudice to the results of the investigation, it is obvious that this atmosphere provided the backdrop for the assassination of Mr. Hariri.

It became clear to the Mission that the Lebanese investigation process suffers from serious flaws and has neither the capacity nor the commitment to reach a satisfactory and credible conclusion. To find the truth, it would be necessary to entrust the investigation to an international independent commission, comprising the different fields of expertise that are usually involved in carrying out similarly large investigations in national systems, with the necessary executive authority to carry out interrogations, searches, and other relevant tasks. Furthermore, it is more than doubtful that such an international commission could carry out its tasks satisfactorily—and receives the necessary active cooperation from local authorities—while the current leadership of the Lebanese security services remains in office.

It is the Mission's conclusion that the restoration of the integrity and credibility of the Lebanese security apparatus is of vital importance to the security and stability of the country. A sustained effort to restructure, reform and retrain the Lebanese security services will be necessary to achieve this end, and will certainly require assistance and active engagement on the part of the international community.

Finally, it is the Mission's view that international and regional political support will be necessary to safeguard Lebanon's national unity and to shield its fragile polity from unwarranted pressure. Improving the prospects of peace and security in the region would offer a more solid ground for restoring normalcy in Lebanon. Report of the Fact-Finding Mission to Lebanon inquiring into the causes, circumstances and consequences of the assassination of former Prime Minister Rafik Hariri 25 February–24 March 2005

DOCUMENT 4

United Nations Security Council Resolution 1701

August 11, 2006
The Security Council,
Determining that the situation in Lebanon constitutes a threat to international peace and security;
1. Calls for a full cessation of hostilities based upon, in particular, the immediate cessation by Hizbollah of all attacks and the immediate cessation by Israel of all offensive military operations;

2. Upon full cessation of hostilities, calls upon the government of Lebanon and UNIFIL (The U.N. Interim Force in Lebanon) as authorized by paragraph 11 to deploy their forces together throughout the south and calls upon the government of Israel, as that deployment begins, to withdraw all of its forces from southern Lebanon in parallel;

3. Emphasizes the importance of the extension of the control of the government of Lebanon over all Lebanese territory in accordance with the provisions of resolution 1559 (2004) and resolution 1680 (2006), and of the relevant provisions of the Ta'if Accords, for it to exercise its full sovereignty, so that there will be no weapons without the consent of the government of Lebanon and no authority other than that of the government of Lebanon;

4. Reiterates its strong support for full respect for the Blue Line (separating Israel and Lebanon);

5. Also reiterates its strong support, as recalled in all its previous relevant resolutions, for the territorial integrity, sovereignty and political independence of Lebanon within its internationally recognized borders, as contemplated by the Israeli-Lebanese General Armistice Agreement of 23 March 1949;

6. Calls on the international community to take immediate steps to extend its financial and humanitarian assistance to the Lebanese people, including through facilitating the safe return of displaced persons and, under the authority of the government of Lebanon, reopening airports and harbors, consistent with paragraphs 14 and 15, and calls on it also to consider further assistance in the future to contribute to the reconstruction and development of Lebanon;

7. Affirms that all parties are responsible for ensuring that no action is taken contrary to paragraph 1 that might adversely affect the search for a long-term solution, humanitarian access to civilian populations, including safe passage for humanitarian convoys, or the voluntary and safe return of displaced persons, and calls on all parties to comply with this responsibility and to cooperate with the Security Council; humanitarian convoys, or the voluntary and safe return of displaced persons, and calls on all parties to comply with this responsibility and to cooperate with the Security Council;

8. Calls for Israel and Lebanon to support a permanent cease-fire and a long-term solution based on the following principles and elements:
   - full respect for the Blue Line by both parties,
   - security arrangements to prevent the resumption of hostilities, including the establishment between the Blue Line and the Litani River of an area free of any armed personnel, assets and weapons other than those of the government of Lebanon and of UNIFIL as authorized in paragraph 11, deployed in this area,
   - full implementation of the relevant provisions of the Ta'if Accords, and of resolutions 1559 (2004) and 1680 (2006), that require the disarmament

of all armed groups in Lebanon, so that, pursuant to the Lebanese cabinet decision of July 27, 2006, there will be no weapons or authority in Lebanon other than that of the Lebanese state,

- no foreign forces in Lebanon without the consent of its government,
- no sales or supply of arms and related materiel to Lebanon except as authorized by its government,
- provision to the United Nations of all remaining maps of land mines in Lebanon in Israel's possession;

9. Invites the Secretary-General (Kofi Annan) to support efforts to secure as soon as possible agreements in principle from the government of Lebanon and the government of Israel to the principles and elements for a long-term solution as set forth in paragraph 8, and expresses its intention to be actively involved;

10. Requests the secretary-general to develop, in liaison with relevant international actors and the concerned parties, proposals to implement the relevant provisions of the Ta'if Accords, and resolutions 1559 (2004) and 1680 (2006), including disarmament, and for delineation of the international borders of Lebanon, especially in those areas where the border is disputed or uncertain, including by dealing with the Shebaa farms area, and to present to the Security Council those proposals within thirty days;

11. Decides, in order to supplement and enhance the force in numbers, equipment, mandate and scope of operations, to authorize an increase in the force strength of UNIFIL to a maximum of 15,000 troops, and that the force shall, in addition to carrying out its mandate under resolutions 425 and 426 (1978):

   a. Monitor the cessation of hostilities;
   b. Accompany and support the Lebanese armed forces as they deploy throughout the south, including along the Blue Line, as Israel withdraws its armed forces from Lebanon as provided in paragraph 2;
   c. Coordinate its activities related to paragraph 11 (b) with the government of Lebanon and the government of Israel;
   d. Extend its assistance to help ensure humanitarian access to civilian populations and the voluntary and safe return of displaced persons;
   e. Assist the Lebanese armed forces in taking steps towards the establishment of the area as referred to in paragraph 8;
   f. Assist the government of Lebanon, at its request, to implement paragraph 14;

12. Acting in support of a request from the government of Lebanon to deploy an international force to assist it to exercise its authority throughout the territory, authorizes UNIFIL to take all necessary action in areas of deployment of its forces and as it deems within its capabilities, to ensure that its area of operations is not utilized for hostile activities of any kind, to resist attempts by forceful means to prevent it from discharging its duties under the mandate

of the Security Council, and to protect United Nations personnel, facilities, installations and equipment, ensure the security and freedom of movement of United Nations personnel, humanitarian workers, and, without prejudice to the responsibility of the government of Lebanon, to protect civilians under imminent threat of physical violence;

13. Requests the secretary general urgently to put in place measures to ensure UNIFIL is able to carry out the functions envisaged in this resolution, urges member states to consider making appropriate contributions to UNIFIL and to respond positively to requests for assistance from the force, and expresses its strong appreciation to those who have contributed to UNIFIL in the past;

14. Calls upon the government of Lebanon to secure its borders and other entry points to prevent the entry in Lebanon without its consent of arms or related materiel and requests UNIFIL as authorized in paragraph 11 to assist the government of Lebanon at its request;

15. Decides further that all states shall take the necessary measures to prevent, by their nationals or from their territories or using their flag vessels or aircraft,

 (a) the sale or supply to any entity or individual in Lebanon of arms and related materiel of all types, including weapons and ammunition, military vehicles and equipment, paramilitary equipment, and spare parts for the aforementioned, whether or not originating in their territories, and

 (b) the provision to any entity or individual in Lebanon of any technical training or assistance related to the provision, manufacture, maintenance or use of the items listed in subparagraph (a) above, except that these prohibitions shall not apply to arms, related material, training or assistance authorized by the government of Lebanon or by UNIFIL as authorized in paragraph 11;

16. Decides to extend the mandate of UNIFIL until 31 August 2007, and expresses its intention to consider in a later resolution further enhancements to the mandate and other steps to contribute to the implementation of a permanent cease-fire and a long-term solution;

17. Requests the secretary-general to report to the council within one week on the implementation of this resolution and subsequently on a regular basis;

18. Stresses the importance of, and the need to achieve, a comprehensive, just and lasting peace in the Middle East, based on all its relevant resolutions including its resolutions 242 (1967) of 22 November 1967 and 338 (1973) of 22 October 1973;

19. Decides to remain actively seized of the matter.

Presidents and Prime Ministers of Lebanon

PRESIDENTS

French Mandate

Charles Debbas	September 1926–January 1934
Antoine Privat-Aubourard (acting)	January 1934
Habib Pacha es-Saad	January 1934–January 1936
Émile Eddé	January 1936–April 1941
Pierre-Georges Arlabosse (acting)	April 1941
Alfred Georges Naqqache	April 1943–March 1943
Ayub Thabit (acting)	July 1943
Petro Trad	September 1943

Lebanese Republic

Bechara al-Khoury	September–November 1943
Émile Eddé	November 1943
Bechara al-Khoury	November 1943–September 1952
Fuad Chehab (acting)	September 1952
Camille Chamoun	September 1952–September 1958
Fuad Chehab	September 1958–September 1964
Charles Helou	September 1964–September 1970
Suleiman Frangieh	September 1970–September 1976
Elias Sarkis	September 1976–August 1982
Bashar Gemayel	August–September 1982
Amin Gemayel	September 1982–September 1988

Michel Aoun (acting)	September 1988–October 1990
René Moawad	November 1989
Selim al-Hoss (acting)	November 1989
Elias Hrawi	November 1989–November 1998
Emile Lahoud	November 1998–November 2007
Fouad Siniora (acting)	November 2007–May 2008
Michel Suleiman	May 2008–

PRIME MINISTERS

French Mandate

Auguste Adib Pacha	May 1926–May 1927
Bechara al-Khoury	May 1927–August 1928
Habib Pacha el-Saad	August 1928–May 1929
Bechara al-Khoury	May–October 1929
Emile Edde	October 1929–March 1930
Auguste Adib Pacha	March 1930–March 1932
Charles Debbas	March 1932–January 1934
Abdullah Bayhum	January 1934–January 1936
Ayub Thabit	January 1936–January 1937
Khayreddin al-Ahdab	January 1937–March 1938
Khaled Chehab	March–October 1938
Abdallah al-Yafi	October 1938–September 1939
Abdullah Bayhum	September 1939–April 1941
Alfred Georges Naqqache	April 1941–November 1941
Ahmed Daouk	December 1941–July 1942
Sami al-Solh	July 1942–March 1943
Ayub Thabit	March–July 1943
Petro Trad	August–September 1943

Lebanese Republic

Riad al-Solh	September 1943–January 1945
Abdul Hamid Karami	January–August 1945
Sami al-Solh	August 1945–May 1946
Saadi al-Munla	May–December 1946
Riad al-Solh	December 1946–February 1951
Hussein al-Oweini	February–April 1951
Abdallah al-Yafi	April 1951–February 1952
Sami al-Solh	February–September 1952
Nazim al-Akkari	September 1952
Saeb Salam	September 1952
Abdallah al-Yafi	September 1952

Khaled Chehab	October 1952–May 1953
Saeb Salam	May–August 1953
Abdallah al-Yafi	August 1953–September 1954
Sami al-Solh	September 1954–September 1955
Rashid Karami	September 1955–March 1956
Abdallah al-Yafi	March–November 1956
Sami al-Solh	November 1956–September 1958
Khalil al-Hibri	September 1958
Rashid Karami	September 1958–May 1960
Ahmed Daouk	May–August 1960
Saleb Salem	August 1960–October 1961
Rashid Karami	October 1961–February 1964
Hussein al-Oweini	February 1964–February 1965
Rashid Karami	July 1965–April 1966
Abdullah al-Yafi	April–December 1966
Rashid Karami	December 1966–February 1968
Abdallah al-Yafi	February 1968–January 1969
Rashid Karami	February 1969–October 1970
Saeb Salam	October 1970–April 1973
Amin al-Hafez	April–June 1973
Takieddin al-Solh	June 1973–October 1974
Rashid al-Solh	October 1974–May 1975
Nureddin Rifai	May–June 1975
Rashid Karami	July 1975–December 1976
Selim al-Hoss	December 1976–July 1980
Takieddin al-Solh	July–October 1980
Shafik Wazzan	October 1980–April 1984
Rashid Karami	April 1984–June 1987
Selim al-Hoss	June 1987– September 1988
Michel Aoun	September 1988–October 1990
Selim al-Hoss	October–December 1990
Omar Karami	December 1990–May 1992
Rashid al-Solh	May–October 1992
Rafiq al-Hariri	October 1992–December 1998
Selim al-Hoss	December 1998–October 2000
Rafiq al-Hariri	October 2000–October 2004
Omar Karami	October 2004–April 2005
Najib Mikati	April–June 2005
Fouad Siniora	June 2005–

Glossary

Ali ibn-Talib — Son-in-law and cousin of the Prophet Muhammad, Fourth Caliph, and inspiration for the Shi'a.

Amal — *Afwaj al-Muqawmat al-Lubnaniyya*, or "Lebanese Resistance Detachments," or, taken as a whole word, "Hope." Amal is a Shi'a militia first associated with Musa Al-Sadr's "Movement of the Disinherited," founded in 1975.

Arab — A person whose native language is Arabic.

Arab Deterrent Force (ADF) — Peacekeeping force authorized by the League of Arab States to intervene in Lebanon in 1971.

Ayyubid — Islamic dynasty founded in Cairo by Salah ad-Din, 1171–1260.

Ba'ath — In Arabic, "renaissance," political parties organized around Arab nationalism; ruling party in Syria.

Bey — Ottoman rank for district governors, right under the rank of Pasha.

Confessional — System of government that distributes political power in accordance with religious identity.

Druze — Derivation of Ismaili Shi'a, found mostly in Lebanon, Syria, and Israel.

Fatwa — A religious advisory opinion.

GDP — Gross domestic product, a measure of economic performance, summary of the total national economic activity.

Hezbollah — "Party of God" in Arabic. Political movement originating in Shi'a resistance to Israel; later became a complex organization with a military wing and a social wing.

Hussein ibn Ali — Son of Ali ibn Talib, a major figure in Shi'a religion.

Imam — Muslim prayer leader; spiritual leader in Shi'a communities.

IMF — International Monetary Fund

Islam — Religion based on the Quran and on the life of the Prophet Muhammad.

Ismailis ("Seveners") — Shi'a followers of the seventh Imam, Ismail.

Ithna Asharis ("Twelvers") — Shi'a followers of the twelfth Imam, born Abu-Qasim Muhammad ibn Hasan, or "Mahdi," the "Hidden Imam."

Jihad — Literally, "struggle" or "striving" in Arabic.

Kahan Commission — Israeli commission that investigated the Sabra-Shatila refugee camp massacres.

Kataeb Party — Another name for the Phalange Party.

Levant — Eastern Mediterranean region.

Maronite — An old Christian faith based initially on the teachings of St. Maron, which has historical ties to the Roman Catholic Church.

MEPI — Middle East Partnership Initiative, initiated by President George W. Bush in 2002 to foster democratization in the Middle East.

Muhammad — The person that Muslims believe received revelations from God (Allah) that became the Quran.

Ottoman Empire — Turkish Empire, late 13th century to the end of World War I.

Palestinian — Persons who trace their ancestry to the former area of Palestine, most formally defined by the borders of the British Mandate after World War I, but extending earlier to parts of Syria, Lebanon, Jordan, and Israel.

Phalange Party — Secular, though Maronite Christian-oriented political party of the Gemayel family, currently a part of the March 14 Alliance (see also Kataeb Party).

Quran — Text Muslims believe to be collected revelations from God given to Muhammad (literally "recitation" in Arabic).

Sabra-Shatila — Two Palestinian refugee camps attacked by Phalangist militia while under Israeli control in September 1982.

Salafiyya — Literally "pious" or "venerated ancestors," a term for those who turn to the earliest Islamic community for current inspiration and guidance.

Security Council Resolution 1701 — Resolution that ended the conflict between Israel and Hezbollah in 2006.

Shi'a — Sect of Islam whose followers claim that Ali ibn Talib, the cousin and son-in-law of the Prophet Muhammad, should have become the successor (caliph) to the Prophet, now around 40 percent of the Lebanese population.

South Lebanon Army — Pro-Israeli militia founded and led by Major Saad Hadad.

Sunni — Sect of Islam whose followers argued that the succession to the Prophet Muhammad should be determined by consensus of the Muslim community.

Takfir — In Islam, a declaration of Muslim heresy, or excommunication.

UNFIL — United Nations Forces in Lebanon, created in 1978 to monitor Israeli withdrawal from Lebanon, later empowered by Security Council Resolution 1701 to monitor end of hostilities and to support Lebanese forces in their deployment in south Lebanon.

Index

About the Author

DAVID S. SORENSON (Ph.D. Graduate School of International Studies, University of Denver) is Professor of International Security Studies at the U.S. Air War College. He has previously published *An Introduction to the Modern Middle East: History, Religion, Economics, and Politics* (2008), *The Politics and Process of Defense Acquisition: A Reference Handbook* (2009), *Military Base Closure: A Reference Book* (2006), *Shutting Down the Cold War: The Politics of Military Base Closure* (1998), and *The Politics of Strategic Aircraft Modernization* (1995) and co-edited three other books, along with numerous articles and book chapters on Middle East politics, defense budget politics, and national security affairs. He served previously on the faculties of Denison University and the Mershon Center at the Ohio State University.